MW01579007

CONTEMPLATING CURRICULUM

Contemplating Curriculum takes up world-renowned curricular scholar, teacher, and mentor Ted T. Aoki's invitation to contemplate where curriculum scholars situate themselves in their work. At the same time, it probes into the historical and present conditions that make it both possible and impossible to attend to this work in classrooms and communities in mindful, embodied, and aesthetic ways, both locally and globally. The book offers a strong representative sampling of contemporary thinking in the field with a focus on contemplative approaches to curriculum. In their theorizing, contributors call on literary and other mixed-genre formats, such as creative nonfiction, poetry, and essay. They acknowledge the importance of intergenerational dialogue and recognize the importance of time and place in curricular, pedagogical, and personal sense making. These written and visual texts invite contemplation on notions of curriculum, both planned and lived, in an Aokian spirit of intertextuality.

Wanda Hurren is Associate Dean, Faculty of Education, University of Victoria, Canada.

Erika Hasebe-Ludt is Professor, Faculty of Education, University of Lethbridge, Canada.

Studies in Curriculum Theory

William F. Pinar, Series Editor

For additional information on titles in the Studies in Curriculum Theory series, visit
www.routledge.com/education

CONTEMPLATING CURRICULUM

Genealogies/Times/Places

Edited by
Wanda Hurren and
Erika Hasebe-Ludt

 Routledge
Taylor & Francis Group
NEW YORK AND LONDON

First published 2014
by Routledge
711 Third Avenue, New York, NY 10017

Simultaneously published in the UK
by Routledge
2 Park Square, Milton Park, Abingdon, Oxon OX14 4RN

Routledge is an imprint of the Taylor & Francis Group, an informa business

© 2014 Taylor & Francis

Library of Congress Cataloging-in-Publication Data

Comptemplating curriculum / edited by Wanda Hurren and Erika Hasebe–Ludt.
    pages cm. — (Studies in curriculum theory)
  Includes bibliographical references and index.
  1. Curriculum planning—Philosophy.   2. Postmodernism and education.
I. Hurren, Wanda, 1957–   II. Hasebe–Ludt, Erika, 1951–
LB2806.15.C745   2013
375'.001—dc23   2013008119

ISBN: 978-0-415-64058-9 (hbk)
ISBN: 978-0-203-08267-6 (ebk)

Typeset in Bembo
by Apex CoVantage, LLC

Printed and bound in the United States of America by Publishers Graphics, LLC on sustainably sourced paper.

For Ted Tetsuo Aoki
Teacher still . . .

CONTENTS

PREFACE

An Invitation to Contemplate the *Topos* and *Humus*
of Curriculum on Genealogical Grounds:
A *Festschrift/Gedenkschrift* for Ted Tetsuo Aoki

> . . . the taste of life and for life comes to its own as a gift through the grace of the
> piety of thinking that is truly of the earth—the earth that knows the sun of the
> dawn, the calm of the morn, the silence of its mystery. . . . For is it not true that
> face to face with the primal mystery of being, we are brought to an awareness that
> language which has served us well to describe the phenomena of the world begins
> to falter; at best it merely points and then passes into silence.
>
> —Ted Tetsuo Aoki, from "The Sound of Pedagogy
> in the Silence of the Morning Calm"

This book celebrates the life and work of renowned curriculum theorist Ted
Tetsuo Aoki. Any attempt to fully describe the influence of this eminent scholar,
inspiriting teacher, and beloved human being seems an impossible task, one for
which words alone are not enough. Ted Aoki has shaped the field of curriculum
and the discipline of education in significant ways in Canada, North America,
and international contexts. His publications and public lectures,[1] and his teaching in public schools and education faculties across Canada and beyond, were
deeply thought provoking. He was the first director of the Centre for the Study
of Curriculum and Instruction at the University of British Columbia, and
he was professor and chair of the Department of Secondary Education at the
University of Alberta. Through such leadership roles, as well as his work with

graduate students, Ted influenced curriculum studies in innovative, provocative ways. He inspired generations of curriculum scholars, students, teachers, and administrators by always provoking them to "let learn," to dwell in curriculum as both a lived and planned *topos,* and to remember that human identities are shaped by the nourishing gifts of the *humus* they share with other living beings on this earth.

When contemplating the genealogy of this book, we trace its birth back to the idea for a *Festschrift,* a celebratory "feast of writing," conceived at a birthday party, and not just any birthday party. In October 2009, friends and family from near and far gathered together in Vancouver to celebrate with Ted Aoki on his 90th birthday. At that birthday party there were several obvious genealogical connections: Ted's close family members who were able to attend were present, and members from Ted's academic family who were able to attend were also present. As we looked around the tables, it was possible to detect a certain academic lineage and a common denominator: *curriculum.* In the tributes to Ted that afternoon, there was a celebration of shared intellectual pursuits, and many spoke of how Ted had inspired them to think more deeply about curriculum. Words and concepts that characterized Ted's work and life were spoken: *curriculum-as-lived, curriculum-as-plan, curriculum in a new key, hermeneutic inquiry, metonymic moments, in-dwelling/indwelling, lingering,* and *inspiriting pedagogy.*

In the days following Ted's birthday party, as we talked together about the celebration and the far-reaching influence of Ted's life and work, our plans unfolded to honour Ted with an anthology. We approached Ted, and as a result of our conversations, we envisioned a collection of writing that would take up curriculum inquiry as a *contemplative* endeavor, framed within *genealogical* themes, and considerations of *time* and *place.* So, we sent out an invitation that went something like this:

> We invite you to contribute to a new anthology that focuses on the work/life world of scholars situated within curriculum studies. Following an earlier anthology,[2] we intend to once again contemplate notions of intertextuality in an Aokian spirit of curriculum and *currere.* For more established scholars, we ask what is "still current" for you, what are the "still currents" that flow through your *currere?* For scholars situated at the beginning or in the middle of your curricular theorizing and pedagogical imagining, what provokes you at this time to engage with the field? And we ask all, wherever you are in your geo-cultural place(s), to contemplate your interpretation of the Aokian *humus* you dwell in. What questions do you linger with while tracing Aokian pedagogy and other ancestral connections?

The response was overwhelming. Not only did we get replies from the list of invitees, but also many invited contributors suggested other people to invite.

Former students of Ted suggested their own students who might contribute, since their students were reading Ted's work and had thoughts to contribute as well. A strong ancestral lineage was beginning to spread its rhizomean shoots in this new intertextual *humus* and *topos* of Canadian curriculum studies.

Then one afternoon in July 2011, we sat with Ted and June in the resident suite of their South Granville care home, and Ted listened with great interest as we shared the table of contents and the abstracts of each of the chapters in this newly configured anthology. His "oh yes" came after we read out each scholar's name. Together with Ted, we were once again mindful of the importance of intergenerational relations and genealogical connections in our life worlds.

We have noticed, in the field and in our own work, an increasing awareness of understanding curriculum as a genealogical intertext, one that requires a relational praxis on the part of teachers and researchers. In Canada where we both live and work, this understanding and agency has brought with it a commitment to being mindful of ancestral relations, both collectively and personally. As curriculum scholars, arts-based practitioners, and editors of this collection, we are encouraged by the ways this relational praxis is unfolding and strengthening the field and the local and global commons we share.

We hope that this collection will be helpful for curriculum scholars in multiple scholarly and pedagogical contexts and with a wide range of professional experiences and expertise. What makes it particularly valuable and unique is that the writing illustrates an orientation to curriculum studies that acknowledges the context of our times, the history of the field, and the people who shape it. This is a collection that invites you to linger, to take the time to contemplate curriculum before you rush off to continue the various formal and informal enactings of curriculum in which you may be involved. The 26 contributions represent a wide range of situations and places. The authors employed various (mixed) formats and genres of creative nonfiction in their writing: personal or expository essay, photo essay, letter, narrative, poetry, memoir, and tribute. Not only is the Aokian ancestry and scholarship traceable, but there are also familial genealogies structuring the collection: father/son, mother/son, student/teacher, apprentice/elder, colleague/friend, among others.

Our call to contributors attended to notions such as genealogy, time, and place, and living and lingering with curriculum as a somatic, visceral, and earth-bound *intertext*. These are notions that have been nurtured through our decade-long writing and editing collaboration[3] and our mutual learning from and with Ted. As we read and became familiar with each contributor's piece, and as the tones and timbres of these texts emerged and came together, we saw that there was not one best way of organizing them, so what is presented here is only one possible organization. We have organized the anthology into three sections: *Weaving Genealogies; Lingering with Times, Dwelling in Places;* and *Living the Topos.*

In the first section, *Weaving Genealogies,* the authors highlight intergenerational aspects of curricular theorizing and acknowledge how memories, ideas, and conversations within the curricular world have the possibility of being familial as well as familiar. The section begins with a tribute from a son to a father, written by Ted Aoki's son, Douglas Aoki, and continues to weave the *topos* of relationality by attending to specific narratives of ancestry, apprenticeship, mentorship, lineage, love, blood relations, friendship, and following—all in relation to and in homage to the caring parental and humble pedagogical journeying of one "who has gone before."

The writers in the second section, *Lingering With Times, Dwelling in Places,* attend to particular geographical, historical, and/or contemporary elements of curricular theorizing and practice. Notions of place, in particular be/longing and be/coming of/to/from a place, inclusion and exclusion from places such as schools and other institutions and contested landscapes and languages, figure prominently in these selections, in particular with respect to the tensionalities at work between east and west, north and south, home and not-home, foreign and familiar.

The chapters in the final section, *Living the Topos,* focus on issues around contemplation and contemplative practices within curricular deliberations. Ted often encouraged this notion of contemplation through his call to linger and meditate, to notice the present moment, and the reality of where we already are. Authors in this section are attuned to the aesthetics and artistry of curricular theorizing and languaging through metaphor and metonymy, which were prominent features of Ted's writing. With these authors, we listen to strands of *sonare* and *videre,* and we move with the rhythms of poetry and pathos in life writing. We meditate on living with loss and dwelling with obligations in the traditional and contemporary communities of our commons, as members with various racial and ethnic identities. And we return to theorizing from the fragile, shifting ground we live on, to contemplate and re/imagine curriculum as a genealogical intertext.

As we worked to bring this anthology into being, we stayed in touch with Ted. We were hopeful that we would have the opportunity to present the completed *Festschrift* to Ted on a special occasion, in the way that a publication of this kind is usually celebrated in the presence of the honoured scholar. This was not to be. With great sadness, many of us came together to honour Ted's life when he passed away on August 31, 2012. Now, this Festschrift has also become this *Festschrift* has also become a *Gedenkschrift,* a commemorative publication of "thinking and re-membering," as the meaning of the word signifies, that pays homage to Ted Aoki's significant *oeuvre.* We will miss Ted's presence in this world. We hold him in our thoughts and memories with this collection that is not precisely one or the other but both *Festschrift* and *Gedenkschrift.*

It has been our privilege to take up and extend to all of our relations Ted's call to linger, to contemplate our genealogies in the field of curriculum studies and the ways in which our pedagogical practices are both constituted by and contributing to Ted's legacy. *Contemplating Curriculum: Genealogies/Times/Places* is a celebratory collection. Now, as you are about to turn the page and begin to read, it is our pleasure to invite you to join the celebration and to contemplate, as we honour the life and work of Ted Aoki, what it means to dwell together humanly.

Erika Hasebe-Ludt and Wanda Hurren
Lethbridge, Alberta and Victoria, British Columbia
December 2012

Notes

1. See *Curriculum in a New Key: The Collected Works of Ted T. Aoki,* co-edited by William F. Pinar and Rita L. Irwin (Lawrence Erlbaum, 2005).
2. See *Curriculum Intertext: Place/Language/Pedagogy,* co-edited by Erika Hasebe-Ludt and Wanda Hurren (Peter Lang, 2003).
3. See the aforementioned coedited *Curriculum Intertext* anthology, and the 2011 co-authored article *Bringing Curriculum Down to Earth: The Terroir That We Are,* published in *JCT: Journal of Curriculum Theorizing,* 27(2), 17–34.

ACKNOWLEDGMENTS

We thank the Faculties of Education at the University of Victoria and the University of Lethbridge for support. In particular, we acknowledge Adam Steffanick, research assistant, and Bev Asclin, administrative support at the University of Victoria; at the University of Lethbridge we acknowledge Margaret Beintema, administrative support, and Dr. Nané Jordan, postdoctoral researcher.

Thank you to our colleagues, students, and friends who have supported us throughout this project and whose inspiriting ideas found their way into this book.

We extend our deep gratitude to William F. Pinar, series editor of *Studies in Curriculum Theory*, for his much-valued feedback and endorsement of this *Festschrift* and *Gedenkschrift* in honour of Ted T. Aoki. We also appreciate the professional expertise of the production team at Routledge, in particular Naomi Silverman and Andrew Weckenmann.

We are most grateful to our families for their love and support, in particular, Wanda's sons, Mark and Jordan Grimsrud; and Erika's partner, Ken K. Hasebe, and daughter, Charlotte C.L. Hasebe.

PART I
Weaving Genealogies

1

TO MEDITATE ON THOSE WHO HAVE GONE BEFORE

Douglas Sadao Aoki

Ted Aoki was my father. When my son was born in 1996, Dad and Mom were overjoyed, especially since he was their first grandchild. We call him *Alex,* but that's actually his middle name. His first is *Tetsuyoshi* 哲義, a patronymic devised by my father, whose legal name is *Tetsuo* 哲夫. *Ted* is just an example of how *nisei* 二世 (second-generation Japanese Canadians) often reconfigured their given names as near-homophones that are easier for English speakers to pronounce. *Tetsuo* means "philosopher," and 哲 *tetsu* is the first *kanji* 漢字 (Japanese Chinese character) in both my father's and son's names. The other kanji in *Tetsuyoshi* is 義 *yoshi* ("righteousness," "justice," or "honor") and comes from the name of my father's father, *Sadayoshi* 定義. He and my grandmother were schoolteachers who came to Cumberland, British Columbia, after its community sent a request to Japan for someone to teach Japanese to its children. *Tetsuyoshi* can be translated as "obligated to philosophy." My mother, June, rolled her eyes a bit when she heard about Dad's neologism, but she didn't linger on it; she just wanted to be with her grandson as much as possible—so much that Dad usually got crowded out. When we visited, we had to get my wife, Lucy, who Mom adored, to distract her in conversation, and once they were chatting merrily, I could sneak off with Alex and place him in my father's arms. Dad would walk slowly around, cooing to the tiny face that stared up at him. A man with his grandson, such a commonplace scene, nothing special at all, but utterly singular.

I entered graduate studies late—13 years after graduating with a bachelor of science in physics. As an undergraduate, I never considered education as a field of study, though not because of any rebelliousness, and Dad never pushed me towards it. After peregrinations through medical biophysics, postmodern sociology, and a job at a car wash, I was in the fourth year of my doctoral program, studying Lacanian psychoanalytic theory when Alex was born. The same year, I also

FIGURE 1.1 Grandpa teaching Alex, age 3, about *Thomas the Tank Engine*

became a teacher. I was hired as a sessional instructor and discovered the thrall of teaching. Dad and I now had a common passion to talk about, even if my enthusiasm seduced me into thinking I was much better than I really was. And we talked about fatherhood.

Sensei and *Shōgō*

You likely know that the Japanese word for teacher is *sensei* 先制, but perhaps you're not aware it's also the way a medical doctor, lawyer, or clergyperson is addressed. This leveling, compared to the statuses of physician and teacher here in North America, suggests that Rudyard Kipling's "East is East and West is West" still obtains. The English idiom is "Those who can't do, teach," not "Those who can't do, heal," but for the Japanese, it is precisely when you *can* do that you have earned the title of teacher.

    Sensei is an honorific, although it is also used sarcastically to refer to megalomaniacs or couriers of sycophancy. In such cases, it is written as センセイ. The iconic *sensei* of pop culture likely remains the fictional Mr. Miyagi from *The Karate Kid*. Even my friends who grew up in Norway know "Wax on, wax off." The movie was a clichéd coming-of-age story, yet it inspired many parents to enroll their children at the local *dōjō* 道場 (training hall). They intuited that *karatedō*

空手道 (literally, "the way of the empty hand") could teach their sons and daughters to become better people.

In that spirit, Dad got me into jūdō 柔道 at the age of 6, although he was doomed to be disappointed by my lack of talent, which proved to be irremediable. The most I can say about my training is that I kept going. Genuine jūdō or karatedō is so demanding that beginners frequently drop out quickly, and, these days, teenagers find first-person shooter video games such as *Call of Duty: Black Ops* a much easier way to fight. Even so, parents keep trying to introduce their kids to karatedō, out of hope and devotion, though few of them, regardless of ethnicity, know anything substantial of the *budō* 武道 (martial ways) or *bugei* 武芸 (martial arts). Some beginners stick with it, though. Alex has trained since he was 7 years old, and recently he began to teach some classes, which made Grandpa very proud.

Some of the budō and bugei, especially those under the auspices of the esteemed *Dai Nippon Butokukai* 大日本武德會 (Greater Japan Martial Virtues Society) and *Kokusai Budōin* 国際武院 (International Martial Arts Federation), use *shōgō* 称号, a trio of titles recognizing exceptional *sensei*. In ascending order, its levels are *renshi* 錬士, *kyōshi* 教士, and *hanshi* 範士. Historically, a renshi was a samurai who led soldiers by virtue of his exceptional mental, physical, and technical abilities (Chambers, 2005, p. 2). Kyōshi moved explicitly from leading to teaching; a kyōshi was responsible for training soldiers. The most venerated level was hanshi, commonly translated as "teacher of teachers." In the past, shōgō were rarely awarded. Only a handful of *karateka* were so honored, such as Miyagi Chōjun[1] 宮城長順 (1888–1953), founder of *Gōjū ryū* 剛柔流, and Funakoshi Gichin 船越義珍 (1868–1957), who brought karatedō to mainland Japan from Okinawa.

The most familiar emblem of karatedō is the black belt, but at the same time, its misinterpretation is synecdochic of the problems besetting karatedō in North America. Here, the black belt is mistaken as a marker of mastery, when it actually signifies a sufficient readiness to learn. Yes, a real black belt is real achievement, but more because it is such a privilege to be a student of karatedō than because it is any kind of goal. The *koryū* 古流 (literally, "old stream"), the more ancient bugei, admitted applicants only after a scrutiny more rigorous and exclusive than that of an elite modern medical school. The black belt is also a test of character. It is axiomatic that no one who craves a black belt deserves one. The only path to a legitimate black belt is the unrelenting pursuit of *nyūanshin* 初心, the mind of a beginner.

As shōgō have become better known in North American martial arts, the number of renshi, kyōshi, and hanshi has proliferated far beyond those registered by the Kokusai Budōin. Either this generation is blessed with a profusion of karate superteachers or truly great karatedō *sensei* have become vastly outnumbered by those making claims to greatness.

Fields of Dreams

There is a different but resonant problem in pedagogy. Many teachers are plagued by a desire for authority in the classroom, but they rarely consider the ominous politics of that desire. Or perhaps, because they just didn't grow up as the son or student of a Japanese man, they don't realize how a smiling little yellow guy can instantly become formidable when necessary. Authority is no guarantee of respect; instead, authority commands only its semblance, regardless of whether respect is actually there. A case in point, more parallel to shōgō, is the assertion of titles. Many faculty expect their students to address them as *Dr.* X or *Professor* Y. I even know of a school principal with a PhD who signs his name, in longhand, as *Dr.* Z. Titles are always motivated artifices of discourse, so the question begged is the nature of that motivation. It certainly isn't humility. If you insist on being called *Dr.*, at least have the wit and good humor of a friend of mine, whose students call her (not by her suggestion) "Dr. Booty."

The quest for authority is also fraught because it is desire in a classically Lacanian sense: unceasing but never fulfilled. For too many karateka, becoming a *sensei* only kindles the desire for a more magnificent title. Yet the needed response to such sorry epigones of Miyagi and Funakoshi is "Why aren't you satisfied with being a *sensei*?"

The karate lesson for faux hanshi and pretentious academics alike is that respect is real only when it is not demanded. Higaonna Morio 東恩納盛男 (1938–), *jūdan* 十段 (10th-degree black belt), is a revered *sensei*. Donn Draeger (1922–1982), acclaimed as the finest Western exponent of classical Japanese martial traditions to have ever lived, wrote,

> There is no better one for me than the Okinawan Gōjū ryū under Higaonna Morio. . . . Here is a man who exemplifies the word *dō* [道, the way, such as the way of karate]: humble, resilient, skilled, silent, friendly, strong, all at the right times. His technique is the best in Japan, and in a real fight I know nobody, including Ōyama [founder of Kyokushinkai 極真会 karatedō and a famous full-contact fighter], who can best him. He does not go around proselytizing his art . . . and the man, Higaonna, is a gem. (Jarvis, 2010, p. 219)

Yet even today, when Higaonna calls on the phone, he just says, "Higaonna *desu*" ("This is Higaonna") (Chambers, 2005, p. 2).

My father was not a martial artist, although when curfews for Japanese Canadians in Vancouver were implemented after Pearl Harbor, he and his buddies did occasionally sneak out and mug Chinese guys for their IDs. Dad was a tremendous athlete, much better than me, but in saying that, I don't want to repeat the common error of seeing karatedō as a sport or recreation. It's neither. Dad played inside center on the Britannia High School rugby team that, stocked with Asians from the east end, won a Vancouver city championship. Once, he told me with a small grin, "We loved to beat the white boys." When he taught at a small town in southern Alberta, he was a catcher in an amateur baseball league, and to this day he has a finger that bends the wrong way because of an errant pitch. He tried to teach me baseball, but I was too terrified of anything hurtling towards my face. Many years later, I played on a very recreational slow-pitch team, and a friend watching said, "I feel so *bad* for your father."

After Dad retired, he and I went to see *Field of Dreams*. At the end of the film, when the protagonist, played by Kevin Costner, called after the spectre of his father and asked if he wanted to play catch, I glanced at Dad, and his eyes were glistening. I felt bad for him too.

Being Silent at the Right Time

Dad taught social studies and coached basketball at the Lethbridge Collegiate Institute in Lethbridge, Alberta. Rugby, baseball, social studies, and basketball are very different from karatedō. Yet coaching is a kind of teaching, and any dō is much more encompassing and subtle than the concrete specifics of its defining *waza* 技 (techniques), whether kicks, throws, or cuts with a sword. As the very existence of shōgō suggests, at the heart of dō is teaching, and, as Draeger points out, the embodiment of dō is a teacher's humility, resilience, skill, friendliness, and strength (see Jarvis, 2010). My father was not a karateka, although he did fight the good fight. Yet he was a *sensei*, even in terms of karatedō. The way of teaching for him wended from Normal School in Calgary, where he was allowed to attend only if he lived outside the city limits, through his first teaching job in a colony of Hutterites, the only people in Alberta who would hire him, to the Universities of Alberta and British Columbia, where he taught several generations of teachers. My father was a respected curriculum theorist. Yet when he called someone, he said, "This is Ted."

Despite my quotation of Kipling, the critical difference between Higaonna and the hanshi wannabes isn't ethnic. *Nihonjin* 日本人 (Japanese people) are not superior to *gaijin* 外人 (non-Japanese), and unfortunately, there are karateka from all cultures, including the Japanese, who avidly collect titles and awards, as if those were sports trophies or highlights of a curriculum vitae. As Konishi Yasuhiro 小西康裕 (1893–1983), founder of *Shindō Jinen ryū* 神道自然流, observed, "Karate-dō aims to build character, improve human behavior, and cultivate modesty; it does not, however, guarantee it" (as cited in McCarthy, 2007). And of course it is not necessary to be Japanese to understand karatedō. Draeger, who fought and killed Japanese as a marine in World War II, then moved to Japan, learned its language, and became an expert in multiple fighting traditions, was the dynamic refutation. The best proof is neither his high ranks in multiple budō, his several *menkyo* 免許 (licenses to teach specific bugei), nor his authorship of landmark books on the martial arts. It is that he knew learning and teaching the way meant being silent at the right time.

Dad knew too. He taught it to me through jūdō. He took me to watch an adult tournament where one particular *jūdōka* 柔道家 (jūdō practitioner) stood out. He was powerfully built and preternaturally agile, and although he didn't play a crude defensive game, he thwarted every attempt to throw him. Everyone in the gymnasium took notice. In one of the final matches, someone finally knocked him partially off his feet and the crowd roared. I started to clap, but my father instantly rebuked me. He said, quietly, "Never applaud a man's defeat."

Often, the very dedication of teachers surfaces in an anxiety over silence, because their ideal pedagogy is students engaged enough to speak. If there is a time to be silent, then there must be a time *not* to be as well. Yet there is a particular silence of the dō. The trite adage is "If you can't say anything nice about someone, don't say anything at all," but the karatedō version is "If you can say something nice about yourself, don't." Don't applaud a man's defeat, and don't applaud yourself. If you're an award-winning teacher whose honors came from judiciously speaking well of yourself—even if that was crafting a successful nomination for a 3M Teaching Fellowship—you should stay well clear of the dōjō floor. There,

FIGURE 1.2 Grandpa being guided by Alex, age 13

regardless of your reputation, you will be regarded as a センセイ, not a 先生, and will receive very concrete correction. As Homma 本間学 (1994) says,

> Accomplishment means ascending the peak, but it does not mean that one will stay there. What's left after reaching . . . the peak is the climb down. If [someone] tries to stay at the top, he will soon be escorted once again to the bottom. (p. 52)

I will not rehearse the critique of teaching awards I have made elsewhere (Aoki, 2010), but I will point out there are better ways to honor teaching than honoring yourself. If you want to convince me you're a good teacher, don't tell me about yourself—tell me about your students. Good teaching is infinitely variable and complex, but it does have a simple principle: Pay attention to those you teach. You're not paying attention anytime you're making sure someone else knows how good you are. Lowry (2005), whose writing on the budō and bugei is nonpareil, notes that "the first hurdle [a *sensei*] must overcome is his own ego" (p. 98).

To Meditate on Those Who Came Before

I recently had to reset an online password, and to do so, I had to answer a security question: "Who was your favorite teacher?" For me, it was Mrs. Hemingway, who taught me junior-high English. Now, the point is not what made her so memorable, like her firm kindness, intelligence, edgy wit, and glorious legs. The point is that I remember Mrs. Hemingway 43 years later. The poet Philip Larkin, upon finally meeting Cyril Connolly, whose writing has influenced him tremendously, said, "Sir, you formed me" (as cited in Longley, 2000, p. 32). You don't forget the teachers who formed you. You can't forget because you have the obligation to remember.

Britzman (2003) has been much more gracefully intelligent than I could ever be on teaching as a practice, but I will add that the Japanese word for practice is *keiko* 稽古, which literally means "to meditate on the old." In karatedō, each practice, every movement and every stillness, should embody a tribute to the teachers who have come before (Ohshima, 1998, p. 4). A thoughtful karateka of my acquaintance once condemned the autobiography of a martial arts movie star. The problem wasn't the ghostwriting, even though that was execrable. The problem was that the book was nearly 250 pages long but the actor's *sensei* was mentioned in but one paragraph. So many pages with the actor talking about himself; so little acknowledgment of his teacher.

I am grateful that so many of Dad's ex-students visited him and Mom. Those visits are what he enjoyed most, and each time I was there, he told me who had come by. One visitor was Bob Christie, who was Dad's student in 1961. I thank Bob, as I thank Wanda and Erika and everyone else who has contributed to this volume. And I thank you for reading. Thank you for not forgetting my father. The literal meaning of *sensei* is "one who came before." The practice of teaching should be animated by the spirit of karatedō, which obliges us to remember and pay attention. Dad was a devoted teacher of teachers, a genuine hanshi. But the self-indulgent eagerness for shōgō gets the rank order wrong—hanshi is ostensibly the highest title, but the very modesty of *teacher* makes it much more significant.

My father was a teacher.

References

Aoki, D. (2010). The need to express dignity in an institution bent on wrestling it away: The kata of teaching. In J. Maudlin, B. Stodghill, & M. He (Eds.), *Engaging the possibilities & complexities of hope: Utterances of curriculum and pedagogy's past, present, and future* (pp. 3–17). Troy, NY: Educator's International Press.

Britzman, D. (2003). *Practice makes practice: A critical study of learning to teach.* Albany: State University of New York Press.

Chambers, D. (2005). From the publisher's desk. *Classical Fighting Arts, 7,* 1–2.

Homma, G. (1994). *Aikido sketch diary.* Berkeley, CA: Frog.

Jarvis, J. (2010). *Kurosaki killed the cat.* LaVergne, TN: Gulliver Press.

Longley, E. (2000). Larkin, decadence and the lyric poem. In J. Booth (Ed.), *New Larkins for old: Critical essays* (pp. 29–50). New York, NY: Palgrave Macmillan.

Lowry, D. (2005). *Clouds in the west: Lessons from the martial arts of Japan.* Guilford, CT: The Lyons Press.

McCarthy, P. (2007). Myth busting. Retrieved from http://www.koryu-uchinadi.com/Myth_Busting.htm

Ohshima, T. (1998). *Notes on training.* Enumclaw, WA: Idyll Arbor.

Note

1. Japanese names are given in the traditional order, with the family name first.

2

A DAY IN THE LIFE OF TED AOKI

Wm E. Doll Jr.

The day sweltered. Moisture hung in the air like a wet towel. The sun blistered. Nothing moved. Sounds fell dead. The compound guard slouched. She looked young for this job. I approached and gave my name. She checked my credentials, and with guests, I was admitted. While heads hardly turned, one could feel pairs of eyes looking at three newcomers entering the country club pool enclosure. I had recently purchased a house within the club grounds—on the 14th tee— and by fiat was a club member. This was a new and somewhat uncomfortable experience for me. I did not *belong* to the country club set, and it showed. It certainly showed this hot, summer day in Louisiana. I brought two guests with me: Bill Pinar and Ted Aoki. If Bill and I looked odd—while large in build, neither of us had the stereotypical potbelly of so many middle-aged Louisiana men—Ted, small in stature and wiry, was definitely a *foreigner*. The club did not discriminate; it just had no Asian, African American, or Jewish members. This was Louisiana, a gumbo of cultures, not a melting pot. A good gumbo has distinctive flavours, each of which can be savoured, each needing its own place. The club community in which I resided was a white, upwardly mobile enclave. The housewarming my wife and I gave upon our arrival was attended by neighbours, all comfortable with themselves and quite shocked when in breezed a parade of African American students from New Orleans, singing, dancing, reciting poetry, and waving multicoloured scarves. The party was great, the drumming electric, and the neighbours, ever so polite, just a bit astonished. What was happening in their enclave! What was Louisiana State University coming to!

The summer of our pool entrance, Bill had invited Ted down to teach a course. It was, as all who knew Ted will understand, fantastic. He touched on themes of curriculum, particularly the tensions between *curriculum-as-lived* and *curriculum-as-planned* (Aoki, 1986/2005). That curriculum could be lived brought forth astonishment from the students, and with this astonishment came a new appreciation of Pinar's *currere*. In his own quiet, dare I say humble, way, Ted encouraged our students *to think*. He took to heart Martin Heidegger's statement, "The most thought-provoking thing about our thought-provoking times is that we are not yet thinking" (as cited in Aoki, 1993/2005, p. 298).[1]

I liked going to the pool after a day of teaching in Baton Rouge. The country club subdivision in which I lived was literally a drained Louisiana swamp, with a small levee around it. It was located partway between New Orleans and Baton Rouge. Bill Pinar would sometimes join me for an afternoon swim, and my wife and I often hosted visiting scholars for dinner at our house. On this day, Ted came down and, before dinner, he, Bill, and I went swimming. Mothers quietly told their children that it was "adult time" in the pool, but no adults joined us; the pool was ours, and we enjoyed floating on our backs, relaxing as we looked up at the blue, cloudless Louisiana sky. The issue of racism remained sotto voce. Only years later, reading Bill and Rita Irwin's book of Ted's writings (Pinar & Irwin, 2005), did I realize the hurt and humiliation Ted suffered during World War II. During this time, as an "other," he and his family were shipped off to a "camp," far from major Canadian cities. What they left was taken from them— by others. I know little of Ted's feelings about that time; he spoke sparingly of it. He certainly would not embarrass me by mentioning the obvious connection that must have come to his mind about the odd similarity between his "camp" days and the enclosure of the country club pool—both designed to separate, exclude, humiliate.

In his writings, Ted played with the word *humiliation*—the attempt to make one feel that his or her "otherness" is really an inferiorness (Aoki, 1993/2005). He asked us to imagine a different sense of humiliation, one "humiliating humiliation," one where "*humour, human, humus, humility* live together" (p. 300). These four signifiers, and others such as *humilitas,* live in a special place, a place where the "arrogant I . . . of human-centeredness dissolves," leaving "room for the emergence of new lines of meaning" (p. 300). This place—a "third space," Serres (1991/1997) would say—broad enough to allow tensions to play and interact—provides a repositioning of humiliation so that it can operate, not as a negation but as a "sign of our humanness" (p. 300).

Serres (1991/1997, p. 166) captures the humanity of this space well, I believe, when he says of his *troubadour,* who lives in the third space:

> *Reborn, he knows, he takes pity.*
> *Finally, he can teach.*

References

Aoki, T.T. (1986/2005). Teaching as indwelling between two curriculum worlds. In W.F. Pinar & R.L. Irwin (Eds.), *Curriculum in a new key: The collected works of Ted Aoki* (pp. 159–166). Mahwah, NJ: Lawrence Erlbaum.

Aoki, T.T. (1993/2005). Humiliating the Cartesian ego. In W.F. Pinar & R.L. Irwin (Eds.), *Curriculum in a new key: The collected works of Ted T. Aoki* (pp. 291–301). Mahwah, NJ: Lawrence Erlbaum.

Pinar, W.F., & Irwin, R.L. (Eds.). (2005). *Curriculum in a new key: The collected works of Ted T. Aoki*. Mahwah, NJ: Lawrence Erlbaum.

Serres, M. (1991/1997). *The troubadour of knowledge* (S. Glaser, Trans.). Ann Arbor: University of Michigan Press.

Note

1. It is worth noting that the Provoking Curriculum Conference was first held at the University of British Columbia in honour of Ted Aoki.

3

REGARDING TED AOKI

On Love and Learning to Listen in the Curriculum Studies Field

Kathryn Jones

Heart rushing naughty
crushing over
unrequited love.
A charismatic stranger,
on the page,
all-consuming wooing.
Enlivening and delicious
curriculum world reading.

Awakening thinking,
reading me, back to me.
His teacherly presence,
on the page
before me, a world.
Ted Aoki
becoming himself,
listening to us
speaking to me.

I confess: I have a crush on Ted Aoki. There's something intoxicating about the act or experience of "crushing." It's all-consuming. The "crusher" is transported into fantasy. It seems a little naughty to be crushing on a male academic when one is a grown and married lesbian woman, but it is exhilarating having one's thoughts taken up and read back to them by another human being. Ted's words have begun to echo through my own thoughts and quite profoundly through the works of other theorists I am reading as a graduate student. The intertextual and conversational nature of curriculum studies is seducing me.

Presence

Ted Aoki's writing is powerful. Encountering his work, readers are captivated. Great pedagogues connect with their students by virtue of their presence and felt intention. Ted's *embodiment* in his writing leads me to agree with Pinar and Irwin's (2005) description of him as a "giant" who continues to help define the curriculum studies field. No wonder I find myself falling in love with Ted as he presents himself to me through his life's work.

Ted's work does not resonate because he idealizes or romanticizes the suffering that can take place in educational spaces. He embodies Loy's (1993) observation that "to become enlightened is to forget one's own suffering only to wake up in or rather *one with* a world of suffering" (p. 502). Ted suffered state-sanctioned discrimination against Japanese Canadians during his lifetime. He was relocated and interned during World War II and treated as an enemy alien who needed to apply to live within the city of Calgary when he chose to retrain as a teacher in the late 1940s. And yet Ted never appears bitter or resentful. His suffering has heightened his ability to take a compassionate stance as a teacher.

Ted's compassion is evident in his description of teachers such as Miss O. He describes the competing demands of the "lived" (present, embodied, intimate, situated) and "planned" (detached, disembodied, imposed, external) curriculums and acknowledges Miss O's (and, in fact, all) pedagogical situation(s) as a "living in tensionality" (Aoki, 1986/2005, p. 159). His deep respect and appreciation for all teachers is evident in his description of the difficult space Miss O finds herself living in. Ted's description of teaching as a "mode of being," one that involves "face-to-face living with" (p. 160) students and is guided by a sense of the "pedagogic good" (p. 164), resonates with me.

Ted cultivates himself and his own beliefs about teaching through his work. He does not profess to be an "expert," nor does his work attempt to disseminate the knowledge he has collected over time. He shares his insights by lending *himself* to us (me!). Readers can witness him becoming more of himself through his work. Ted entices readers with his own questions, wonderings, and ruminations. Describing what it means to teach (well) is an elusive and slippery task. He is highly attuned to the practice of trying to treat a thing (teaching) so that its nature can show. Ted's work points to, rather than pins down, what good teaching *is,* looks like, or, perhaps more aptly, *sounds* like.

Ted's work is predicated on an ethics of "connection and intimacy rather than separation and estrangement" (Noddings, as cited in Grumet, 1989, p. 177). In his pedagogical stories, he emphasizes engrossment, presence, and "receptivity." He retells his wife June's experience of her teacher Mr. McNab (Aoki, 1992) silently and thoughtfully watching over his Japanese Canadian students as they were removed from his care during World War II. This story is an example of the difficulty of giving voice to exactly what (good, lasting, memorable) teaching *is.* In fact, it is ironically Mr. McNab's *silence* in that moment of powerless yet protective watching that speaks profoundly to the experience of *being* a teacher.

In Ted's work, the question of *what* a good/effective teacher *does* shifts to a consideration of *who* a good/effective teacher *is*.

We live in a world focused more on doing than being. Our collective obsessions in capitalist Western industrialized nations are productivity, accumulation, and competition. Educational research and policy are also caught up in what Smith (2008) describes as the "limits of Western intellectual paradigms" (p. 5). What makes Ted's work so beautiful and compelling is his quiet refusal to be caught up in modern discourses of attempting to pin down, describe, and define exactly what (good/effective/efficient) teaching *does* so that we might attempt to replicate, reproduce, and profit from it. He reminds us that our "concern for *doing* needs to be accompanied by a concern for *not doing,* for holding back, for withdrawing, for letting go, for letting be" (Aoki, 1991/2005, p. 386). Ted suggests that authentic teaching might consist less of action and more of "watchfulness, a mindful watching overflowing from the good in the situation that the good teacher sees. In this sense, good teachers are more than they do; they are the teaching" (Aoki, 1992, p. 26). His quiet willingness to share who he *is* enables readers to feel that he is watching quietly over us (me!).

Losing me to find us
together with the young
in familiar classrooms
before us.
Entering conversations
still beginning,
flourishing and
ever-emerging.

Echoing calls.
Responding, rendering me
response-able.
A scholarly ancestor
still emerging
sounding, and bridging,
dovetailing into
lightening.

Hearing

Ted contemplates the ways in which teaching involves musical acts such as practice, pausing, tension, calling, responding, bridging, lingering, and voice. In a culture that does not deeply value or respect teachers, I often find myself struggling to explain why I teach. I tend to fall upon (sometimes seemingly empty) clichés such as my love of working with the young, passion for learning, and desire to protect and nurture our world. I also call upon my own experiences with wonderful teachers whose *beings* resonate with me and echo in my life years after our face-to-face encounters. Contemplating this idea of *resonance,* I begin to understand why Ted employs auditory metaphors.

Musical instruments require tension in order to resonate. Ted's description of pedagogical situations as sites of tension is alluring. Teachers are familiar with tension as they attempt, daily, to negotiate and fulfill the competing demands of students, curriculum, administration, parents, and society. Ted invites me to consider that tension is, in some senses, *the* (unavoidable and essential) "mode of being of a teacher, a mode that could be oppressive and depressive, marked by despair and hopelessness, and at other times stimulating, evoking hopefulness for venturing forth" (Aoki, 1986/2005, p. 162). He invites educators to "attune ourselves to the *call* of what teaching is" (Aoki, 1986/2005, p. 162), and we respond to his call.

In his discussion of the ways in which the "East" deeply inhabits, informs, and intertwines with the Western imaginary, Smith (2008) acknowledges the fact that "sound structure is always related to social structure" (p. 20). He emphasizes the importance of engaging in new *conversations* and of cultivating an ability to *listen.* Smith (2009) himself employs an auditory metaphor when he "calls" readers to "see the material world as itself pedagogical, that is, instructive of our basic human condition, particularly its qualities of impermanence, ambiguity and mystery constrained in the tension between birth and death, arising and dying" (p. 99). As soon as I began to see this motif of the auditory in Ted's work, it began to make itself recognizable to me in the works of others. Doll (1993) speaks about the importance of cultivating pedagogical spaces based on "dialoguing, negotiating, interacting" (p. 286), and Jardine (2008) talks about being "always ready to hesitate and cup my ear again, not just toward the voice of another, but again toward the ghosts howling in my own voice" (p xi). After encountering Ted's idea of allowing the essence of what teaching is to "sound," I have begun to "hear" responses to his call in other scholarship I encounter. Being able to hear these conversations (echoes/calls/responses) is exciting and exhilarating.

> *Entering a field,*
> *coming home.*
> *An enlightenment that*
> *frees me from me.*

Dwelling

The experience of being inducted into the field of curriculum studies by a mentor such as Ted is a homecoming. As such, it is not surprising that so many curriculum theorists speak to the notion of *dwelling* in educational spaces. The connotations of dwelling with human desires for security, comfort, and nourishment are not inconsequential here. This sense of dwelling is apparent to me in scholarly invocations of pedagogical landscapes or topographies. Curriculum theorists prior to the reconceptualization of the 1970s tended (in the tradition of Tyler) to approach curriculum as material to be "covered" by teachers in a very formulaic manner so that students would "progress" in very normative and functional ways (Kliebard, 1970). Ted Aoki, like other more contemporary theorists such as Jardine, Friesen, and Clifford (2006), suggests that educational spaces are sites of "abundance" in which we must seek to *live* together with students. Smith (2008) calls upon readers to begin to see the "entire world" for what it really is: "an integrated field" (p. 13). What an honor to be invited to dwell together with others deeply invested in (or perhaps more aptly *entrusted with*) educating our young. These scholars are leading me away from simple considerations of how I/we might *survive* in education spaces and to remember to "ask the question, Survive? What for?—the fundamental question of the meaning of what it is to live life, including school life" (Aoki, 1986/2005, p. 163).

> *Not here or there*
> *but now.*
> *Coming to see, to celebrate*
> *the other already in me.*

Bridging

Ted Aoki's scholarship comes together in his descriptions of the auditory and his invoking of dwelling in educational spaces. The site of this coalescence is the musical and structural image of the *bridge*. A bridge connects, joins, and supports two otherwise unconnected or oppositional sides. Ted's interest in the bridge (as both a noun and a verb) seems to stem from his criticism of and discomfort with what he describes as the "Western imaginary that has created the notion of the individual" (Aoki, 1999, p. 33). In late modernity there continues to be comfort with (and indeed dependence upon) upholding dualisms between such notions as self and other, teacher and student, East and West, mother tongue and other tongue, past and future, theory and practice. Ted suggests that we need to shift our attention toward "a generative space of difference, an enunciatory space of becoming, a space where newness emerges" (Aoki, 1999, p. 35). The bridge is an in-between or interspace through which we might dwell, together, not only as teachers and students but also as human beings in (with!) *our* world.

In Smith's (2008) invitation to participate in a new kind of conversation, he asks readers to contemplate what it means to meet those we have been traditionally taught to believe are outside of us but in fact constitute significant parts of who we *actually* are. In his exploration of the ways in which the "West" has constructed itself around narratives that exclude an imaginary "East," Smith uncovers a series of fascinating "parallels, common sources, and lines of influence" (p. 11) that have been hidden from us by virtue of what he describes as the "deep phenomenology of exclusion in the heart of the Euro-American tradition" (p. 24). The bridges Ted speaks about are not sites we need to construct but parts of who we *already actually are* as human beings *sharing* this world.

Ted is not advocating that the disorder and deterioration we are confronting in educational spaces, and in the world today, will be solved by simply crossing over the bridges that connect and divide us. Approaching bridges in this way would be antithetical to his call for us to "indwell between two horizons" (Aoki, 1986/2005, p. 161). Instead of seeing bridges as passages from here to there, from self to other, from inside to outside, or from West to East, Ted suggests that we seek to dwell in the inter or in-between spaces that bind us together. This idea of living with an awareness of our connections is essential. Loy (1993) goes so far as to suggest that "awareness of mutual identity and interpenetration is rapidly developing into the only doctrine that makes sense anymore, perhaps the only one that can save us from ourselves" (p. 483).

Ted's concept of the bridge resounds in my life and my practice. I hope I can continue to dwell in the space Ted and his (my!) scholarly family are helping to clear for me, and live here, together with my students, remembering the power that might come from facing our shared horizons.

> *Awakening again*
> *to all the ways in which we are broken,*
> *crushed by love, honouring*
> *our ancestors who render us who we are.*

Renewal

A fellow graduate student recently informed me that she has been instructed to disregard "older" scholarship and to focus only on what is most recent (published in the last 5 years) in her research. This advice points to a (dangerous, limiting) cultural (capitalist) obsession with the young, the new, and the soon to be obsolete. The idea that new scholars should forsake the foundations upon which new work depends speaks to a contemporary state of disembodiment and detachment. I would have lost so much had I been discouraged from falling in love with an elder like Ted Aoki!

The pressure new scholars feel to forsake old(er) ideas for newer ones points to an academic world caught up in the very world (of planned obsolescence, disposability, and consumerism) that it should be attempting to critique. It is an act of self-deception to assume that the best indicator of quality is the "youthfulness" of scholarship and that it is possible for the "new" to exist in isolation from scholarship that precedes it. If we refuse to acknowledge the very conversational nature of academic work, then we sever the call from the response, and our ability to make sense of what we read becomes increasingly detached, distorted, and disembodied—an active and artificial choice to "forget" that all new scholarship is a response to the call(s) of our ancestors.

Ted speaks *to me* about the educational tensions in *today's* classrooms. He helps me to interpret the work of others who have taken up, responded to, and engaged with his ideas. Ted shows us that the act of teaching can occur very effectively in the physical absence of a teacher. Of course, this teacher is a remarkable one. Even though I've never met him and will never sit in on one of his classes, his impact on my life and my view of the pedagogical spaces I inhabit has been life changing.

It seems appropriate to return now to the beginning, to the "heart rushing" crush I have on Ted Aoki. The word *crush* is a variant of the French word *croissir* (to gnash or break teeth), is figuratively associated with humiliating, and is also associated with *infatuation*. How could a word associated with being broken and demoralized ever be appropriate when talking about the experience of love?

And Yet . . .

Wilde (2010) reminds us "feelings of anger and despair at the state of things is perhaps a necessary part of our collective awakening" (para. 34). Coming face-to-face with the ways in which our schools (and world) have been and continue to be "broken" is painful. But Wilde goes on to suggest that "such awakening must not end here: One must transform one's own suffering so that it does not contribute to increased suffering in the world" (para. 34). So the experience of crushing on or being crushed by Ted Aoki has been bittersweet. He has demanded that I see and listen to the ways in which our educational and human worlds are sites of tension, breakdown, and suffering. And yet his view of these fractured or tension-filled worlds is to see them as sites of compassion, hope, and possibility.

Perhaps the sweetest part of my crush is that it has presented me with an opportunity, as a student, teacher, and human being in our world, to be put back together. Ted himself implores me to remember "the experience of breaking can help us in breaking out of the seductive hold of an orientation to which we are beholden" (Aoki, 1992, p. 20). I move forward in my work *with* him, able to see/hear the tenuous ties that bind *all of us,* and aware of the importance of keeping these ties intact so that we can live well together in *our* world, live better than we are living right now.

References

Aoki, T.T. (1986/2005). Teaching as indwelling between two curriculum worlds. In W.F. Pinar & R.L. Irwin (Eds.), *Curriculum in a new key: The collected works of Ted Aoki* (pp. 159–166). Mahwah, NJ: Lawrence Erlbaum.

Aoki, T.T. (1991/2005). Taiko drums and sushi, perogies and sauerkraut: Mirroring a half-life in multicultural education. In W.F. Pinar & R.L. Irwin (Eds.), *Curriculum in a new key: The collected works of Ted T. Aoki* (pp. 377–388). Mahwah, NJ: Lawrence Erlbaum.

Aoki, T.T. (1992). Layered voices of teaching: The uncannily correct and the elusively true. In W.F. Pinar & W.M. Reynolds (Eds), *Understanding curriculum as phenomenological and deconstructed text* (pp. 17–27). New York, NY: Teachers College Press.

Aoki, T.T. (1999). In the midst of doubled imaginaries: The Pacific community as diversity and difference. *Interchange, 20*(1), 27–38.

Doll, W. (1993). Curriculum possibilities in a "post"-future. *Journal of Curriculum and Supervision, 8*(4), 277–292.

Grumet, M. (1989). Other people's children. In *Bitter milk: Women and teaching* (pp. 164–182). Amherst: University of Massachusetts Press.

Jardine. D. (2008). Foreword: The sickness of the West. In. C. Eppert & H. Wang (Eds.), *Cross- cultural studies in curriculum: Eastern thought, educational insights* (pp. ix–xv). New York, NY: Lawrence Erlbaum.

Jardine, D., Friesen, S., & Clifford, P. (2006). *Curriculum in abundance.* Mahwah, NJ: Lawrence Erlbaum.

Kliebard, H.M. (1970). Reappraisal: The Tyler rationale. *School Review, 73*(2), 259–272.

Loy, D. (1993). Indra's postmodern net. *Philosophy East and West, 43*(3), 481–510.

Pinar, W.F., & Irwin, R.L. (Eds.). (2005). *Curriculum in a new key: The collected works of Ted Aoki.* Mahwah, NJ: Lawrence Erlbaum.

Smith, D.G. (2008). "The farthest West is but the farthest East": The long way of Oriental/ occidental engagement. In C. Eppert & H. Wang (Eds.), *Cross-cultural studies in curriculum: Eastern thought, educational insights* (pp. 1–34). New York, NY: Lawrence Erlbaum.

Smith, D.G. (2009). Critical notice: Engaging Peter McLaren and the new Marxism in education. *Interchange, 40*(1), 93–117.

Wilde, S. (2010, February). In conversation with Eppert and Wang's *Cross-cultural studies in curriculum: Eastern thought, educational insights. Journal of the American Association for the Advancement of Curriculum Studies, 6.* Retrieved from http://www2.uwstout.edu/content/jaaacs/vol6/Wilde htm

4

AS NEITHER/BOTH TEDS

Theodore Reflects Upon Tetsuo

Ted Riecken

It's odd how particular comments or brief conversations can somehow secure a lasting hold in one's memory, while other exchanges are almost instantly forgotten. One such lasting exchange that I can clearly recall is a short conversation I had more than 20 years ago while a graduate student at the University of British Columbia (UBC). I was talking with Jim Sherrill, who was then associate dean of graduate programs. Dr. Sherrill had asked me about my program of study and what brought me to UBC to do my doctoral work. I told him about being a student in the Centre for the Study of Curriculum and Instruction, that I was taking courses from Walt Werner and that I had an interest in curriculum studies and program evaluation. Dr. Sherrill asked if I was familiar with the work of Ted Aoki. I replied that I had read some of Ted's work but had not met him. (At the time, Ted was at the University of Alberta.) Dr. Sherrill's response was something to the effect of, "So if you are studying with Walter Werner, then that sort of makes Ted Aoki your academic grandfather."

In that instant I had my academic lineage both ascribed and described, and it is an association that I have held to ever since. Now admittedly, it is an ascribed status that I have embraced without any sort of consent from Ted Aoki, given his own ascribed status as a kind of *pater familias* for curriculum theory. But then, that is how fandom seems to work. People acquire followers who identify with some aspect or another of their creative output, and those followers remain in that sphere of influence for as long as there is a resonance with their ideas and worldview. One can think of it as intertextuality personified. Influence on one's thinking grows subtly and is brought into life one experience at a time. Ideas ripple through time and across generations. In the case of education, ideas ricochet between conversations and classrooms, then into contemplation and practice, and back again into spoken and written discourse and the minds of students. It is intersubjectivity loping across the lifeworld, leaving its impact in subtle and unpredictable ways.

For me, over the course of nearly three decades, my resonance with Ted Aoki's ideas has continued in such a manner. Initially, as a doctoral student at UBC, then as a beginning assistant professor of social studies education at the University of Victoria, through midcareer as an associate and a full professor, and now, as a dean of education, Ted Aoki's ideas have continued to underpin not only my sense of what it means to be an educator but also my sense of how we can live in the world.

While a graduate student at UBC, I learned about Ted's tri-paradigmatic framework for curriculum evaluation. His reworking and applications of Habermas's ideas of knowledge and human interests to the field of curriculum theory provided me with an important pathway to understanding (Aoki, 1991/2005). His theorizing in this area helped me to make sense of what, to that point, had remained largely for me an intuited critique of schools and schooling. The nagging worry that had troubled me through a preservice teacher education program, and then into my initial years of teaching—that schooling was as much about an ideology of control as it was about real learning—was legitimized for me through Ted's writings. Add to that his concern for the primacy of lived experience as a way to understand teaching and learning, and I felt better equipped to make sense of my own initial (and disorienting) experiences as a beginning teacher.

For me, one of the most powerful distinctions Ted has illuminated is the difference between *curriculum-as-planned* and *curriculum-as-lived* (Aoki, 1986/1991/2005). Not only did this distinction equip me with an analytic construct that validated and explained my own initial teaching experiences, but also, as a beginning assistant professor, I was able to use this distinction to prepare preservice teachers for what they would encounter as they moved between the theory and practice of education. Ted's simple but powerful acknowledgment that plans are only plans, and that the complexities of life and human interaction are largely unpredictable but nonetheless impactful, was liberating for me.

I have long believed that within our teacher education programs, we too often reify planning as a key component of preparation for teaching. The educational liturgies of planning—lesson planning, term planning, unit planning, practicum planning, individual educational planning—all contribute to a kind of curriculum-planning idolatry. We school preservice teachers in what they ultimately discover to be an imperfect *techne* designed to instill a kind of pedagogical orthodoxy that yields a sense of security. We do so partly at our students' insistence, owing to their belief in the existence of a grail of failure-proof lesson structures. And yet, if we promulgate a liturgy of planning in the absence of any critical discourse about the limitations of technical and industrial models of education, we set neophytes up for shock and disappointment. For me, Ted Aoki's conception of curriculum-as-planned, and curriculum-as-lived, serves as such a critical counterpoint.

Another powerful idea of Ted's that has served me well over my career is the related notion of the "third space" (Aoki, 1996/2005, p. 318). His notion that we are sometimes required to live in a place of "betweeness" acknowledges that life is not lived in the spaces of either/or dichotomies. Rather, it is about the transitions from one place of being to another, with the transitional spaces in between being representing an enriching "overlappingness." The third space represents a fluid intermingling of different kinds of experiences. For me, it is not one place or the other but a fluid mixing of the possibilities inherent in both. It allows for the possibility of difference and change, with an acceptance that such spaces are often the way of life itself.

I recall Ted giving a talk to one of my social studies curriculum classes in which he used the notion of betweeness to illustrate what he saw as the hidden or missed potential of Canada's policies of multiculturalism. His point to the students was that we could learn even more about what it means to be Canadian by looking at the hyphenated spaces that we all occupy as Canadians from diverse ethnicities and cultures. There is a contradiction, he noted, in a multiculturalism policy that asks us all to self-identify as "hyphenated Canadians" of whatever background we might be, whether that be as Japanese Canadians, Chinese Canadians, German Canadians, Indo-Canadians, Polish Canadians, and so on. Ted's point was that highlighting our differences, and then asking us all to "go ahead and mix," is counterintuitive. He asked the students to consider how much more might we learn about what it means to be Canadian if we collectively looked at what was common to our shared experiences of the hyphenated spaces between our places of ancestral origin and our diverse experiences as Canadians. It was a perfect example of the insights that one can arrive at through entering some sort of third space. I thought it was a brilliant example.

I remember another presentation in which Ted's insightful and playful attention to language and its structure yielded a similarly powerful reframing of one of our many taken-for-granted assumptions. He was reflecting on the term we use to describe ourselves—"human beings"—and pointed out to the class that conjugating the verb "to be" yields an inaccurate descriptor of us as living entities. Using the chalkboard, he showed how conjugating the verb "to be" yields "I am," "You are," "She is," "He is," "We are," "They are." Ted noted that each of these linguistic states of being points to a fixed and static point in time, as distinct from something that is always shifting, growing, and changing. Ted said that a more accurate and appropriate description for us would be "human becomings." I read the smiles and nods that greeted his presentation as an indication that his thinking struck a chord among the students.

I continue to draw upon many of Ted's ideas in my role as dean of education at the University of Victoria. Educational leadership is a complex mix of many things, including big-picture and detailed strategic planning, building and maintaining relationships, and paying close attention to cultural values and mores. In a decanal role, decision making and the necessary consultations that must underlie those decisions are sometimes anything but simple or straightforward.

Ted Aoki's notions of the differences between "planned" and "lived" have proven as powerful for me as a dean as when I was teaching undergraduate preservice teachers. Just as the carefully wrought plans of student teachers face the complexities of the classroom, so too can the best made plans of educational administrators go awry. Ted's work tells us there is much that lies beyond our abilities to predict and control. His curriculum theorizing has shone a much-needed light into the dusty crevices of technical rationality. In that light, we see not only the limitations of our organizational thinking but also the richness of their human constituents, as well as the possibilities they offer for other ways of thinking and knowing.

In a similar way, Ted's notion of a third space has served me well in my role as dean. I interact with his idea of a third space as a kind of mental place for contemplation and sense making, on both a personal and professional level. In some ways, it represents that place of compromise where leaders are often required to be. It is a space for a coming together of ideas so as to integrate the best of different worlds and build solutions from diverse contributions. And as each of us enter such spaces, we do so not in search of stasis or certainty but rather with a momentum that is generated by difference itself and propelled by our own becomings. It is through my exposure to Ted's thought and insight that I am able to experience and think about the world in this way. His impact on me has been tremendous. Ted Aoki's ideas continue to resonate with me to this day, and I appreciate the opportunity to respectfully acknowledge his influence in this way.

References

Aoki, T.T. (1986/1991/2005). Teaching as in-dwelling between two curriculum worlds. In W.F. Pinar & R.L. Irwin (Eds.), *Curriculum in a new key: The collected works of Ted T. Aoki* (pp. 159–165). Mahwah, NJ: Lawrence Erlbaum.

Aoki, T.T. (1991/2005). Layered understandings of orientations in social studies program evaluation. In W.F. Pinar & R.L. Irwin (Eds.), *Curriculum in a new key: The collected works of Ted T. Aoki* (pp. 167–186). Mahwah, NJ: Lawrence Erlbaum.

Aoki, T.T. (1996/2005). Imaginaries of ' East" and "West": Slippery curricular signifiers in education. In W.F. Pinar & R.L. Irwin (Eds.), *Curriculum in a new key: The collected works of Ted T. Aoki* (pp. 313–319). Mahwah, NJ: Lawrence Erlbaum.

5

CURRICULUM COOL

Alison Pryer

A few years ago, Ted Aoki was awarded an honorary doctorate from the University of Western Ontario. The university also awarded a doctorate to Oscar Peterson around the same time. My first thought was, *How fitting!* My mind made a lazy connection between these two men, even though they are from different walks of life. As an educator, Ted was a technical virtuoso. He did more than hold the line of a melody; he was a master of improvisation. Each one of his pedagogical gestures was played simply and was always understated, but just one of his subtle shifts in key could change everything. When I was his student, Ted once said to me, "Your work is so hot. Try to make it more cool." Ted always played his curriculum theory cool—never, ever hot.

I clearly remember my first class with Ted. As every graduate student knows, each new course begins with a round of introductions. The teacher usually says, "Why don't we go around the class and each say something about ourselves, about who we are?" When I began a graduate course with Ted Aoki, he started the first class not by asking, "Who are you?" but rather, "What conditions make it possible for us to ask the question 'Who are you?'" It was one of those questions that Ted liked to ask in his laid-back, humble way.

This question fascinated me during the course and continued to haunt me long afterward when I began to explore my family's history as part of my doctoral research. My family's stories weave a complex dance around the colonial axes of English and Irish identity. There are the "British narratives" of propriety and gentility, middle-class status, and modest inherited wealth, which were much beloved, and oft repeated, by both my parents. And then there are "Irish narratives" of immigration and hardship, struggle, oppression, marginalization, and upward social mobility born out of prudence, cultural adaptation, and hard work. My mother and father, preferring to think of themselves as British, chose to disregard the Irishness. Yet, the Irish narratives that they tried to conceal from my sister and me simply would not fade away. They were revealed to us in throwaway snippets of conversation, in unguarded asides. in papers that were stashed away secretly for years, in tall tales spun after a drink or two, and in the muttering of one parent complaining about the other's damned Irish blood. My parents' marriage reflected the clash of two incommensurable cultures. Often seemingly contrary, their actions in everyday life were a vital embodiment of the struggles of their hybrid identities. Their conflictive belief systems were those of colonizer and colonized, citizen and immigrant, Roman Catholic and Protestant.

I discovered that Ted's opening question allowed for the possibility of an anti-essentialist view of my own identity: What conditions make it possible for us to ask the question "Who are you?" Revolutionary for me, it turned the concept of ethnicity "out of its anti-racist paradigm, where it connotes the immutable difference of minority experience, and into a term which addresses the historical positions, cultural conditions and political conjectures through which all identity is constructed" (Papastergiadis, 2000, p. 190). Rather than locating identity in those all-too-familiar, fixed binaries—the polarities of black and white, Jew and gentile, hetero- and homosexual, and so on—with Ted's question, identity may be conceived as an ongoing process of hybridity, in which one's sense of self is continuously made and remade. In such a paradigm, each person's particular, subjective understanding of their ethnic, cultural, gender, and class locations provides a narrative wellspring of stories of self, which flow into and constitute the vast delta of broader cultural narrative.

Introduced by Ted to the work of van Herk (1991), I was able to employ her notion of the doubleness of "overt" and "covert" stories—in particular, the doubleness of immigrant family narratives—when exploring my family's stories. In seeking the truths of my identity in the overt and covert stories of my family history, I came to recognize that our stories had been told and retold in ways that changed and reshaped the meanings of events. These repeated tellings thrust certain characters, themes, and family triumphs and sufferings to the fore while pushing others out of sight. Indeed, I discovered many broken places in these ancestral lifelines and wondered how they could ever be mended. My family story is not a narrative of love flowing gently and steadily from one generation to the next, although this is how I would like to tell the story and have it be known. It is more a story of interrupted love and unknown love, early death and tragic death, abandoned hope, and abandoned children: a succession of orphaned generations.

The word *orphan* has more than one meaning. According to my dictionary (Pearsall & Trumble, 1995), it can mean:

1. a child bereaved of a parent or usually both parents.
2. a person bereft of previous protection, advantages, etc.
3. the first line of a paragraph at the foot of a page or column. (p. 1026)

A *narrative* orphan is a story that is left hanging at the bottom of the page, a fragmented or erased story, one that is perhaps too horrible, shameful, or sad to tell, incommensurable with the public face of a family or the expectations of a community, nation, or church—a story with nowhere to go.

The limited dualistic polarities of my Anglo-Irish family history, the overt and covert narratives that struggled to hold themselves together despite incoherences and inconsistencies, could not contain one further dangerous chaotic element— that of Jewishness. In my family's narratives of binarized identity, this third ele- ment seemed untenable, dangerous even, and would have acted as an explosive counternarrative to the tales that had been carefully spun by my family members over generations. In continuing the intergenerational suppression of the narratives of our Jewish bloodlines, my family members chose not to know, did not seek to ask, and decided never to tell.

Ted also introduced our class to the work of Bhabha (1990), who reminds us that different forms of culture do not fit together well and do not easily coexist. I now understand that in order to construct a coherent, consistent, less chaotic sense of family identity in solidarity with the myths of nationhood and empire that constitute England, my family *had to* actively "disappear" in many narrative strands, rendering certain "untouchable" family members invisible.

The remaining traces and fragments of my orphaned family narratives pull me into the realm of the ambivalent, the imaginary, the speculative, and the desired, drawing attention to the fictional, chaotic, problematic qualities of my under- standings of self and hybrid identity. I am left with the dissatisfying understanding that my ancestors—their motives, actions, choices, thoughts, battles, and dreams— remain foreign to me, known only partially through incomplete glimpses and within silences. So how can I come to know these ancestors who seem such a vital part of my identity? In Ted's class, I came to see that in seeking to know my family, I must change my conception of what it is to know: Is knowing an act of seizing, fixing, defining, or pinning down? Or is knowing more of a gentle movement toward a stranger, a slow opening up toward that which is always necessarily foreign and unknowable?

My relationship toward my ancestors changes whenever I change, whenever I discover another snippet of family history about "how things were," thereby triggering a myriad of subjective memories, associations, and responses. This recognition permits an identity that is "a continual process of assemblage, of location, relocation and recollection, rather than as something fixed and self- evident" (Solie, 1998, p. 3). Clearly, the quest for the origin of the self, the longed- for immaculate, singular *I* is futile.

I have made some peace with my family's orphaned stories and now feel that perhaps they do not constitute a narrative failure. With Ted's help, I am now able to see these orphaned stories as mysterious catalysts that spark narrative energy through their very absence. I now see that a narrative friction, created by the clash of hybrid cultures, can be used to thrust future generations toward alternative possibilities for living and loving. "What conditions make it possible for us to ask the question 'Who are you?'" asked Ted. This one question allowed a process to unfold and afforded me the possibility of theoretical cross-pollination.

Many years passed, and I went on to teach students of my own. After teaching a week of classes in a course where we learned about and struggled with the legacy of the residential schooling of aboriginal students in British Columbia, one of my students, an articulate, accomplished white woman, raised her hand and told us all that her grandparents ran a residential school. Everyone in the room turned to look at her. A silent, but palpable, revulsion filled the air. My heart skipped a beat. The student wanted the class to know that her grandparents were not "bad people." She was struggling to form her feelings into words—her love for her grandparents, her knowledge of the cultural genocide of aboriginal peoples, the darkness of our colonial history, and how this history has shadowed our nation's (and her own) identity. Her confusion, her shame, and her determination to speak about her family history were all palpable. She said she wanted to be a good mother, a good educator, a good citizen. So what was she to do with her family history? I tried to hold a space for her, in the way that I am sure Ted would have done. Something was happening there between all of us . . . I held my breath, waited for her to articulate the unspeakable in this space of not knowing—a small, shared moment of terror. I allowed myself the Aokian pleasure of dwelling within pedagogical difficulty and impossibility and tried to keep my curriculum cool.

What followed was the beginning of a difficult, but careful and respectful, conversation among the members of our diverse classroom community about the legacies of colonization that have been passed down to the descendants of Canada's European colonizers. We talked about the tension between knowing and not knowing, about half knowing, dealing with shame and guilt in a way that could be productive, how to stay present when teasing out fragments of almost-forgotten or orphan narratives. We discussed how we might work consciously with these orphan narratives and how we might go about weaving them into the threads of our current personal and collective understandings in order to engage with them in meaningful ways—meaningful for ourselves, our families and communities, and the children and adults with whom we work in pedagogical contexts. The problem of coping with the narrative dissonance between competing histories, mythologies, family stories, and paradigms of knowledge arose and led to further conversation.

We did not seek answers. We seemed to be reaching more for understandings through the sometimes-tense back-and-forth of our conversation. As our hour and a half together drew to a close, the students began to shift in their seats, rustling papers as they packed up to move on to their next class. We all knew that something of importance had happened in class that day.

I have often heard bachelor of education students talk about the "real world." The real world for them is always something that happens elsewhere—on practicum, at home, or in their workplaces. The real word never happens in class. But that day, we all knew that something "real" had happened. Unknown to my students, I felt Ted's presence in the classroom accompanying me every step of that uneasy, but honest, pedagogical way.

References

Bhabha, H. (1990). The third space. In J. Rutherford (Ed.), *Identity: Community, culture, difference* (pp. 207–221). London, United Kingdom: Lawrence & Wishart.

Papastergiadis, N. (2000). *The turbulence of migration: Globalizing, deterritorialization, and hybridity*. Cambridge, United Kingdom: Polity.

Pearsall, J., & Trumble, B. (Eds.). (1995). *The Oxford English reference dictionary*. Oxford, United Kingdom: Oxford University Press.

Solie, K. (1998). *Wayne Arsenault and Nancy Duff: Between landscapes*. Victoria, British Columbia: Open Space Gallery.

van Herk, A. (1991). *In visible ink: Crypto-frictions*. Edmonton, Alberta: NeWest Press.

6

CALLING UPSTREAM/DREAM

Sheena Koops

Summer 2000: Remembering Lethbridge

I remember the road trip westward along the Trans-Canada Highway from Regina: wide-open lanes, fields of flax, and beehives; July heat. We theorized hope, chatted landscape, recorded dialogue, my professor, classmate, and I. The field trip flew, and I felt only a little guilt for missing my kissing cousin's wedding that weekend in Victoria, although I had little romance for our destination, the University of Lethbridge, home of my Alberta-raised redneck cousins. Yet, somehow I knew that this journey—an optional part of my first curriculum class at the University of Regina—was not optional.

We rode the elevator up to a carpeted room that spanned the length of the building, ceiling-high windows looking onto a desert canyon-like valley, horsetail clouds in a summer-blue sky, deer and coyotes on a winding path. Dr. Hurren led me to her sibling symposium presenters: Drs. David Jardine, Cynthia Chambers, Erika Hasebe-Ludt, David Smith, and Carl Leggo, who each welcomed my hand. Then my professor brought me to a small man, Dr. Ted Aoki. In his outstretched palm, a deep current pulsed. Throughout the weekend, I watched Aoki and those sitting at his feet. I harvested every gentle word. Dr. Aoki was no sibling. He was a teacher. He was the teaching.

Here began the awakening of my post-bachelor-of-education, post-6-years-in-the-classroom, post-disillusioned teacher's soul. That was 13 years ago, the summer of 2000. I finished my master of education in curriculum and instruction in 2006. In 2013, I am 21 years into the living waters of my curriculum, and once again I am undereducated, young, disillusioned.

Reading Dr. Hurren and Dr. Hasebe-Ludt's invitation to swim into Aokian *currere* was a calling home into a sweet dream, a sweet stream. There is a possibility that things are not as cut and dry as the Friday morning English tests on my desk, held in place by rocks collected along my path or fished from a current. (So often people ask, "What's with the rocks?" and I point to the window at my left. "Sometimes the wind blows." I want to tell them more, but it's never the right time . . .)

Fall 2010: Current Rocks and Poetry

I'm at home today in bed. The yellow and orange leaves of the Qu'Appelle Valley are in stages between the branches and the ground. It's raining again. I'm sick of my school. I'm sick of myself. My lack of confidence is like a smooth stone, like many smooth stones drowning in a swift current. Like the one from my childhood pasture found sparkling on a walk in the rain. (I lick my finger and wipe the stone. "Look," I tell a student, "it sparkles when it's wet.") I had to get off the tall horse to collect the rock brought back from the trail ride and climb way back into the saddle. Sometimes I give a fidgety student a rock, and I say, "Here, squeeze it. It helps." And what about those students who believe you shouldn't pick up stones from where they lie?

I'm a fool in my classroom, a fool among my colleagues. I look around my high-school English classroom and take inventory: 2 whiteboards; 1 chalkboard; 3 bulletin boards (no SMART Board); 2 tall windows; 14 octagon tables; 38 brown chairs (well, a few are black); 2 music stands; 3 acoustic guitars; 1 electric guitar; 2 bass guitars; 1 guitar stand for seven; 1 Cajon drum; 1 neck drum; 1 mixer; 2 amps; 2 stools; 1 electric organ; 1 piano; binders; books; dictionaries; posters of Canada Reads, the Globe Theatre, and First Nation Children in powwow regalia; Canada's flag; clock; teacher desk; computer desk; computer; 2 comfy chairs by my desk; 1 swivel chair; 1 computer cart with 36 mini computers; headset and speaker; 1 phone; 1 television and VCR/DVD player; 4 filing cabinets (2 beige and 2 black); 3 years' backlog of student portfolios and exams; shelves; drawers; cupboards; a costume tub; 2 pastels; and 2 charcoal pictures by my husband . . .

Visitors to my classroom will say, "Oh, you must teach music." During homeroom, breaks, and sometimes at lunch, crazy, unmelodic banging or electric rock screeches from my classroom; however, once in a while that student who has his Grade 8 piano will venture in and start playing, or a young man will pick quietly on the guitar, or my daughter in Grade 8, who just started lessons this year, pops in to play her latest song by heart. I even had a young man singing gospel this past fall, me practicing my harmony, another girl reading her Bible. (Both these kids' parents attend the Full Gospel Indian Bible School.) I nearly cried saying good-bye to a former student this past week as his family moved back to northern Manitoba. I gave him a copy of my novel and wrote in the front cover, "I will miss your smile, voice, and music."

He turned the book over, flipped through the pages. "Sheena Koops," he said, reading the spine. Then he looked up and smiled. "I didn't know you wrote a book."

I tell visitors, "No. I don't teach music."

This is the classroom-scape in which my students and I find one another. And here on my desk under a rock lies the invitation from Dr. Hurren and Dr. Hasebe-Ludt, my teachers who, in turn, are students of Professor Aoki.

I have phoned the University of Regina bookstore three times. Once they were closed. Once from a bus full of students, and the answering machine was full and nobody would pick up. Once home sick in bed, and no answer. How will I get *Curriculum in a New Key* (Pinar & Irwin, 2005)? I don't live in the city. It's too late to order from the Internet. I have been writing, playing with this *Festschrift,* but what if I'm off pitch, dissonant, too melancholy in my minor chords? Then I remember the controversial Google Books. And here he is: Aoki's heart through Pinar's eyes. I begin reading, and my throat tenses as though I've found a lost love letter.

I found Pinar found Aoki found Poem

Competent Teacher

on one side management, planning, discipline

the far side playing a new key
or is it ancient
competere,
com means *together*
petere to seek
competence
to seek together
Aoki
holds promise
of what it means
reimagined the world of school

every day to go beyond
technique on one side
praxis on the other

Tensionality

employee of an institution
fiction of sameness
trust her to do what she must do as their teacher
to lead them into possibilities, to educate them

between two horizons
third space in-between
the aliveness of school life
uniqueness of every teaching situation
such sensitivity requires humility
      curriculum builders, beware sick buildings
      shrill claims to know what teaching is
      reduced to doing

truly good teacher of yours is the measure of the immeasurable
he is the teaching
she is the teaching

lingering Episteme and Sophia
growing from the middle of their conversation
Oh Miss O
I can see the twinkle in his eye

conversation in our reaching
never fully reach

to teach
jump up and down
in the AND
more ANDs tumble out
between the child
between the teacher
between the curriculum
it will have to be a language of humility
of humour AND human AND humus
AND humility

does not come easy
to someone flowing within the mainstream
more readily
to one at the margin

Winter 2011: Hyphens, Hallways, Breaks, and Bridges

It's Sunday night, and my husband has spent much of the afternoon marking
Grade 8 and 9 math and social studies exams in the pulsing, colored glow of

Batman cartoons. Earlier in the evening he'd said, "I suck as a teacher." Now he comes into the bedroom where I type and says, "I didn't get near what I wanted accomplished." This from the man who has inspired his Grade 8s in our community high school to formal debates: Be it resolved that school attendance should be voluntary; be it resolved that school is no longer a valid educational institution. Our exceptional teacher librarian, a former debate champion herself, has been equipping the students with resources and fresh angles. For heaven's sake, he invited the mayor to be one of the judges, and the mayor is coming. If my husband doesn't see himself as a competent teacher, who would?

AND this is just what I struggle with: competence. I walk through our school's hallways and spy my colleagues breathing their classrooms to life. I see fellow teachers look into my classroom and my own alliterated list the length of my culpable conscious unscrolls of messy management, poor planning, and lame lessons. But then at the break, Kelsey flies into my room and calls, "You owe me."

And I say, "I know, I know." Another student is playing "Chopsticks" on the piano and another is noodling on the electric guitar. I grab my copy of *A Book of Good Poems* and flip pages to the poem I've dog-eared for Kelsey.

She says, "Do you have a sticky note?"

I say, "Top drawer."

She opens her copy of *A Book of Good Poems*—which her father left her in his will—and sticky-notes the poem. Ever since she brought the book to school last fall, a few weeks after the funeral, we've been giving each other poems. We're supposed to take turns, but sometimes one of us stalls for a day or two, and then the other nags.

Kelsey reads the poem, we discuss back and forth, and then she says, "Well, I better get going." She pauses at the doorway. "I love you, Mrs. Koops."

"Love you, too." I collapse into my rolly chair, piano banging, guitar whining, and my competency is off the courtroom floor, at least for the moment.

Easter 2011: Last Spring

After school on the last day before the Easter holidays, a fight with my husband spills into the parking lot of the Esso station. My daughters are crying, I am yelling, and my husband leaves on foot. My oldest daughter takes the keys and drives us home so that I can get my bags for my trip to Hong Kong, the flight leaving Regina that evening. I sob to my mother on the phone, "How can I go to Hong Kong now?" My sister takes my girls and me for supper, a movie, and then to the airport. She assures me everything is okay, reminding me of other fights on the last day of school, before summer and Christmas holidays. (Lucky us, my sister is a social worker.)

A cool shadow follows me across the ocean for my 8-day reunion with Hong Kong friends, celebrating 25 years since our graduation (back in Saskatchewan). We hike and tour and eat and play table tennis. I even begin writing an article for *Fine Lifestyles Regina* and *Fine Lifestyles Saskatoon* with the lead, "Every world traveller should be able to say, 'When I was in Hong Kong.'" But I leave out the part that, when I was in Hong Kong, my heart was broken. My Hong Kong girlfriends hear confession from wife, mother, and teacher as we eat sushi and drink Japanese coffee.

On the last leg home (after 13 hours to Vancouver), I start visiting with the man in the aisle seat. We quickly find shared ground; I'd taught on a First Nations reserve for 5 years; he's Lakota, so he knows about Standing Buffalo First Nation (where many of my current students come from). He is a professor; I am a teacher. He is a writer, and so am I. He tells me about his surprise when he started working at the university that professors had so little understanding of pedagogy. I tell him about research we did while living and teaching on a Dene First Nations reserve and how the community informed us that there were two categories for skills such as beading or starting a fire: *do you know* and *can you teach*. He thinks this is insightful. We discuss youth at risk, and I spout, "It doesn't really matter what I buy into. If I don't have relationships with the kids, nothing matters."

He says, "That's exactly right. We advocate relationships" (M. Brokenleg, personal communication, April 24, 2011).

He is Martin Brokenleg, world-famous educator, psychologist, lecturer . . . We visit some more and then I let Mr. Brokenleg have some time with the conference notes he is preparing. I pull out my travel journal and write. I hear echoes of our visit, and I realize that I, too, am at risk, just like my students. And the answer is in relationship. This is how I will go back to my husband, even as I remember that my husband was one of these youths at risk, from a single-mother home, my uncle his father figure, my kissing cousins his brothers.

As the plane descends onto my prairie, I say to Mr. Brokenleg, "You are the perfect ending to my trip. When I left for Hong Kong I was broken, but with the adventures and tests of my travels, and this visit with you, I remember who I am and what I believe."

He smiles.

I continue, "And your name . . . it's broken . . . that means so much to me."

"We're all broken people," he says (M. Brokenleg, personal communication, April 24, 2011).

So I go back to my family, school, and community, mended with Brokenleg's golden words, stronger, yet fragile enough.

Summer 2012

And sure enough, I'm cracking again, but here comes Aoki, paddling upriver, calling his old song in a forever-new key. And I can't help smiling, knowing this lingering note started in Lethbridge, the last place on earth I thought I'd find poetry or healing or beauty; and listen, Aoki is still current, even as he once flowed deeply through the Lethbridge badlands, humbling and freeing me to sing along the river in my own Qu'Appelle Valley, listening for the legendary calling, in Cree, *Katapaweo;* in French, *Qu'Appelle;* in English, "Who calls?" And now as I fall asleep, I hear coyotes howling in the hills, my brokenness glinting along this stream, this dream in the moonlight

References

Pinar, W.F., & Irwin, R.L. (Eds.). (2005). *Curriculum in a new key: The collected works of Ted T. Aoki.* Mahwah, NJ: Lawrence Erlbaum.

7

WAITING FOR MY SON'S CALL

Invitation to Contemplate Possible/ Impossible

Lynn Fels

> To be awake is to be alive. . . . We must learn to reawaken and keep our-
> selves awake, not by mechanical aids, but by an infinite expectation of the
> dawn, which does not forsake us in our soundest sleep.
> —Henry David Thoreau, as cited in Maxine Greene,
> *Landscapes of Learning*

In a basket of saved letters, I retrieved the sole personal letter that Dr. Ted Aoki wrote to me, on December 28, 2001: a single page, handwritten, enclosed with a xeroxed copy of an interview,[1] with permission to republish it in a special issue of *Educational Insights* (Wiebe, 2003).[2] His handwriting was like an old friend's conversation; I recognized his voice in the familiar loops of blue ink. His letter reminded me of another time, when professors had office hours and the faculty club was a place for lingering conversations. His gracious wisdom is embodied in the letter that I now hold in my hands. A memory tugs at my sleeve . . .

"Lynn, you talk a lot about possibility," Dr. Aoki notes, "but what about impossibility?"

I laugh. This is why I had wanted him at my doctoral defense, to offer the unexpected. I stall for time.

"I've spent all these years thinking about possibility," I tell him. "It's impossible to contemplate impossibility." But it seems that now I must.

Procrastination is like a lover who overstays his welcome, neither of us willing to untangle ourselves from the sheets to display our nakedness in awkward re-treat to the bathroom. We no longer belong to each other. Instead of rising and attending to my work, I read the newspaper, column by column, pages strewn about the bed. The traffic outside my window signals a morning unraveling.

I am sidestepping time. My life, this emergent curriculum of lived experience that dances me from one obligation to the next, is one long to-do list. A common complaint. And who has not entertained fantasies of escape? Funny, really, as a curriculum scholar, to have ranted against *curriculum-as-planned,* only to now resent *curriculum-as-lived* (Aoki, 1986/1991/2005), in search of—?

When did I become so stuck?

Something is missing that needs attention . . .

Reading through Dr. Aoki's letter, I wonder, should I revisit his question? Contemplate impossibility? Why is it so impossible to engage in my work? What (or whom) am I avoiding? Why do I lie in bed, reading the newspaper, morning after morning, reluctant to get up, waiting for my son's call? I recognize that I am stopped: "Between closing and beginning lives a gap, a caesura, a discontinuity. The betweenness is a hinge that belongs to neither one nor the other. It is neither poised nor unpoised, yet moves both ways. . . . It is the stop" (Appelbaum, 1995, pp. 15–16).

A stop, a moment of risk, a moment of opportunity, occurs when we come to witness or experience an event, an encounter, an action, a relationship that calls us to attention, illuminating those habits of engagement that cause unease, moments that leave us wondering. Who am I?

Within this stop of recognized procrastination, I note two things:

> *Resistance is what matters.*
> *I am waiting for my son's call.*

Some mornings—I never know which one or at what time, although the weather is often a clue—my son yells up the stairs, "Mom, what are your plans today?" and I know he is asking if I am free. At the sound of his voice, I am propelled out of bed, in a flurry of clothes gathered, feet shoved into running shoes, clearing of windshield from winter rains, doors locked, turn of the key, and now, wide-awake, I execute a 180—the car, a 1989 Toyota Corolla—and we are off to his workplace downtown in a litany of maternal exhaust: *Put on your seatbelt, you should take the bus, get up earlier, be responsible, don't tell me how to drive! Are you okay?* He slouches beside me, morning stubble on his chin, *I don't want to talk about it.*

He listens impatiently as I launch into one of my stories—complaining about an overdue article, a dysfunctional relationship, or sharing of experience lived so as to impart a moral or teaching, a telling of what to do, or not—as we weave our way through traffic.

"You're taking too long to tell your story," he complains. "Turn left, here. Not right! Left! I just need the synopsis."

"But I have to give you the context—" I lean on the horn.

"Mom, your stories are like a long-term investment: Listeners have to stay in for the long haul and hope they get a decent return."

"Funny guy. Here's your stop. Hey! Stop! You forgot your lunch!"

He taps on the window of the car door—a signal of *thanks, sorry I slammed the door, see you,* or maybe, *I love you,* and my heart stops. When did he begin doing that? This unexpected gesture that had always been my signal to the driver—friend, colleague, lover—who has given me a ride home as he or she prepares to drive off: a Morse code tap on the car window meaning *drive carefully, thank you, thanks for being my friend, I love . . . you.*

Could gestures be genetic?

He disappears behind reflective glass doors, and I face a 20-minute drive home that, like my stories, extends another 30, as I linger over a latte at my local café. Delaying tactics, I know. Why am I avoiding my work—in this case, this chapter, which is refusing to allow itself to be written? What am I missing?

In the interview Dr. Aoki sent me, he writes that in our enthusiasm for metaphor, we have forgotten to pay attention to the "pedagogy of metonymic moments" that calls us to attend to our own tensions of engagement. To call our attention to such moments, Aoki places a rhetorical device—the slash (/)—between words, things, relationships, concepts such as *planned/unplanned, curriculum/instruction,* or *student/teacher* and invites us to dwell in the space between, "a tensioned space of ambiguity, ambivalence, and uncertainty but simultaneously a vibrant site" ("Interview With Ted," 1999, p. 181). The site of the slash, says Aoki, "looks like a simple oppositional binary space, but it is not. It is a space of doubling, where we slip into the language of both this and that, but neither this nor that" (p. 181). Aoki's slash is an invitation to dwell in the generative space between words, actions, encounters juxtaposed. Possible/impossible.

In the conceptualization and articulation of performative inquiry, I inserted Aoki's slashes in the word *per/form/ance* to signal how the words inform and perform one other. It is a clever etymological trick that places us in the playground of complexity theorists and grants me license to speak to performative inquiry as an action site of research and learning (Fels, 1999; Fels, 2011; Fels & Stothers, 1996). Similarly, metonymic moments call us to attention, like a child's tug on the sleeve, offering an opportunity for inquiry and learning. Aoki reminds educators,

> It is in this space of between that our teachers, sensitive to both curriculum-as-planned and curriculum-as-lived, dwell, likely finding it a tensioned space of ambiguity, ambivalence, and uncertainty but simultaneously a vibrant site. . . . Confusing? Yes. Confusingly complex? Yes. But it is nevertheless a site that beckons pedagogic struggle, for such a human site promises generative possibilities and hope. It is, indeed, a site of becoming, where newness can come into being. (Interview With Ted Aoki, 1999, p. 181)

How could I have forgotten Ted Aoki's invitation to attend to the slash as it plays through and within my life? Aoki's pedagogy of metonymic moments—attending to the spaces in between—speaks of a living inquiry: a way of being in research that attends with mindful awareness to place, time, language, and self/other.[3] I need to dwell in contemplation in the space(s) between lying in bed with the newspaper/ sitting down to my computer. I must (re)turn my attention to the slash between possible/impossible. What will move me from the dis-ease of procrastination to active engagement in my work? What catalyst calls me to action? What was it I wrote earlier?

> *Resistance matters.*
> *I am waiting for my son's call.*

This is a metonymic moment—a pedagogical inquiry within which dwells possible understanding and renewal.

To contemplate a slash between what is desired and what is lived, what is planned and what is unplanned, requires that I willingly dwell within an uncomfortable site of ambiguity, ambivalence, and uncertainty—embracing that which invites disruption from my state of procrastination, a son's call, to engage in a vibrant if troubling site of performing absence/presence.

I am waiting for my son's call, his invitation to engage. He calls me into presence. This moment of recognition matters. Natality, as imagined by philosopher Arendt (1958), invites us to come to thoughtful awareness and action in the presence of others, to engage anew in mindful ways, to release others and ourselves from expectation, to reimagine *who we may become in each other's presence*. To come to a moment of recognition and be startled awake. Natality offers a reconsideration of the impossibility/possibility of belonging that is humankind, an opportunity to reclaim what has been lost, to contemplate what is, to reimagine ourselves anew, to breathe deeply within the moments that stop us. As philosopher Gordon (2001) writes,

> Natality stands for those moments in our lives when we take responsibility for ourselves in relation to others. In this way, natality initiates an active relation to the world. It signifies those moments in our lives (and there are many) in which we attempt to answer the question that Arendt argues is at the basis of all action and that is posed to every newcomer to the world: "Who are you?" (p. 21)

Aoki's metonymic moments may be thus understood as performative and pedagogical action/sites of natality—requiring our mindful engagement, a calling for respect, compassion, reciprocity. Embraced within the action site of natality is vulnerability, belonging, compassion, responsibility, imagination. Yet here, too, within metonymic moments of encounter, are possible complicity and betrayal.

And it is at this moment that I stop and pull my thesis from the bookshelf that stands behind my computer. I have just recalled another moment in my doctoral defense in which Dr. Aoki questioned me about my understanding of the Japanese scholar Yuasa's concept of *shinshin,* or bodymind oneness.

I explain, "Yuasa translates the Japanese *shinshin* as bodymind, with 'body' preceding 'mind,' in order to avoid the dualism implied in the hyphenated 'mind-body'" (Fels & Stothers, 1996, pp. 258–259).

Ah, but shinshin also embraces the heart. Dr. Aoki gently calls my attention to the absence of heart in my interpretation. His wife, June, a generous artist, paints the Japanese characters of shinshin for me, a doubled gift that I insert into my doctoral thesis (Fels, 1999, p. 45) and frame for my office. How could I have forgotten? So many years ago, Dr. Aoki called me to the absence of heart in my understanding of bodymind oneness, and here, now, in this moment of writing, I am reminded again: "It is only with the heart that one can see rightly; what is essential is invisible to the eye" (de Saint-Exupéry, 1982, p. 70).

Greene (1978) advises that we must be wide-awake if we are to attend to the moral responsibilities that are the challenges that scholars and educators encounter in their work, within those moments that trouble us. In the absence of heart and wide-awakeness, our work fails to engage us. We become weary. We become complicit. Or we may withdraw. Procrastination.

This awakening to the generative space of learning is the impossibility/possibility between; it is Aoki's pedagogy of metonymic moments, inviting us to dwell in ambiguity, ambivalence, and uncertainty, recognizing a vibrant action site of learning and inquiry. And thus, we (re)turn again and again to love of our work, our lives, ourselves, in our relationships with each other. This is the lesson of my son's call.

> *We dwell in the presence/absence of each other*
> *within the possibility/impossibility of love,*
> *and in our actions of how we choose to do so,*
> *we become who we are.*

If we sleepwalk through our lives, our work, our relationships with each other, we become lost. Our wide-awakeness is engaged through dwelling within Aoki's pedagogy of metonymic moments; reflectively dwelling in metonymic moments of possible/impossible calls us from the brink of losing ourselves, shakes us by the shoulders, and says, *Be present to this moment, here, now.*

And this wide-awakeness to what matters is Ted Aoki's gift to me, his invitation to contemplate the impossible, not as one half of a dichotomy but to dwell within the space of the slash, coupled with the offering of June Aoki's gift of art. Ted understood I would need to attend to the space in between, and be alert to the absence of heart, if I was to come to renewed understanding.

I am waiting for my son's call.

In my act of driving him to work, we reach out to each other, he listens to the stories I tell, so that I might become present in the telling and he in the listening. And he tells his own stories, between the silences, driving critiques, and Morse code of his tapping on my car window, and I listen in return. Our narratives and presence together interweave a delicate text of tenderness and belonging. This too is the possibility/impossibility of scholarship, the research of the bodymindheart that is our inquiry. His call wakes me up. The intersection of procrastination and a tap at a car window awakens me.

As a scholar, I had lost my way. In returning to my work, I am reminded of what matters: As Aoki reminded me, as scholars and educators, we are invited to dwell in the spaces of "ambiguity, ambivalence, and uncertainty" and must learn to recognize such spaces as they are, as vibrant action sites of possibility/impossibility. Listening for my son's call, calling me again and again into presence, into action, awakened me to the cause of my procrastination, revealing an absence of heart, a hunger for belonging—a desire for reciprocal engagement that breathes love into being, as we become present in the presence/absence of each other.

Through this writing, I navigate my way to heart; so that now, leaping out of bed first thing in the morning—so that I might attend to my work, with love, with renewal, with hope—is no longer impossible but a matter of pedagogical desire, in the dawning of my awakening.

"Hey, Mom! What are your plans today?"

References

Aoki, T.T. (1986/1991/2005). Teaching as indwelling between two curriculum worlds. In W.F. Pinar & R.L. Irwin (Eds.), *Curriculum in a new key: The collected works of Ted Aoki* (pp. 159–166). Mahwah, NJ: Lawrence Erlbaum.

Appelbaum, D. (1995). *The stop.* Albany: State University of New York Press.

Arendt, H. (1958). *The human condition.* Chicago, IL: University of Chicago Press.

de Saint-Exupéry, A. (1982). *The little prince* (K. Woods, Trans.). New York, NY: Harcourt Brace Jovanovich.

Fels, L. (1999). *In the wind clothes dance on a line. Performative inquiry—a (re)search methodology* (Doctoral dissertation, University of British Columbia). Retrieved from https://circle.ubc.ca/handle/2429/9839

Fels, L. (2011). A dead man's sweater: Performative inquiry embodied and recognized. In S. Schonmann (Ed.), *Key concepts in theatre drama education* (pp. 339–343). Netherlands: Sense.

Fels, L., & Stothers, L. (1996). Academic performance: Between theory and praxis. In J. O'Toole & K. Donelan (Eds.), *Drama, culture and education* (pp. 255–261). Brisbane, Australia: IDEAS.

Gordon, M. (2001). Hannah Arendt on authority: Conservatism in education reconsidered. In M. Gordon (Ed.), *Hannah Arendt and education: Renewing our common world* (pp. 11–36). Boulder, CO: Westview Press.

Greene, M. (1978). *Landscapes of learning*. New York, NY: Teachers College Press.
Interview with Ted Aoki: Rethinking curriculum and pedagogy. (1999). *Kappa Delta Pi Record, 34*(4), 180–181.
Meyer, K. (2006). Living inquiry—a gateless gate and a beach. In W. Ashton & D. Denton (Eds.), *Spirituality, ethnography, and teaching: Stories from within* (pp. 156–166). New York, NY: Peter Lang.
Wiebe, S. (Ed.). (2003). E-voking curriculum [Special issue]. *Educational Insights, 8*(2). Retrieved from http://www.ccfi.educ.ubc.ca/publication/insights/v08n02/intro/welcome.html

Notes

1. The interview was published in the summer 1999 issue of *Kapa Delta Pi Record*.
2. This special issue of *Educational Insights* celebrated the work of Dr. Aoki and those inspired by his scholarship (Wiebe, 2003).
3. Living inquiry is conceptualized and practiced by Meyer (2006), who has been a mentor in my own understanding of learning and teaching as a practice of care and compassion, reciprocity and vulnerability. Living inquiry, like performative inquiry, requires that, as scholars, educators, human beings, we attend to the events, encounters, environments, and relationships experienced in our lives. Through the practice of polished field notes of reflective writing, we may come to new meaning-making and understanding.

8

APPRENTICING WITH TED

Leah C. Fowler

When contemplating curriculum theory and studies as a Canadian professor in education, two specific moments in my educational experience still remain with me as profoundly significant: meeting Ted Tetsuo Aoki and meeting William F. Pinar. These two people and their work continue to influence my thinking, my theorizing, my pedagogy, and my being in education. This writing focuses on my experience of learning with Professor Aoki because I met him first, and he was my introduction into the field of curriculum studies. My educational apprenticeships with him, first in 1985 and then again in 1994, served as a kind of DNA substrate for my still-abiding life in curriculum theory.

It was 1985 in Edmonton, Alberta, that I first met Ted Aoki. He was the professor for a summer course in curriculum studies for master's students. The first thing I heard in his course started even before he arrived: A koto and flute were playing a Japanese folksong as I entered the classroom that first day. It was a sound different than any I had heard before in my life and signaled a new key of listening and paying attention.

That curriculum studies course must have been only three weeks, but in terms of my intellectual development, it was more like three centuries. Until that summer, my understanding of curriculum included only the program of studies. Before studying with Ted Aoki, I had not heard the words *intercultural, multiplicities, interpretation, metanarrative, Cartesian binary, intertextuality, horizontality, verticality, reconceptualism,* or *currere.* I was in a state of not yet, unaware of what it meant to "experience theoretically." I had not yet learned to call concepts of educational experience into question, nor had I considered the relations between voice and understanding or that there may be fertile space and ground that can arise between *I* and *Not-I.* Reflection-in-action started to make its way to the foreground of my potential praxis.

Ted Aoki asked me to consider the idea that to be *thought-full* as a scholar, it was important to know that problems are not the same as questions. It was important for me to see, as a science scholar and educator, that in focusing on problem solving, I was attached to using a method. I re/searched the notion that the approach to much of the science I was trained in was abstractive, calculative, and exacting and that the goal in science is closure, not opening. Answers to problems concern *what* we do, not *who* or *how* are we in the world. Problems concern objects that can be held in view and set off from ourselves and *dealt with*. We pose or posit problems from positions of grasp and control, which do not allow the unexpected, the new, the generative qualities that foster beneficial change.

In contrast, the inquiry or questioning approach pertains to the way we *are* in the world. Inquiry has to do with us as nonobjects and eludes our grasp. One thinks upon, and seeks, deeper contexts of understanding. Authentic inquiry is about opening up, about dis/closure. There are no goals beyond ongoing and open-ended venture of self-understanding and self-appropriation, and opening and closing go together. An inquiry concerns questions about who we *are*, as humans. It is our having, doing, thinking, being together that are at issue. In questioning, there is a being in transformation. This works against the Cartesian binary of "I think/I am" that separates subject and object.

Before meeting Ted Aoki, I had not been provoked to ask, *Who am I to teach?* or, *Whose interests might be served in having separate and boundaried knowledge?* I had not considered the experience of being in the midst of (rhizomatic) interests. I did not think yet about the tension, grief, and possibility between *curriculum-as-planned* and *curriculum-as-lived* (Aoki, 1986/1991/2005). I had not wrestled with contemplating how our (per/sonal) commitments can complement our curriculum and pedagogy or how we might cultivate thoughtful, deliberate relationships in teaching, as in life.

In 1985, I had just begun to experiment with the idea that there may be no need for hostility amid difference. I had begun to see that all of us have narrative "mattering" within a larger, cultural, and contextual metanarrative. But before that first summer with Ted, I was not yet conscious about who gets to decide what stories do and do not count. I still did not know that we craft selves within processes of work and matrices of "authority" and identity, multiple and fraught with tension and power. Still, I remained asleep to the fact that there is always a relentless shuttle between centers and margins. I could not have articulated the capacity and effect of the degree to which hegemonic curricula colonize.

However, during that first three-week-long encounter with Ted and our dialogue journals, he replied to my inchoate musings in his precise script with kind but provocative questions, noticings, insights, and comments. It was the first time I did group projects in my educational experience. (Hitherto, I was the solitary scholar in science and English literature doing experiments, readings, and papers. In the traditions I experienced before Aoki, working with others was called cheating: We kept our "knowledge," "facts," "information" to ourselves to be strategically revealed when called upon by "someone in power.") Instead, his teachings helped me change my pronouns from *I* to *We*, pre/positions from *to, against,* and *at* toward the educational relationship of *with*. Examinations of epistemology and deep relations with language and the internal grammar of my consciousness produced tectonic shifts of a personal and public reformation.

Ted seemed to alter the pace of ordinary life and slow down the class, with tea and time to linger in conversation about essential matters. In studying with him (and it was *with* him, as he brought his own real questions and inquiry into the midst of the discussions we were having), he skillfully led us into questions about the nature and purposes of postmodernism—to rewrite cultural geographies. He spoke mysteriously about how, living ungrammatically, we write the world and about how metaphors of geography shape us.

He used a postcolonial perspective to force us to rethink the limitations of liberalism. He spoke about cultural and political identity construction that occurred/occurs through a process of *othering*. In short, he started serious Kuhnian revolutions in my consciousness and actions.

Ted also invited us into more of these conversations by including us in something called a "curriculum studies conference" related to what we had been studying. He seemed excited that some of the people he introduced us to in the readings were coming to speak and talk together. Apparently, some famous somebodies were to be there: curriculum theorist William F. Pinar and educational philosopher Maxine Greene from New York! A buzz of expectation and interest began to develop. (Did I also imagine Madeleine Grumet was there too? If not present in person, certainly she was present in text.) We did go to the conference like grown-up scholars—class time given for sessions, we apprenticed and participated by hearing good scholars think out loud and talk with each other in front of us. The result of being part of this summer course and conference launched me on a path that changed my life. Until then, I was always torn between sciences and literature and composition, but this conference opened up larger frames of thinking and research that were inclusive of all knowledge that may arise. It felt like a family reunion where Outsider-I finally found an intellectual living room that welcomed me home.

In preparation for these *complicated conversations* (Pinar, 2004), Ted Aoki handed us selected intertextual readings by very few names, but what names! Pinar, Huebner, Greene, Grumet, and Noddings along with other new-to-me thinkers like Schleiermacher, Schön, Husserl, Heidegger, Derrida, and Kierkegaard appeared for the first time in my notebooks. I felt myself begin to wake up in my thinking, my personal study, and in the quality of my internal dialogue and seeing. My own *Being and Time* changed (Heidegger, 1962). This new intellectual work cured a particular set of grief bundles I had been carrying and tumbled me out of the classroom or conference sessions every day, into sunlight and joy. The experience was literally enlightening and exhilarating. I felt so alive, engaged, committed to seeing what was possible and what generative contributions I might be able to make with others in this complicated world.

The second meeting in 1994 with Professor Aoki, during my doctoral studies at the University of Victoria, was equally significant. This second "course" occurred over a term with four face-to-face (whole-afternoon) conversations with him in his Vancouver home. A dialectic apprenticeship was set up again through dialogue journals and reflective papers in between, focused on hermeneutics readings recommended by Ted and particularly the *radical hermeneutics* of Caputo (1987). For many reasons, 1994 was a difficult time in my life, yet with Ted, I began to understand the potential of theory to heal and restore and provide a deep well from which to draw insight, new interpretive understanding, and courage. This encounter was where I stumbled into fearful places of the abyss, the deconstruction of core beliefs and assumptions, disrupting dogma, habitual thinking, and taking things for granted. I began to call everything into question. In this radical hermeneutics apprenticeship with Ted, I developed a courage and honesty and humility that still keeps me open to the mystery of being alive with other mortals, amid profound difficulty and challenge, when we no longer know what to do and/or have answers to crucial questions. I learned more tolerance for ambiguity, space, and uncertainty, learned gratitude for complexity and experiencing life with less judgment and more interest. In 1994, I developed inner tools so that I still do not look away from difficulty but stand with an abiding commitment to cultivating a steady hermeneutic gaze of a wider and more patient and discerning work of perception regarding the way things actually are. There is deep work in noticing as many voices and interpretations as possible, meaning that can be made and interrogated in the ground of the soul, along with other generative mortals in this difficult and multi-narratived life.

After our last meeting in 1994, Ted took me to visit the Japanese garden on the University of British Columbia campus; we lingered in silence and ease, and we both seemed to experience peace that late afternoon. He deepened sentient awareness and introduced phenomenology into my frames of hermeneutics. Again he invited me to conferences and symposia during summer sessions. I met Dwayne Heubner and studied some of his work that appeared later in the *The Lure of the Transcendent* (Pinar & Hillis, 1999). Because of Ted, I met Bill Pinar again after reading more of his astounding papers and books. Until I met Ted and Bill, I had never, in my life of being *other,* felt at home, but again in 1994, this intellectual home and sense of theoretical family where I might belong was a remarkable encounter. I found new meaning and places to explore being, possibility, and experience. Ted welcomed me to narrative research and writing honestly and with careful cognitive and metacognitive tools about difficulty, about my life, and about my intellectual development as it pertained to teaching and learning.

These skills and ways of working from that apprenticehship continue to be a deep current in my work. I invite people in my own graduate and undergraduate classes to write, think, and call being into question regarding living well together in this new century.

Postscript:

In my Lethbridge, Alberta, meditation room at home, between my working and sleeping rooms, my grandmother's small cherrywood rocker rests next to a small Japanese lamp and woodblock print. It is the chair I sat in as a child long before my feet could touch the ground. It is the chair I sat in afterward on the night I was with my grandmother when she suffered her fatal surprise heart attack at age 88. It is the chair I sit in every morning with my green tea, and each evening for 15 minutes before mindfully setting down the day, sometimes with sweet grass, but always with silence and gratitude.

It is the chair I sit in when I sometimes listen to visiting teachers at risk who ask to talk with me about the broken curricula of their teaching lives. Their teaching theory and practice begins to stammer, so they come to hear their own voice outside of schools, out of administrative earshot. We look for new keys together in that room that was designed for dwelling in between waking and sleeping, working and resting, planning and forgetting, teaching and learning, thinking and acting.

Apprenticing with Ted has made all the difference.

References

Aoki, T. (1986/1991/2005). Teaching as in-dwelling between two curriculum worlds. In W.F. Pinar & R.L. Irwin (Eds.), *Curriculum in a new key: The collected works of Ted T. Aoki* (pp. 159–166). Mahwah, NJ: Lawrence Erlbaum.

Caputo, J. (1987). *Radical hermeneutics: Repetition, deconstruction, and the hermeneutic project.* Bloomington: Indiana University Press.

Heidegger, M. (1962). *Being and time* (J. Macquarrie & E. Robinson, Trans.). Oxford, United Kingdom: Blackwell Press.

Pinar, W. (2004). *What is curriculum theory?* Mahwah, NJ: Lawrence Erlbaum.

Pinar, W. F., & Hillis, V. (Eds.). (1999). *The lure of the transcendent: Collected essays by Dwayne E. Huebner.* Mahwah, NJ: Lawrence Erlbaum.

9

STORIED MEMORIES, COLONIAL EXPERIENCES, AND CURRICULAR IMAGININGS

Ingrid Johnston

In his work on teaching and curriculum, Aoki (1987/2005) emphasizes the significance of telling and reflecting on our personal stories of experience. We cannot understand our place in the world and our relationship to others without first acknowledging the significance of these narratives and the tensions and wonderings that they raise. As Aoki questions,

> What are the personal and communal stories that have been told, are being told, and will yet be told? Who are we that tell these stories, and what indeed do these stories tell? And, I add, what are the questions to which these stories are answers? . . . I present myself not so much to tell stories, but rather to participate in a questioning of the questions we typically ask when we, in and through our very living, tell our stories—stories that inevitably tell who we are and, as well, our understanding of how our world is. (p. 349)

For Aoki, as a Japanese Canadian, these stories intersect with disturbing experiences of discrimination and encounters with those who fear difference. Yet his narratives resonate with hope and optimism. "In my being and becoming," he writes, "the tensions that were there created a dynamic world within which I acted which has, after all is said and done, turned out to be my life as I have experienced it" (Aoki, 1979/2005, p. 348). Aoki's privileging of the personal in his reflections on life as a teacher, academic, and curriculum developer serve as an inspiration for the personal nature of my chapter in this book. As I reflect on my family experiences in Nazi Germany and my privileged life as a student and teacher in apartheid South Africa, I am mindful of the need to confront my involvement with discriminatory practices and the role that imaginative literature, media, and artefacts have played in bringing these into focus.

"You are not welcome here" is the tagline from *District 9,* a 2009 science-fictional movie about aliens in Johannesburg, South Africa, who are being forcibly evicted from their militarized ghetto (Blomkamp, 2009). The movie is an evocative reminder of an actual forcible evacuation of occupants of "District Six" in apartheid South Africa. Immortalized in Rive's (1985) fictionalized memoir *Buckingham Palace, District Six,* this vibrant, mixed-race community was razed in the mid-1960s under the government's notorious Group Areas Act that forced physical separation between races by creating separate residential areas. The "palace" in the title refers to a row of five run-down houses in District Six, which housed many of the area's distinctive characters that enliven the stories in the book with their humour and friendship. Stories, such as those told in Rive's book and in the film *District 9,* have the imaginative ability to evoke memories of a colonial past and to raise significant questions of identity, power relations, and subjectivity.

In my discussion here, I probe personal memories of life in postwar Germany and apartheid South Africa, considering ways in which these memories are represented and contextualized through narratives and artefacts, and how such representations might be significant for us as teachers when we engage students in reflections on their own positioning in the world.

Said (2000) suggests, "Memory and its representation touch very significantly upon questions of identity, of nationalism, of power and authority" (p. 176). Questions about who we are, what our place in the world is, are inevitably tied in with issues of national identity. And, as Said explains, "National identity always involves narratives—of the nation's past, its founding fathers and documents, seminal events, and so on. But these narratives are never undisputed or merely a matter of the neutral recitation of facts" (p. 177). So I am reminded that my own early childhood memories of living in postwar Germany and my teenaged memories of life in apartheid South Africa are filtered through the family stories I have heard, the books I have read, and the memorabilia that remain from those times. Such stories are then necessarily subjective and selective. As Razack (1998) reminds us,

> When we depend on storytelling, either to reach each other across differences or to resist patriarchal and racial constructs, we must overcome at least one difficulty: the difference in position between the teller and the listener, between telling the tale and hearing it. Being all about subjectivity, storytelling is often uncritically understood as sentimental, personal and individual horizon as opposed to objective, universal, societal, limitless horizon. (pp. 36–37)

My personal narrative begins with a love story across enemy lines at the close of World War II. My father, a dispatch rider with the British army, was stationed in the German city of Essen, home of the Krupp steel factories that supplied many of the armaments for the war and, consequently, the scene of heavy Allied bombing. My mother lived in the city with her family and had seen their house bombed during the closing months of the war just before meeting my father. Though neither could speak each other's language, their friendship blossomed into love and developed into a lasting relationship that defied the rules of British authority against "fraternization with the enemy."

How was it that among the horrors of war, the atrocities of the Holocaust, and the general fear of the "other" embodied by constructions of the "enemy," their relationship could develop and thrive? I am reminded of the work of Emmanuel Lévinas, who did much of his writing during this time of war. He suffered imprisonment himself for being Jewish, and six members of his family were killed by Nazi officials or by pro-Nazi Lithuanian anti-Semites. Yet his philosophy remained focused on the "wisdom of love" and the ethics of responsibility to others. As Hamblet (2006) comments,

> The natural drives and emotions, for Levinas, provide the person with valuable guides to the Good, pointing the way to spiritual and moral fulfilment. A positive view of the passions, a rarity in ethical philosophy, composes not simply a bold innovation but a highly puzzling one, given the dark backdrop of the atrocities of the twentieth century against which Levinas

FIGURE 9.1 My father in 1945

is staging his work. Perhaps the greatest paradox concerning Emmanuel Levinas resides in his ability to maintain, in the wake of the Holocaust, such a sympathetic view of human existence that he can claim his utterly idealistic account to be a phenomenology rather than a religious sermon, a description rather than a prescription of human encounter. (p. 173)

My parents' love affair created concern and anger among many of my mother's friends and relatives. But, although my mother's sister and mother were at first taken aback at this "foreigner" who had been thrust upon them, they soon accepted my father as part of their family When I was born in late 1946, my aunt agreed that her husband, my uncle, who was still a German prisoner of war in Italy at the time, should become my godfather. So when he was finally able to return home, my uncle discovered he had an English brother-in-law and a half-English goddaughter.

When I was 2 years old, my parents and I moved to England. I came to know my godfather only on our occasional visits to Germany to spend time with my mother's family. By then, I was the "English girl" speaking accented and awkward

FIGURE 9.2 My uncle in 1944

German, but my relationship with my godfather remained strong. My mother's two brothers had died fighting for Hitler, and several of my mother's cousins had been members of the Hitler Youth movement, an organization designed to indoctrinate boys and girls with Hitler's National Socialist ideology and racial doctrines, but these topics were rarely discussed in my immediate family.

It was 5 decades later before I learned my father's regiment had liberated the Bergen-Belsen Concentration Camp in 1945, an experience he recalled as "the most traumatic event of my life." This was the camp where an estimated 50,000 inmates and an additional 50,000 Russian prisoners of war died, with many more near death from starvation and typhus at the time of liberation. Among the thousands of Jewish prisoners who died was the now-famous Anne Frank. I clearly remember reading *The Diary of Anne Frank* as a teenager in England, and being filled with grief at the senselessness of her fate, but with no real understanding of the part my family on both sides of the war had played, even inadvertently, in the tragedy that led to her death (Frank, 1952).

Another memorable experience related to my family's war experiences occurred in 1955 when my father wanted to see the newly released film *The Dam Busters*. The film dramatized the attack on the Möhne and Edersee Dams near Essen, Germany, carried out in May 1943 by a Royal Air Force Squadron, subsequently known as the "Dambusters," using a specially developed "bouncing bomb" (Anderson, 1955). The breaching of the dams caused catastrophic flooding of the Ruhr valley where my mother lived. I remember that she refused to go and see the movie, saying that it was "bad enough to have lived through the bombing without having to see it replayed on the screen." I went to see the film with my father and began to understand a little more about the different war experiences of my mother and father.

Other, more recent texts have played a role in re-creating my own and my family's wartime experiences. One example was reading Boyne's (2006) novel *The Boy in the Striped Pajamas*. The novel's simple language and the naïve viewpoint of a 9-year-old child disguise a deftly constructed storyline of Bruno, a young German boy trying to make the best of his boring new life at a place he understands to be called "Out With," where his father has a new position. A tall fence stretches as far as he can see and cuts him off from the strange people he can see in the distance. His friendship with a starving and scared boy in a striped uniform on the other side of the fence, whose life and circumstances are very different to his own, leads to a shocking climax. Bruno's naïvety and lack of awareness of what is happening around him parallels to some extent my own lack of attention to my family's experiences during the war.

Memorabilia have also played a part in re-experiencing my relationship with my godfather and my family connections with Germany and World War II. Searching for some files in my office at home recently, I came across a tattered cardboard box that contained the old coins I had collected as a child. Among these were many

coins that my godfather had given me on one of my visits to Germany, including two that immediately reminded me of the context of the times into which I'd been born. One 5 Mark coin from 1936 shows the traditional Weimar eagle of the German Republic. Although Adolf Hitler had been in power in Germany since 1933, it was only after 1936 that the Nazi party changed the insignia on coins to a black eagle above a stylized oak wreath, with a swastika, its party symbol, at its centre, as shown in my 2 Reichspfennig coin from 1937. This insignia remained on coins until the end of the Nazi regime in 1945 ("Coats of arms," 2011).

Artefacts such as these coins have a particular power to help reimagine significant experiences in one's life. Strong-Wilson (2008) suggests that

> remembering entails recalling events perceived as at a distance. Re-experiencing, by contrast, draws memory close, such that the remembering becomes an event. . . . Whereas remembering represents a conscious effort on the part of the intellect, re-experiencing occurs more naturally, involuntarily and is typically provoked by a non-random prompt or cue; that is, the cue is non-random in relation to the particularized history of the individual. (pp. 78–79)

Fifteen years after leaving Germany for a life in England, my parents and I moved countries again, this time across the world to apartheid South Africa. Under the dictates of the Nationalist party, all aspects of government, society, and schooling were divided on the basis of race. Racial discrimination permeated all of life. As an immigrant of European heritage, I was immediately considered to be among the "elite" in the country. Under the government policy of separate development, "White" South Africans lived a privileged life while those who were classified as "Black," "coloured," or "Indian" were excluded from participating in much of the life of the country, forced to live in particular areas of the country and to attend separate schools with very limited resources. A cartoon from a Cape Town newspaper (Marais, 1962) that I pasted into my scrapbook en route to our new home in Durban captures the irony and tragedy of the apartheid situation with its portrayal of two out-of-work men, one White and one Black, sitting on a park bench that states in Afrikaans (one of the two official languages of the time) "Net vir Blankes" (Only for Whites). The White man is saying, "Van der Merwe, you may be poor, but by gum, you're white."

As a White person, I was allowed to attend a well-resourced school and university and to become a teacher in an all-White girls' school. The required curriculum, titled "National Christian Education," encouraged us to teach the same canon of European literature I had grown up reading in England and in my university classes in Durban. It was evident that the apartheid government feared the power of any critical imaginative literature to disrupt a society built on racism and effectively banned any texts that were deemed in any way critical of government policies or that promoted indigenous writers.

It was only once I left South Africa to move to Canada that I began to read authors such as Njabulo Ndebele, Nadine Gordimer, and Bessie Head, whose writings unmasked what was hidden in the country at the time. It was ironic that at the same time that I was teaching English literature in a Durban high school, Bessie Head, classified as "coloured" under apartheid, who had grown up close to where I was teaching, was receiving accolades in London and New York for her first novel, titled *When Rain Clouds Gather*. Yet I had never heard of her writing. Her novel relates the story of a troubled young Zulu man called Makhaya who runs away from South Africa, to become a refugee in a little village in neighbouring Botswana. The opening of the book captures the essence of what life was like in South Africa at that time for anyone not White:

> In this hut a man was waiting until dark when he would try to spring across the half-mile gap of no-man's land to the Botswana border fence and then on to whatever illusion of freedom lay ahead. . . . Every half hour the patrol van of the South African border police sped past with sirens wailing, and this caused an unpleasant sensation in his stomach. (Head, 1995, p. 1)

In 1971, I also left South Africa, but as a White person, my travel was unrestricted. I moved with my husband to live in Canada, but our links with South Africa remained strong as we frequently returned with our children to visit family. I remember our first visit in 1973 when we spent Christmas in Durban at the home of my in-laws with our 1-year-old daughter. Their Black maid's little girl, Audrey, was the same age and was invited to play with our daughter's toys while her mother prepared our breakfast.

I think back with shame of the life Audrey's mother must have had, separated from her own family most of the year to live in a small room in the back garden of my in-laws' house, where she cooked and cleaned for them while her own children were left in the care of relatives in the countryside. The South

African pass laws forbade Black people to live permanently in so-called White areas, and they were forced to carry a pass to show they were legally employed in the cities.

Many South African writers have sought to bring these experiences alive for contemporary readers. The South African author, playwright, poet, and storyteller Gcina Mhlophe's (1987) short story "The Toilet" is one of the most poignant. Based on Mhlophe's own life experiences as an aspiring writer, her memoir describes her efforts to realize her desire to write and to resist her class, racial, and gendered discrimination during apartheid. In the story, she recalls moving as a teenager to the city of Johannesburg where her sister worked as a domestic worker for a wealthy White family. Forbidden under the laws of apartheid to live in the city without a work permit, Mhlophe stayed illegally in her sister's room but had to sneak in and out to keep the White owners from finding out. The only place she could call her own was a public toilet in a park. There, she found space and solitude to begin her life as a writer.

Storied recollections such as Mhlophe's short story and Rive's memoir of life in *District Six* stand alongside fiction such as Boyne's *The Boy in the Striped Pajamas* and Head's *When Rain Clouds Gather,* movies such as *District 9,* and artefacts such as family photos and old coins, to re-memory past events and remind us as teachers of the power of these "texts" to interrogate issues of power, identity, and stereotype.

My personal landscapes of living in postwar Germany and apartheid South Africa have encouraged me to consider ways of bringing social justice issues to the fore in my teaching. I have learned it's not possible to be an innocent bystander and to pretend I have no accountability for the past or how it is implicated in the present. As Razack (1998) reminds me,

> We need to direct our efforts to the conditions of communication and knowledge production that prevail, calculating not only who can speak and how they are likely to be heard but also how we know what we know and the interest we protect through our knowing. . . . These pedagogical directions make it clear that education for social change is not so much about new information as it is about disrupting the hegemonic ways of seeing through which subjects make themselves dominant. When we go about the business of subjecting these dominant frames to scrutiny in the classroom . . . , we should be aware of how deeply connected these ways of seeing are to identity. (p. 10)

As teachers, we can look for curricular opportunities that might help us and our students reflect on the "dominant frames" that have shaped our identities. We can look to the work of mentors such as Ted Aoki, whose thoughtful and inspirational personal narratives encourage us to reflect on how our own stories of experience have shaped our teacher identities. And we can draw on the imaginative power of literature, films, and artefacts to look back to what has been and to consider new possibilities for the future.

References

Anderson, M. (Director). (1955). *The dam busters* [Motion picture]. United Kingdom: Pathé Films.

Aoki, T.T. (1979/2005). Reflections of a Japanese Canadian teacher experiencing ethnicity. In W.F. Pinar & R.L. Irwin (Eds.), *Curriculum in a new key: The collected works of Ted T. Aoki* (pp. 333–348). Mahwah, NJ: Lawrence Erlbaum.

Aoki, T.T. (1987/2005). Revisiting the notions of leadership and identity. In W.F. Pinar & R.L. Irwin (Eds.), *Curriculum in a new key: The collected works of Ted T. Aoki* (pp. 349–355). Mahwah, NJ: Lawrence Erlbaum.

Blomkamp, N. (Director). (2009). *District 9* [Motion picture]. United States: Tristar Pictures.

Boyne, J. (2006). *The boy in the striped pajamas*. New York, NY: David Fickling.

Coats of arms of Germany. (2011). *Wikipedia*. Retrieved from http://en.wikipedia.org/wiki/Coat_of_arms_of_Germany

Frank, A. (1952). *The diary of Anne Frank*. New York, NY: Doubleday.

Hamblet, W.C. (2006). A pathological goodness: Emmanuel Levinas' post-Holocaust ethics. *Minerva—An Internet Journal of Philosophy, 10,* 172–196.

Head, B. (1995). *When rain clouds gather*. Oxford, United Kingdom: Heinemann Educational.

Marais, D. (1962). *I got a licence: A new collection of cartoons*. Cape Town, South Africa: Books of Africa.

Mhlophe, G. (1987). The toilet. In A. Oosthuizen (Ed.), *Sometimes when it rains: Writings by South African women* (pp. 1–7). London, United Kingdom: Pandora.

Razack, S. (1998). *Looking White people in the eye: Gender, race, and culture in courtrooms and classrooms*. Toronto, Ontario: University of Toronto Press.

Rive, R. (1985). *Buckingham palace, District six*. New York, NY: Ballantine Books.

Said, E. (2000). Invention, memory, and place. *Critical Inquiry, 26*(2), 175–192.

Strong-Wilson, T. (2008). *Bringing memory forward: Storied remembrance in social justice education with teachers*. New York, NY: Peter Lang.

PART II

Lingering With Times, Dwelling in Places

10

FIVE PETALS OF THOUGHT FALL ON BROKEN GROUND

To Walk With Ted Aoki

Erika Hasebe-Ludt

> You asked of us then: "Walk with me now." We have walked with you, Ted Aoki, ennobled by your teaching, your ethics, your dignity. We will walk with you always. Please linger with us longer.
>
> —William F. Pinar, from "A Lingering Note"

In this chapter, I reflect on some of the paths I have walked and the places I have encountered, both physically and theoretically, while learning and living in relation with Ted Aoki's teaching. I pick up the motif of a "petal of thought" (Aoki, 1991/2005, p. 400), through which Ted pondered the pedagogical relationship between teacher and student and the theme of *belonging together* in the Heideggerian sense of *Kehre*, signifying a turn toward thinking the unthought (Heidegger, 1954/1968).

First Petal of Thought: Prairie Pedagogy

The date was Friday, July 13, 2012. A warm rain was soaking the parched ground of the southern Alberta prairie landscape. I was teaching a graduate Living Literacies summer institute on pedagogy and curriculum at the University of Lethbridge. All of us—the students, my co-instructor Cynthia Chambers, and I—were immersed in life writing. The exercise entailed composing a letter to someone who matters in our lives, to say what we really wanted to say to that person about what was on our minds and in our hearts. The writers were dipping and diving into emotions, mining their memories, conjuring up connections to past and present others with whom they felt a need to connect or reconnect, or redress grief and reiterate joy through this dialogical genre of address. The idea was to get to the truths that sit in our hearts and that are often difficult to face and to enact; truths that hold a significant value for our sense of self, other, and the world. These are truths that often are the "sources of our personal and collective pain" (Smith, 2009, p. 93). As instructors, we hoped that this writing would allow us each to open up deeply meaningful connections and let go of the fears that rule our lives and that prevent us from speaking truthfully. We also hoped that this creative nonfiction writing would "give [us] the courage to say the next hard thing," in the poet Mairs's (1994, p. 25) words. At the heart of this exercise in life writing was the contemplation of *self in relation* and of writing one's self into a more generative way of living our relationships with others and with the world.

Second Petal of Thought: Pacific Poetry

As prompts for this free-writing activity, we used some of Richard Hugo's letters, from his poetic collection "31 Letters and 13 Dreams" (Hugo, 1991). We read aloud selections of the letters to initiate the creative flow and stir the imaginative spirit of writing. In his poems, often about specific places in the Pacific Northwest, Richard Hugo practiced self-examination with poetic sensibility, and with often-brutal honesty. He wrote that he wanted his "life inside to go on as long as I do" (Hugo, 1991, p. 308). In his letters, Loucks (2007) notes, "[He] was able to write about his private life for a public sphere, to take very personal thoughts and offer them up for our consumption. I can think of no more noble and honest approach to art" (para. 11).

I believe that everyone, and especially teachers, need take Hugo's wish to heart and practice poetic, creative life writing as an artful way to develop a rich, meaningful inner life and to help others, especially young people, do so. In his letter poems to friends and fellow writers, Hugo delivered life lessons through a remarkable authenticity of experience:

> Honesty was the keystone of his aesthetic. "How you feel about yourself," he once wrote, "is probably the most important feeling you have." To "let go"—of bitterness, of hatred, of blame—is as important, perhaps more important, as cataloging the indignities of childhood. (Pinsker, as cited in Loucks, 2007, para. 18)

Hugo's own childhood was one of abandonment and isolation. The lessons and experiences he carried with him from the time his Seattle grandparents raised him, a lonely sibling-less boy, were formative for his writing. In her "Letter to Hugo from Later," the poet Hirshfield (1997) acknowledged that "to get the life of anything it seems you have to let some part be broken" (p. 84); she admired and envied his ability, by attending to the particular, "to pack so many parts of the world in such a little space" (p. 84).

Third Petal of Thought: West Coast Living

I wrote my letter to Ted Aoki, beloved curriculum elder and poetic sensei. I met Ted in Vancouver almost two decades ago, at the University of British Columbia, where he taught courses postretirement and I enrolled in one of them as part of my doctoral studies. My *curriculum-as-lived*, my walking on the ground of Aokian pedagogy and poetry, started then. Through his wise words and patient actions—such as choosing literature that he considered of interest to his students—I understood for the first time the power and potential of the hyphen as a signifier of a *third space*, echoing Homi Bhabha's work; subsequently, my own choice of a hyphenated family name took on a deeper meaning. Ted's living pedagogy opened up curriculum as a fertile field of study in that course, and I became familiar with the writing of people with whom he had "talked freely about many things" (Aoki, 2000, p. 61), such as aboriginal elders, other curriculum scholars across Canada, and international—especially Asian—educators. Among them, Ted introduced me to the scholarship of David G. Smith and Cynthia M. Chambers, who became beloved personal and curricular kindred spirits (Hasebe-Ludt, 2004).

Ted practiced an ethos of truth telling and poetic writing throughout his long life. He was a scholar who composed a rich inner life until he passed away on August 31, 2012, at age 92. Ted first became a teacher in Lethbridge in 1945, the closing year of World War II. He lived in the city for 13 years (Aoki, 2000) before moving on to the University of Alberta and becoming a renowned curriculum scholar and teacher in many parts of Canada, especially in Alberta and British Columbia, and in many other parts of the world. In those war-torn times, his life was broken many times by the cruel injustices inflicted on persons of the Japanese race (Miki, 2004).

I used to visit with Ted and his wife, June, whenever I was in Vancouver, where I also live when not teaching in Lethbridge. Over the last years of his life, we read and talked with each other, in the care home where he and June lived. Today, I am still learning from him, soaking in his wisdom gathered throughout his long life, lingering with his humility of being human amid other humans in an unjust world. During his last decade, he suffered from macular degeneration; he was no longer able to read the literature he was so passionate about. Regardless of these physical restrictions, he was still the sensei.

Fourth Petal of Thought: Prairie/Pacific Sensei

This past summer, shortly before Ted passed away, I learned the meaning of this Japanese word for teacher, *sensei*, from Joanne Polec, a Lethbridge Japanese Polish Canadian teacher who participated in our life writing institute and whose Japanese ancestry stems from her father's lineage (J. Polec, personal communication, July 13, 2012). The word is composed of the two *kanji* parts of *sen* (meaning "ahead" or "before") and *sei* (signifying "life" or "birth"): someone who was born ahead of the other; someone who walked his life ahead of another, someone in whose footsteps one can follow and, if fortunate enough, walk alongside for a while. This embodied act of teaching and living, or teaching as living—a hermeneutic approach to curriculum as a lived/living act—is what Ted modeled so well throughout his many years as a teacher.

I now know that it mattered *where* these relationships began and developed and *how* they were connected to my experiences of living and teaching in both Vancouver and Lethbridge. The specifics of this *topos* of here *and* there mattered, in the way that it mattered that Richard Hugo's letter poems were written *from* a particular place and took into account political, social, cultural, ethical, and spiritual conditions of life in that place (Loucks, 2007), such as "Letter to Bell from Missoula," "Letter to Reed from Lolo," or "Letter to Snyder from Montana" (Hugo, 1991). Hugo's poetry haunts towns and landmarks across Montana, especially Missoula, where he taught creative writing at the University of Montana, and all over the Pacific Northwest, especially Washington and Idaho. "When Hugo wrote a poem about a place, he made the place a part of himself, and now that he's gone, a part of him remains in those places," Bolin (2012, para. 2) wrote.

Ted Aoki's expansive ways of walking the topos of pedagogy and curriculum were dynamic and tensioned at the same time, shaped by a deep phenomenological awareness of place and the presence of humans in those places: "In my being and becoming, the tensions that were there created a dynamic world within which I acted" (Aoki, 2000, p. 70). He characterized this world, the places within it, and the experiences shaped by places—such as the sugar beet farms in Southern Alberta and the forced labor that Japanese Canadians and aboriginal peoples were subjected to, or the Marquis Hotel in Lethbridge, where he was denied service as a "Jap"—as phenomena of being "unwanted strangers in our own homeland" (Aoki, 2000, p. 67). Patiently, he walked this landscape of racial and ethnic discrimination with perseverance and dignity, and with a keen pedagogical sensitivity to prejudice and inequity borne out of this own lived experience during the harsh and hostile decades of his long life during the war-torn 20th century, and the 1940 and 1950s, in particular.

Fifth Petal of Thought: Pacific Piety

Ted Aoki's humanity and humility were inspiriting, and his love of others generous and without discrimination. He became a mentor and a father to me, standing in for my own father, whom I lost too soon. He died in 1979, a few months before the birth of his granddaughter, my daughter Charlotte. I am saddened that he never got to know her and that Charlotte's grandfather lived in my daughter's mind only through the stories and memories of others. Ted and June's life together was also shaped by a premature death. Their only daughter, Michelle, died suddenly at age 19. In 1979, Ted referred to this tragic event in a "lingering note" when writing about his life and his experiences as a Japanese Canadian teacher in Alberta:

> We have taken her home and have buried her on the coast. Beside her is a plot. It is mine. I intend to come home to BC and when I come home, I will want to see the *sakura* and the rose so beautiful and bountiful are they in British Columbia. But seeing them, I will be seeing myself—for I know that what I see and how I see is because of who I am. I am what I see. I am how I see. (Aoki, 1979/2005, p. 343)

In the muted light of the approaching winter season, I now stand at the grave of Ted Aoki, located beside that of his daughter's. He has come home. I surrender to the stillness that surrounds this place, and I hear "the sound of pedagogy in the silence of the morning calm" (Aoki, 1991/2005, p. 389). A memory surfaces, of reading "Anjin's story" in Ted's class and contemplating what it means to be truly pedagogical, along with pondering the theme of pedagogical leave taking with regard to "the true relation between teacher and taught" (Aoki, 1991/2005, p. 395) that he wanted us to consider then. In his discussion of Anjin's story, Ted also meditated on the notions of "belonging together" and Heidegger's notion of Kehre as an unexpected turn, "an attempt to think the unthought" (Aoki, 1991/2005, p. 395). Rather than highlighting the traditional primacy of *togetherness* in this notion, Ted asked us to rethink what it means to *belong* together in a pedagogical relationship. Rereading his words, I am reminded of the German words for this notion, *zusammen gehören*, and that the stem of the verb, *hören*, means "to listen." In this way, an attunement to listening, and being present in the hermeneutic event of relating to an other, is the primary responsibility of both teacher and student.

I linger in my renewed awareness of the meaning of these notions now that this beloved teacher has taken his leave from us. My Kehre moves with a slowly emerging understanding, that, much like the beloved teacher in Anjin's story, Ted has drawn the topos of curriculum for us, his students, with inspiriting thinking, poetic tact, and deep attunement to the call of teaching he heard arising from each one of us. He has walked this ground for us so we in turn could walk the *humus* of our work freely on our own while still dwelling in the metonymic relational space of "coming to where one truly belongs" (Aoki, 1991/2005, p. 397), where we already are, in a pedagogical *Ereignis*, an event that signifies an attunement to Being and dwelling on the earth. Remembering Anjin, the storyteller, and his response to her pedagogical thinking, Ted concluded his essay with these words:

I am left with a petal of thought that the appropriate topos for such piety of thinking is the silence of the morning calm. . . . And at this moment in the shimmering presence of her absence, I stand—midst the silence—alone but not alone. (p. 400)

Returning to this Pacific place where my pedagogy has come into Being, I am grateful for the gifts from this inspiriting pedagogue who walked this broken ground before me, nourished by the humus my feet are touching. In the shimmering presence of his absence, between the *sakura* and the rose, the sweetgrass and the cedar, I stand and walk with Ted Aoki, alone and not alone. Although Ted has taken leave of us, he remains a cherished part of this place, and of the prairie and coastal places where he taught and lived, between the Alberta prairies and the West Coast Pacific Rim. He lingers with us all, as we linger with him, unfolding petals of thinking the unthought, between teacher and taught.

> Mile after mile
> falls away each day I search
> for cherry blossoms
>
> —Matsuo Bashō, from *Narrow Road to the Interior*

References

Aoki, T.T. (1979/2005). Reflections of a Japanese Canadian teacher experiencing ethnicity. In W.F. Pinar & R.L. Irwin (Eds.), *Curriculum in a new key: The collected works of Ted T. Aoki* (pp. 333–348). Mahwah, NJ: Lawrence Erlbaum.

Aoki, T.T. (1991/2005). The sound of pedagogy in the silence of the morning calm. In W.F. Pinar & R.L. Irwin (Eds.), *Curriculum in a new key: The collected works of Ted T. Aoki* (pp. 389–401). Mahwah, NJ: Lawrence Erlbaum.

Aoki, T.T. (2000). On being and becoming a teacher in Alberta. In J.M. Iseke-Barnes & N.N. Wane (Eds.), *Equity in schools and society* (pp. 61–71). Toronto, Ontario: Canadian Scholars' Press.

Bashō, M. (2000). *Narrow road to the interior and other writings* (S. Hamill, Trans.). Boston, MA: Shambhala.

Bolin, A. (2012, May 14). At the grave of Richard Hugo [Web log post]. Retrieved from http://www.theparisreview.org/blog/2012/05/14/at-the-grave-of-richard-hugo/

Hasebe-Ludt, E. (2004). "We talked freely of many things": Writing home/away from home. In A.L. Cole, L. Neilsen, J.G. Knowles, & T.C. Luciani (Eds.), *Provoked by art: Theorizing arts-informed research* (pp. 203–213). Halifax, Nova Scotia: Backalong Books.

Heidegger, M. (1954/1968). *What is called thinking?* (J. Glenn, Trans.). New York, NY: Harper & Row.

Hirshfield, J. (1997). Letter to Hugo from later. In *The Lives of the heart* (pp. 84–85). New York, NY: Harper Perennial.

Hugo, R. (1991). 31 letters and 13 dreams. In *Making certain it goes on: The collected poems of Richard Hugo* (pp. 273–319). New York, NY: W.W. Norton.

Loucks, J. (2007, Summer). Recovering Richard Hugo: Confessionalism, the authority of experience, trout fishing, and politics in "31 Letters and 13 Dreams." *The New Yinzer, 13*. Retrieved from http://www.newyinzer.com/archive/summer07/13.html

Mairs, N. (1994). *Voice lessons: On becoming a (woman) writer*. Boston, MA: Beacon Press.

Miki, R. (2004). *Redress: Inside the Japanese Canadian call for justice*. Vancouver, British Columbia: Raincoast Books.

Pinar, W.F. (2003, December). "A lingering note": Comments on the collected works of Ted T. Aoki. *Educational Insights, 8*(2). Retrieved from http://www.ccfi.educ.ubc.ca/publication/insights/v08n02/celebrate/pinar.html

Smith, D.G. (2009). Engaging Peter McLaren and the new Marxism in education. *Interchange, 40*(1), 93–117.

11

LEARNING TO DWELL ARIGHT IN THE TENSIONALITY OF A SWEAT LODGE

Michele Tanaka

February 13, 2011
Victoria, British Columbia

Dear Dr. Aoki,

Please allow me to introduce myself. I'm Michele Tanaka, a relative new-comer to the field of curriculum studies, and I was delighted to be intro-duced to your work. May I call you Ted?

As a teacher educator, I find much resonance with your thoughts on *indwelling, inspiriting, multiplicity*, and *tensionality*, and I feel fortunate to be following in your thoughtful curricular footsteps. As a teacher educator, I walk alongside preservice teachers as they develop a pedagogical approach I call *transformative inquiry*. I am interested in understanding how teachers develop cross-cultural awareness, and I focus in particular on indigenous ways of being.

Your concepts swirl through my practice, my writing, and even my dreams as they nudge me to engage more mindfully in the field. Your writing echoes through my own lived experiences as a classroom teacher. Additionally, I am drawn to your work because, while I am Caucasian of mixed-European descent, my husband is third-generation Japanese Ameri-can, and our two children are, of course, hapa. We are new Canadian citizens as well, and so I carry many stories of border crossings.

You introduced me to Ms. O[1] (Aoki, 1986/1991/2005, p. 159[2]), a teacher much like myself, concerned with the aliveness of her classroom. We share an unease around how an overemphasis on curriculum-as-plan might limit some of the possible futures of our learners (pp. 162–163). In many educational contexts, I notice how educators often "assume a curriculum of sameness" (p. 161), shying away from appreciating the unknown potential of the many different learners and the richness of relationships in our classrooms. You write, "There is a forgetfulness that teaching is fundamentally a mode of being" (p. 160). We forget that *learning* is also essentially about *beingness*. We objectify learners as "thing beings" (p. 358) rather than acknowledging the endogenous learning impulse inherent within each person. What might learning look like if we were to nourish the learning spirit (Battiste, 2009)? How do we move away from using static labels and embrace instead a more indigenous understanding "that all of life is a process, that every person is seen as a 'thing-which-is-becoming,' as opposed to a 'thing-which-is'" (Ross, 1996/2006, p. 104)?

When Ms. O asks, "How shall I teach?" (p. 161), she is grappling with questions complicated by the multiplicity of life in flux (p. 205), wondering, how do I teach required curriculum effectively? How do I handle behaviours, scheduling, and special learners? What is expected of me from parents, administrators, peers, and politicians? What do children *really* need? Who am I becoming as a teacher? This last question particularly catches my attention. As you describe, "An educated person, first and foremost, understands that one's way of knowing, thinking and doing flow from who one is" (p. 365) Ms. O relies on the quality of her pedagogical being to live within the tensionality of practice. Her pedagogical integrity is pivotal, as the physical classroom and the learners "arrange themselves around [her] intention [and presence]" (p. 159). We teach who we are (Palmer, 1998).

Ted, I wonder if we do enough in teacher education to help preservice teachers "dwell aright" (pp. 163, 365) in the complicated multiplicity of practices they encounter each day. How fully do they understand their intention and what their presence emanates? Within the breakneck pace and pressure of consumerist modernity, it is all too easy to recreate a stale culture of schooling rather than look to possibilities of *curriculum-as-lived*. Unprecedented courage is necessary for teachers as we foster our learners more fully towards "being and becoming" (p. 361).

For me, curriculum-as-lived embodies the notion of *curriculum-as-transforming*. If we teach who we are, then, as teachers (or learners becoming teachers), we need time to be conscious of and sensitive to our essential nature, to know where we dwell before we can "dwell aright in thoughtful living with others" (p. 365). In my Transformative Inquiry course, I mentor learner-teacher-researchers as they become attuned to who they are and to the pedagogical frameworks in which they ground themselves. I encourage them to more fully articulate what matters and to respond to multiplicity with honesty and audacity. This decenters me in my role as instructor and requires a commitment to the work of reflexivity (Tanaka, Nicholson, & Farish, 2012).

I believe I best help learners if I practice what I teach. Like you, in my own search for what it means to be human (and therefore to become a teacher who more fully honours curriculum-as-lived), I find it useful to probe the margins (p. 336). It is an intentional act of stepping away from my comfortable mainstream existence and purposely opening to tensionality. In opening, I must release my preference to what I know in order to embrace new possibilities. As you say, "It is the tensionality that allows good thoughts and actions to arise when properly tensioned chords are struck . . . tension-less strings are not only unable to give voice to songs, but also unable to allow a song to be sung" (p. 162).

Through deeper exploration of my own pedagogical beingness, I seek out tender spaces of tensionality, places where I am in a relationship of awareness with that which surrounds me. From an attuned place of tensionality, I set my moral compass. This deeper awareness of holistic resonance, with the full multiplicity of life in this moment, helps me to decide more appropriately in what direction I might head and to have a greater sense of the implications of my actions. But, in all the busyness of the world, Ted, where might I find appropriate tension?

Soon after arriving in Canada, I began to realize that no matter what my personal epistemological bearings might be, I stood and walked every day on the traditional territory of indigenous peoples. My intuition told me that, somehow, appropriate tension included expanding my awareness beyond my own sense of reality to include the narratives of this place. In particular, I sensed the importance of listening to generations of people who for thousands of years had a sustainable relationship with the planet Earth. I began to research my academic interest in cross-cultural understanding to include indigenous worldviews, to recognize the wisdom of an eco-social-spiritual-awareness of life.

Indigenous elders tell us that everything within the field of time-space-being is in relationship (Little Bear, 2009). There is important spirit knowledge connected with the wisdom of ancestors, moving forward in a way that is at its core useful and sustainable (Aluli-Meyer, 2008). In this worldview, we exist *only* in relationship, and research is about understanding relationships more fully through paying attention with the utmost of care (Wilson, 2008).

A few years back, I was invited to take part in Sioux sweat lodge ceremonies on a quiet piece of land tucked into the abundant greenness of Vancouver Island. I am forever grateful that I was welcomed into that sacred space. My visiting, over the course of two years, inspired my beingness within the context of this place and in relationships with those around me. I use the word *visiting* with the specific intent of moving beyond a touristic frame of mind, into deeper participation where I was able to dwell more fully within the cultural place of another (Chambers, 2006). I was offered a great gift—to cross a border and drop into another way of being. I was, as you describe, Ted, briefly inhabiting a crack between worlds, experiencing the lived curriculum between cultures (p. 327). In that crack, I found an unforgettable sense of integrity upon which to dwell aright.

It is difficult to put this visiting into words without losing the spirit knowing that came from the loamy smells, the resonance of heartbeat to drum, the organic mixing of sweat and stone. I invite you to engage with this story through more than your intellectual understanding, to take a slow breath and blur your eyes to current surroundings, so that you might open your holistic sensitivity and consideration to my words. I hope I tell this story well as I revisit, remember, and research.

~~~~

Walking away
from the warm vibrancy of the fire,
I bend down
and crawl into the womblike quiet of the lodge,
breathing in
the smoky scent
of cedar~ grass~ and te'mexw~earth.[3]

In the muffled silence inside,
I feel
firm suppleness of ground
beneath me.
Breathing out
the arching strength
of surrounding willow branches.

Tucked between sisters,
I sit in stillness.
Feeling trembling heat
of Grandmothers and Grandfathers
brought from fire
placed gently into the centre,
stone stories glowing hot.
Red~ white~ blue~ yellow~ hot.

The heartbeat
of the drum
reverberates through my body
lifting my senses
as steam begins to rise.

Heat brings out salt
sweat~ tears~ stories~ hope~
I begin to understand much
about what I have.
And what I have given up.

~~~~

I feel connected.
Surrounded
by echoing voices of ancestors.
Listening through our feet
and the beat of the drum.
Listening through our hearts
and the beat of soul.

Setting aside reason
and expectation,
opening to possibilities
of those who came before . . .
and seven generations
yet to come.

Sustained teachings,
passed through eons,
stories woven
into fire~ cloth~ sweat~ stones~
Stories intimately entwined.
Liquid stories.
Permeating in
to our very skin.

The air is full.
And I know
in the centre of my being
that I am not alone.
Songs of the Grandfathers and Grandmothers,

forgotten by many,
are songs that keep us alive
on te mexw-earth.

~~~~

I feel our tune
reverberating
with the heartbeat of the drum,
echoing stories
of pain~ hope~ sorrow~ fear~
stories of injustice
stories of separation.
Tender,
often jagged stories,
laid bare for witness.

Soul searching
intermingles
with heartfelt appreciation.
Acknowledgment
towards the goodness
and mystery
of life.

The beat of the drum
lifts our voices
calling out
midst isolation~
kinship~
and wilderness~

Life stories
of those I walk alongside
on this earth.
Clear, unfettered emotional expression.
Honest.
Yet guided gently
away from hurtfulness,
frenzy and rage.

We are encompassed
in a vessel that hears and holds

the rumour
hidden deep in our hearts.

~~~~

I feel my place.
It seeps through the soles of my feet,
from land on which I walk
every day.

This place moves
through to the top of my head.
As the steam rises
I am grounded.

In this moment
I know that I live on this land.
This island.
With cedar~ rain~ salt~ and cool breeze.
I feel extraordinary resiliency
rooted in te'mexw~earth.

Connecting
with the spirit
of those who have come before,
those who are here now,
and those yet to walk
on this good living planet.

My heart~mind knowing
opens
to a deeper,
more nuanced consciousness
of relationships.
I acknowledge
my place
within this web.

~~~~

Briefly,
understanding my holistic
place in the world,

intellect breathes
in balance
with emotional~ spiritual~ physical~ knowing.

My sense of purpose becomes one.
With those around me~
with the blades of grass~
and the teachings of the ancestors.

~~~~

As steam~ offerings~ stories~ settle,
I circle forward,
crawling out of protected space.

Into cool brightness.
Drinking fully,
crisp clear water,
deep blue sky
I lie belly down on te'mexw~earth.
Listening.

Breathing in . . .
breathing out . . .

Faint sun caressing my back
through cool winter mist,
continuing the warmth.

Five bald eagles
circle overhead
calling out.
Echoing
my dreams.

From this place
I live my questions:
How do I take care of this planet?
How do I learn to get along with others?
How do I tend my own soul?[4]

~~~~

Entering the lodge was a deeply humbling and transformative experience. I was fed heart-body-mind-soul by generous relations. It was a holistic, inspirited experience that reattuned me to the world and my sense of place and relationship with it. My lodge visiting reminded me of who I am and renewed my sense of purpose. I bring this knowledge forward into my teaching practice.

I believe I was being appropriately tensioned, Ted, as in your words, like a carefully tuned violin (p. 360). Or like a deer-hide drum, lovingly rubbed to perfect timbre while being warmed near a fire. This tensionality of the lodge continues to open the source of my own understanding. I now carry a more direct awareness of the location from which my beliefs, values, and attitudes emerge. It is, as the editors of this anthology suggest, a "still current" that continues to flow through my practice. The lodge teachings both sustain and move me forward, reminding me of who I am and of the landscape upon which my feet intimately walk. This is the place of integrity within tensionality from which my heart-mind teaches and learns.

FIGURE 11.1 The medicine wheel I wore into the lodge

Here I can hold gently the complexity of multiplicity and dwell in my questions, to be still with them, to remain for a time with them, to attend to them with an open heart.

In order to dwell aright within the messy multiplicity of practice, preservice teachers need support. Without attention to this difficult work, it becomes possible to fall into what Maureen, my retired principal friend, refers to as "the curse of the Bs: bitterness, blame, and burning out." Ted, I think we have both seen the effects of such teachers on the lives of children we care about. The practice of transformative inquiry seeks to balance intellect with other ways of knowing, to dwell in the difficult places we encounter as teachers. To maneuver the messy multilayered "Zone of Between" (p. 164) as we learn, amid the multiplicity of our classrooms, to teach paradoxically (Kumashiro, 2004).

Surely you know that cultural borders are funny things. On the surface, my ways appear very different than those of the Sioux. Yet deep down, I found profound resonance. My intent, in my role as transformative learner-teacher-researcher, is to bring forward awareness of the deep and gentle relationships I witnessed in the lodge. To inspirit my learner-teacher-researcher relationships with a sense of connectedness and humble appreciation to that which surrounds us: our ecology, our community, and each learner's inner-learning direction and spirit. As teachers, we have the possibility and privilege to model and encourage how we "dwell aright in thoughtful living with others" (p. 365). I believe this sense of dwelling extends to *te'mexw*-earth. We hold a responsibility to act in a good way towards all the relationships we engage in throughout our learning-teaching-researching lives.

As time goes on and I no longer participate in that particular border crossing, I know that I am changed. The lodge stories are intimately linked to how I now see the world. I bring forward the memory of that vibrant, sweet tensionality wrought within an encirclement of holistic acknowledgment. I remember who I am in relationship with past-present, me-you, fear-joy, earth-sky. I remember my humanity and my humbleness, that I am simply a two-legged creature, one of so many sentient beings on the planet. I try to honour the importance of expressing what is in my heart and listen without judgment to what is in the hearts of others.

As I walk alongside learner-teacher-researchers who are learning about inquiry, my hope is that my story, now entwined within the stories of the lodge, will somehow resonate with theirs. That our conversations might provide a spark that serves to deepen their personal transformative-inquiry approach. For me, the lodge is a living example of a pedagogical space where we can be deeply human. In your words, it is a sanctified clearing where the teacher and students gather—somewhat like the place before the hearth at home—an extraordinary unique and precious place, a hopeful place, a trusted place, a careful place—essentially a human place dedicated to ventures devoted to leading out, an authentic "e(out)/ducere(lead)," from the "is" to new possibilities yet unknown. (p. 164)

My challenge is to nurture such space and time within the academy where emotions can be fully and honestly acknowledged within the context of our concentric communities on *te'mexw*~earth. Where I as "teacher" can be decentered and trust the "learner" to lead (p. 283). Who knows what promise this might hold?

Thank you, Ted, for the wonderful work you have done and for this chance to express my gratitude for your impact on my journey as I strive to walk on this planet in a good way. In the words of my Irish ancestors,

> May joy and peace surround you,
> contentment latch your door.
> May happiness be with you now,
> and bless you evermore.

Yours in inspirited tensionality,
Michele

References

Aluli-Meyer, M. (2008). Indigenous and authentic: Hawaiian epistemology and the triangulation of meaning. In N.K. Denzin, Y.S. Lincoln, & L.T. Smith (Eds.), *Handbook of critical and indigenous methodologies* (pp. 217–231). Thousand Oaks, CA: Sage.

Aoki, T. (1986/1991/2005). Teaching as indwelling between two curriculum worlds. In W.G. Pinar & R.L. Irwin (Eds.), *Curriculum in a new key: The collected works of Ted T. Aoki* (pp. 159–165). Mahwah, NJ: Lawrence Erlbaum.

Battiste, M. (2009). Nourishing the learning spirit: Living our way to new thinking. *Canadian Educational Association, 50*(1). Retrieved from http://www.cea-ace.ca/education-canada/article/nourishing-learning-spirit-living-our-way-new-thinking

Cajete, G. (2009, April). *Building healthy and sustainable indigenous communities through research.* Paper presented at the American Educational Research Association conference, San Diego, CA.

Chambers, C. (2006). "The land is the best teacher I ever had": Places as pedagogy for precarious times. *Journal of Curriculum Theorizing, 22*(2), 27–37.

Kumashiro, K.K. (2004). Uncertain beginnings: Learning to teach paradoxically. *Theory Into Practice, 43*(2), 111–115.

Little Bear, L. (2009, May). *Indigenous philosophies of land and life.* Public lecture given at the Indigenous Governance Leadership Forum, Victoria, BC.

Palmer, P. (1998). *The courage to teach: Exploring the inner landscape of a teacher's life.* San Francisco, CA: Jossey-Bass.

Ross, R. (1996/2006). *Returning to the teachings: Exploring aboriginal justice.* Toronto, Ontario: Penguin Canada.

Tanaka, M., Nicholson, D., & Farish, M. (2012). Committed to Transformative Inquiry: Three teacher educators' entry points into the mentoring role. *Journal of Transformative Education, 10*(4), 127–274.

Wilson, S. (2008). *Research is ceremony.* Halifax, Nova Scotia: Fernwood.

Notes

1. I hope you don't mind! I've updated "Miss" to "Ms."
2. Unless otherwise noted, all page references are from Aoki (1986/1991/2005).
3. *Te'mexw* is the name used for *sacred earth* in the area where the lodge was set.
4. Here I am echoing questions asked by indigenous science educator Gregory Cajete (2009).

12

THIS PARK HAS SNAKES

Christina Audet

> There is a deeper and more important way of remembering. . . . This is the memory of a past that has written itself on you, in your character and in the life on which you bring that character to bear.
> —Mark Rowlands, from *The Philosopher and the Wolf*

As a rural high-school humanities teacher raised in a number of large cities, I find myself telling stories of adjusting to this isolated world of my husband's family's place. Many of my students have a history as rooted as my husband's family name (and now my family name), and they help me understand what it *is* I belong to.

I belong to a place that was settled only a short time ago by men like my children's great-grandfather, a Catholic, French Canadian carpenter who had enough confidence to believe he could begin again as a cattle rancher in an area not yet even surveyed. I belong to a place that is sacred to the First Nations people, a place they would never presume to claim because it is a place so special it must be shared. I belong to a place near a North West Mounted Police (NWMP) outpost, nestled in a long coulee running across the American border where horse thieves and whiskey traders tried to make their living. I belong to a place where I can walk amongst the rocks and find the names and dates of my old neighbors who walked before me. And, if I walk a little farther, and if the park gives me permission, I can have my lunch by a place the locals call Signature Rock. Here, almost every NWMP stationed to this remote outpost carved their names into the soft sandstone. Many are beautifully crafted testaments to a human need to tell others where they had been. Like a cemetery, the sandstones of my yard are full of such markers; documenting lives lived in the context of a different time and place. I belong to a place that reminds me to linger longer.

As much as I remain the newcomer in this area that is slow to embrace change, many of my students are much newer to this place. Our school also houses an elite girl's sports team, which draws from teams all across Canada, the United States, and sometimes even Europe. This group of about twenty-two 15- to 18-year-olds, come together in a shared residence and, in the course of a school year, learn to make themselves into a family.

In my classroom it seems clear that while many of my students have a perception of a role they are playing ("town kid" or "hockey girl") within the dynamics of our interactions, they are also struggling to belong in a way that crosses these artificial boundaries. When Ted Aoki (1993/2005) spoke to the Association for Supervision and Curriculum Development in 1992, he summarized what I observe on a daily basis: "Identity is not so much *something* already present but, rather as production in the throes of being constituted as we live in the place of difference" (p. 205). As a humanities teacher, the process of finding one's identity in the midst of difference is an enduring theme found throughout my curriculums, both "lived" and "planned." In fact, this *is* the curriculum. So, as I see it, my primary responsibility is to model the importance of being "thoughtful and watchful" (Aoki, as cited in Pinar, 2005, p. 19). I listen, to try and hear how each of these students is understanding his or her world on this particular day. I do so by reading their writing, listening to their stories, and using my own life writing and oral stories to begin our conversations.

Pretty Stories

I

day's first light finds me
inside a picket fence where
I tend my yard
of landscaped happiness
strong brown fingers pinch
wilted blossoms   tie back daisies
bent on messing up my yard

II

wrapped in her favorite crocheted blanket
fluffed into a flowered chair
she sits on the edge of a sunny puddle
and smiles old dreams
while fingers stroke the worn picture
of a beautiful princess

from a storybook
my mother used to read to me

III

spreading out her well-used flannel blanket
she tells pretty stories
to her family dolls
chubby hands set them in a miniature house
complete with Waterford crystal
fine Monet prints
and a Claiborne closet
roads that pass this sunlit house
wind through weedless gardens
scattered with plucked daisies

In our school, there is a place of tension between those whose families have long claimed this place as their prairie home and the sporty female newcomers who come here as a stepping-stone to even better, bigger places. It could even be said that Aoki's (1993/2005) "curriculum-as-lived" (p. 202) is exemplified through the world of the "town" students' 4-H clubs, spring seeding schedules, and annual fall suppers, while the "curriculum-as-plan" is evidenced in a team calendar filled with the daily game/practice schedule, postsecondary admission deadlines, and reminders to book the early flights home. The town students live their lives according to many traditions established long before they were born, and they are most comfortable just *being,* while the hockey girls have clear goals for their futures and parents who have paid significant fees to ensure these goals are achieved.

Both groups appear to be so entrenched in these seemingly diverse positions that they often miss opportunities for exploring each other's situations. Our educational system has helped create a space where the rush toward acquiring a specific knowledge set, as demonstrated by the high-stakes Alberta Diploma Exam system, has compromised the ability for teachers and students to "linger" in an effort to learn as a process of understanding how each other *is.* Like Aoki (1979/2005), "I know that what I see and how I see is because of who I am" (p. 348). The challenge for both myself and, ultimately, my students is to explore and broaden the concept of personal identity so that we are better positioned to really "see."

The Tour

I take my place
among the curious

lined to catch a glimpse
history recounted in bright tones
dressed in a blue uniform   brassy
diamond willow stick
traces the high points
careful not to touch ancient memory
pointed-shoulder man Shoshone
square-shoulder man Blackfoot
round shield man   warriors
now   horses appear
open lines at mouth
tell us this one still lives

two o'clock sun melts my interest
wandering   I hear familiar rattle
dancing instinct   hop   step   and scream
audience moves my way

later they will only remember
this park has snakes

As a teacher, I struggle to create a space where all my students feel comfortable "being in becoming" (Aoki, as cited in Pinar, 2005, p. 12) and often this is achieved by humorous stories that remind us all how this is not always an easy place to live. By opening the door to some of the difficulties we face together, my students begin to feel more comfortable sharing their discomfort. But, like Aoki's Miss O, I "must listen and be attuned to the care that calls from [my] very living" (Aoki, as cited in Pinar, 2005, p. 15). In an effort to create this space, I follow Aoki's advice and speak "so that we may awaken to the truer sense that stirs within each of us" (Aoki, as cited in Pinar, 2005, p. 17). Though mine is not a voice entirely silenced by "the cacophony of voices" (Aoki, as cited in Pinar, 2005, p. 17) in the original sense of "political" constraints, it is a voice struggling to be true to the curriculum of possibility created in a room where I share my own life writing.

The Mothers I Have Known

My Aunt Julie didn't
seem to mind
when her brother dropped us off at their farm
for a spring
he needed to go to Calgary   alone
to find a job

a house
a housekeeper
for three children
only one in school

it was a glorious holiday
we made hay bale forts
jumped from the loft (when nobody was looking)
slid down the silver spouts of junked combines
learned how to save air on the path
to the outhouse
so you didn't have to breathe inside

had scummy Sunday baths in the big copper tub
(littlest ones do go last)
and bread and jam on Monday

I even got to go to school
on a bus
long enough to get a report card
good attitude   tries hard
still no files to say what grades completed
keep up the good work

kick-the-can at nightfall
near-death experiences with the nasty left-over Christmas goose
and dropping the baton in the annual
spring parade
the stuff holidays are made of

skipping school with my cousin
to watch fuzzy television
because we couldn't get close enough to see
when everyone was home

I was never afraid of the dark in those days
so cozy   all seven of us
in the converted basement   now dorm
the bucket in the corner
because the outhouse was too far   too dark   too cold
for night time visits

I never got the feeling
my aunt   minded sharing her holiday life
especially those evenings she gently placed another warm facecloth
over yet another terrible earache.

As I engage my students in conversations, both written and oral, we uncover layers of being and in so doing model an Aokian mindfulness that will allow a space of speech for those students who have been silenced by difference. I am reminded of Aoki in that I "present myself not so much to tell stories, but to participate in a questioning" (Aoki, 1987/2005, p. 349). I am the stories of my youth as my students are creating their own. Many before us have also lived through difficulties related to being separated from family or of just trying to fit into a new place. Life might be simply the process of learning to belong. My hope is that the voices of my students will create conversation that questions why the whispers of others like them in faraway places are barely heard in the imposed silence of our shared humanity, only to be broken periodically by faraway echoes reminding everyone, "We're still here."

References

Aoki, T.T. (1979/2005). Reflections of a Japanese Canadian teacher experiencing ethnicity. In W.F. Pinar & R.L. Irwin (Eds.), *Curriculum in a new key: The collected works of Ted T. Aoki* (pp. 333–348). Mahwah, NJ: Lawrence Erlbaum.

Aoki, T.T. (1987/2005). Revisiting the notions of leadership and identity. In W.F. Pinar & R.L. Irwin (Eds.), *Curriculum in a new key: The collected works of Ted T. Aoki* (pp. 349–355). Mahwah, NJ: Lawrence Erlbaum.

Aoki, T.T. (1993/2005). Legitimating lived curriculum: Toward a curricular landscape of multiplicity. In W.F. Pinar & R.L. Irwin (Eds.), *Curriculum in a new key: The collected works of Ted T. Aoki* (pp. 199–215). Mahwah, NJ: Lawrence Erlbaum.

Pinar, W.F. (2005). "A lingering note" An introduction to the collected works of Ted T. Aoki. In W.F. Pinar & & R.L. Irwin (Eds.), *Curriculum in a new key: The collected works of Ted T. Aoki* (pp. 1–85). Mahwah, NJ: Lawrence Erlbaum.

Rowlands, M. (2008). *The philosopher and the wolf: Lessons from the wild on love, death and happiness.* London, United Kingdom: Granta Books.

13

REASSERTING THE *CURRICULUM-AS-LIVED* UNDER THE CONSTRAINT OF THE INTEREST IN CONTROL

Bruce G. Hill

Since 1976, each spring, as the earth prepares to renew itself, Grades 4, 7, and 10 teachers across British Columbia, Canada, have been required to administer the Foundational Skills Assessment (FSA) in their classrooms. Currently, the FSA is one of a number of mandated assessments, initiated either locally or provincially, that tie into the Accountability Contracts between the ministry of education and the school districts and provide direction for the development of School Improvement Plans (British Columbia Ministry of Education, 2002). Over time, the FSA, if not the entire superstructure of accountability, has become a sore spot in the relations between teachers and the government. The government defends the FSA on the grounds that it provides useful information about student achievement in reading, writing, and math, while teachers argue that it provides at best a fragment of a snapshot of these programs and as such is a waste of time and money. The debate on the FSA drones on, usually spilling over into the airwaves and providing political theater for talk-show audiences.

There is more at stake in this debate than the future of the FSA. In this chapter, I will attempt to situate this debate in the wider North American context of the ongoing and building tension between, on the one hand, the widespread use of mandated assessments and other related instrumental teaching practices and, on the other, the diverse postmodern and ecological trends in curriculum theory (Sumara, Davis, & Laidlaw, 2001). The postmodern trend rejects right answers in favor of situated and provisional ones, while the ecological trend promotes an awareness of the interrelatedness of life on Mother Earth. I follow Pinar (2004) in defining curriculum theory as "the interdisciplinary study of educational experience" (p. 2). To provide an outline of the wider context for the debate, I will draw mainly on Ted T. Aoki's contribution to curriculum theory as articulated in *Curriculum in a New Key: The Collected Works of Ted T. Aoki* (Pinar & Irwin, 2005).

Across North America, from the 1970s forward, Aoki and other scholars have sought to reconceptualize curriculum as a legitimate school-and-classroom-situated alternative to the hegemony of curriculum conceived in the context of management theory. Smith (2006) identified the emancipative reason of Kant and Hegel as a way of knowing that precluded all other ways of knowing. Jardine (2006) connected Smith's notion of the universality of a single logic to the everyday practice of teaching reading through the use of leveled readers, a practice that seeks to define and measure reading competence in terms of predetermined outcomes. Peter M. Taubman used the technique of "painting by numbers" as a metaphor for the reductive practice of "teaching by numbers" generated by mandated assessments (as cited in Boelé, 2010, p. 2). These scholars dwelled in the twilight of modernity, rejecting the certainties of the past.

The struggle for the soul of curriculum plays out in the daily lives of students and teachers. At what threshold does the reconceptualized curriculum become marginalized under pressure from the resurgence of curriculum conceived in the context of management theory? To put the question more bluntly, will a surfeit of mandated assessments and related instrumental evaluation practices turn teachers into installers rather than improvisers of curriculum? I wish to consider this question in the light of Aoki's ideas on curriculum.

For Aoki, lines from *The Anthem* by Leonard Cohen evoke a metaphor for the scholarly work of reconceptualizing curriculum:

> Ring the bells that still can ring
> Forget your perfect offering
> There is a crack, a crack in everything
> That's how the light shines in. (As cited in Aoki, 2003/2005, p. 425)

As part of the reconceptualist effort, Aoki opened up cracks in the words *education, pedagogy,* and *curriculum,* lighting up these words with new meaning. He defined education in terms of its Latin root, *educere,* which he interpreted as a "leading out" into the "not yet" (Aoki, 1987/2005, p. 350). It is the classroom, he said, that is the usual meeting place for teacher and students, where together they "dwell in the present that embraces past experiences but is open to the possibilities of the future yet to be" (Aoki, 1990/2005, p. 365). He defined pedagogy, "in the Greek sense," as "leading children," with leading understood as following the good of care:

> Teaching is truly pedagogic if the leading [of children] grows out of this care that inevitably is filled with the good of care. Teaching then is a tactful leading that knows and follows the pedagogic good in a caring situation. (Aoki, 1992/2005, p. 191)

He defined curriculum as enfolding the "curriculum-as-plan" and the "curriculum-as-lived" where the *curriculum-as-plan* refers to the mandated curriculum of the ministry while the *curriculum-as-lived* refers to the curriculum as experienced by the teacher and his or her students in the classroom. In this newly envisioned curriculum landscape, the teacher dwells in the tensioned space between the curriculum-as-plan and the curriculum-as-lived, well positioned to improvise the curriculum-as-plan to meet the diverse needs of students (Aoki, 1986/1991/2005).

At a deeper level, Aoki theorized that the "irreducible center" of curriculum is the human/world relation, which provides the broadest possible context for the "entertainment of activities we call education" (Aoki, 1978/1980/2005, p. 95). In this view, humans relate to the world through activities driven by interests, including the interest in control of the world, the interest in understanding the human world, and the interest in changing the human world. In the classroom, teachers subscribe to particular interests. In the system, however, others subscribe to particular interests and bring the influence of those interests to bear in the classroom. These interests generate, among other things, particular teaching practices and particular curriculum landscapes. However, at times, and this is my interpretation, there may be one or more interests at play in a teaching practice, though one of these may be predominant, just as there may be one or more interests at play in a particular landscape, though one of these may be predominant. In these cases, it is the predominance of an interest that distinguishes a teaching practice or a curriculum landscape.

In other words, the interest in control generates a curriculum landscape in which the curriculum-as-plan reigns supreme, holding teachers and students on a tight leash, defining success in terms of the achievement of predetermined outcomes (Aoki, 1996/2005). Within this landscape, teachers act as installers of curriculum, locking into a linear process in which all students are regarded as the same, requiring the same recipe for success, the same lesson plans, the same activities, the same predetermined outcomes, and the same evaluation instruments. Teachers as installers use instrumental language that frames the experience of students in terms of a series of problems to be solved. The danger here is that students become things to be manipulated and managed and that, in the relation of teachers to students, all that really matters are the right answers derived from the single logic of so-called best practice.

The interests in understanding and change, on the other hand, generate a curriculum landscape in which the curriculum-as-lived enjoys co-legitimacy with the curriculum-as-plan, allowing teachers and students wide latitude for improvisation and defining success in terms of the transformative possibilities of students and teachers (Aoki, 1993b/2005). Typically, teachers dwelling within this landscape bring into the classroom an object of study, say, a poem, a story, a question, or a math problem, and invite responses from their students (Aoki, 1978/1980/2005). The object of study is the curriculum-as-plan, while the responses of teacher and students to the object generate not one curriculum-as-lived, but multiple curricula-as-lived, a curriculum for each student and the teacher (Aoki, 1993a/2005). Teachers cannot predict what the responses of students to the object of study will be but rather can only improvise in drawing out their responses, encouraging them to make connections and deepen their understanding. Within this multifold curriculum landscape, the emphasis of teachers and students in the classroom is on *human being* understood as *human becoming,* entailing a shift from instrumental language to the nuanced language of being.

In light of Aoki's ideas, I offer a measure of the impact of local manifestations of the interest in control on the lived curriculum. I begin with the FSA. The test items on the FSA, like the test items on a standardized test, are decontextualized in an attempt to provide the student with an objective test of skill. For example, one item from a recent FSA requires the student to plan, write, and edit a piece of writing on a given topic in a given form (British Columbia Ministry of Education, 2012). Teachers cannot offer a choice of forms or topics based on student interests, nor can they help students contextualize the topic, allow students to collaborate, evaluate the writing, or go over results with students. In short, teachers cannot teach and, subsequently, students cannot do their best; this begs the question as to what exactly the FSA seeks to measure and why. In this situation, the space between the curriculum-as-plan and the curriculum-as-lived vanishes, leaving only the curriculum conceived solely as plan, the teacher as its hapless installer, and students as its passive consumers.

Other manifestations of the interest in control may have an impact on the lived curriculum. The interest in control drives school and classroom management practices, such as the organization and deployment of resources, the establishment of classroom routines, and the scheduling of classes and meetings, all of which may be defensible in terms of freeing up teachers to concentrate on curriculum improvisation. The interest in control, though, manifests itself with greater import in key school-wide teaching practices. Allow me to briefly consider two of these practices.

One such practice is the process for the identification of, and programming for, the special needs of students. Typically, in a school district, the process of identification emulates the control-driven diagnostic model used in medical practice whereby a sequence of screens point the practitioner toward the most plausible diagnosis. Classroom teachers may initiate this process for a student by filling out a referral form, indicating, among other things, areas of difficulty, strategies attempted, and outcomes achieved. In acting upon the referral, the support or resource teacher and, later, the school psychologist may proceed to administer standardized tests in order to profile the strengths, weaknesses, intelligence, and aptitudes of the student compared to his or her peer group. However, the results of these tests may fall short of a full accounting of student potential and performance, possibly focusing more on words and numbers than on art, music, or movement. To round out the student's profile, school and district staff attend to the lived world of the student. Through file reviews, interviews, and other means, they gather a wealth of information on the experiences of the student in the classroom, at home, and in the community. For students diagnosed as having a disabling condition generative of special needs, a support team, always including the classroom teacher, develops an Individual Education Plan (IEP) that modifies or adapts the ministry-mandated curriculum-as-plan (British Columbia Ministry of Education, 2011). The IEP may entail objects of study both suited to and not suited to evaluation in terms of predetermined outcomes. Among the former, I would include social skills, communication skills, movement skills, and decoding skills, while, among the latter, I would include regular school subjects understood as narratives calling forth the dialogic responses of teacher and students. Ideally, in following through on their IEP assignments, classroom teachers, resource teachers, or other caregivers translate the language of the object of study into the language of the student and vice versa, an undertaking requiring both expertise in the object of study and insight into the lived world of the student. Behind the scenes, district and school staff strive to ensure caregivers have the resources, including support time, commensurate with the identified needs of students, a degree of expertise commensurate with the objects of study, and an approach to evaluation appropriate to the particular objects of study. From the initial referral to the organization of care, the process of identification and programming features an entanglement of activities generated both by the interest in control and by the interest in understanding the human world. If understood pedagogically, the process would allow accounts of the lived experience of the student to dialectically inform the diagnosis of a disability and the direction of programming and also allow the expression of concerns about the organization of care, specifically, for example, concerns about any mismatch of resources and needs. In this precarious arrangement of interdependent curricular and management interests, there is always a risk that the interest in control will demand efficiencies that overwhelm the pedagogical interest, with the result that IEPs may devolve into a curriculum conceived solely as plan where caregivers merely monitor students as they plow through objects of study presented in workbooks and measured by checklists.

Another control-driven school-wide teaching practice is evident in early literacy programs. All primary students participate in early literacy programming. I was involved in my district's early literacy program for many years and offer my perspective on this program. As a rule of thumb, only about half of our primary students would ever struggle with reading mechanics, yet all primary students were required to participate in the early literacy program. This program required the use of leveled readers in which the word count, sentence structure, words per page, relation of words to text, relation of pictures to text, and the range of phonemes per book were under tight control, allowing for incremental increases in the level of difficulty. In the program, teachers placed students in groups based on ability, ensured all groups had three or four reading sessions per week, and reported student progress at regular intervals to the Board of Education office. Teachers and/or resource teachers led the group sessions and adjusted group composition to allow students to proceed at their own pace. In the course of the sessions, students were asked to demonstrate their mastery of a leveled reader by answering prosaic questions on the literal dimension of the text, the only possible questions since the text has very little in the way of a figurative dimension. The limitations of the leveled reader in terms of language complexity, however, could be offset by other parts of the language arts program. For example, students had the opportunity to respond to a work of literary art read to them at carpet time, select good books from the school or class library, or in later years, participate in a late-literacy program that featured interpretation of more imaginative texts. The interest in control may well drive this early literacy program. But it also placed it in the wider context of the language arts curriculum and allowed it to serve in the capacity of yet another special-needs screen, possibly reducing the demand for special-needs referrals. There remains a risk in this kind of early literacy program, however, that the interest in control, with its emphasis on the mechanics of language along with the ongoing burden of centralized local assessments through the FSA and other concerns for systemic efficiencies, will lead classroom teachers to overvalue predetermined outcomes in comprehension at the expense of interpretation, thereby skewing the language arts program in the direction of curriculum conceived solely as plan.

When the interest in control comes to dominate the curricular landscape at the expense of the other interests, it creates what Aoki, borrowing from Paulo Freire, calls a "limit situation" (Aoki, 1978/1980/2005, p. 94). I adapt the term "limit situation" for use in a school or classroom context in which a surfeit of external or internal instrumental practices diminishes the transformative possibilities of teachers and students. Teachers caught up in a limit situation may grow indifferent to the need, for example, to inquire into or reflect upon the most obvious of all educational experiences in the classroom, and that is the experience of dialogic space.

Aoki cited many voices from diverse disciplines that speak to the dynamics of dialogic space, among them, the philosopher Gilles Deleuze, the psychoanalysts Julia Kristeva and Jacques Lacan, and the linguist Roman Jakobson. Deleuze claims that it is not the elements but the space between the elements that matters most in dialogic space. By the term *elements,* he refers to our perspectives on, or responses to, an object of study. "A multiplicity is not a noun," he says, adding that "multiplicities grow in the middle" (as cited in Aoki, 1993b/2005, p. 269). I take him to mean here that we reposition ourselves at the borders of our perspectives and open ourselves to the influence of the lines of movement, the new ideas or insights, that spring forth in the spaces among and between the elements.

Kristeva claims that the human subject is constituted, not as an undivided individual, but as *self and other.* In her view, there is an unknown part to us, a stranger within, who is this *other*. We will never get along with others in the world, or strangers in our midst, she argues, until we gain awareness of the other who dwells within us (see Aoki, 1993c/2005). I take her to mean that in dialogic space the tendency of the fortress ego to preserve itself, for example, by shutting down the other is, in some form, a shutting down of self, a retreat into subjectivity.

Jakobson describes language as having a *vertical* or *metaphoric* dimension and a *horizontal* or *metonymic* dimension (see Aoki, 2000/2005), while Lacan claims that a *signifier* (a word) can never (re)present the *signified* (the object to which it refers) and that the meaning of the object may only be found in differences along a chain of signifiers, that is, in differences between and among attempts to name the object (see Aoki, 2000/2005). The implication here for dialogic space is that, in accepting the slipperiness of truth, we lighten up on our perspectives and open ourselves more to the influence of others.

In addition to drawing on these and other voices, Aoki used daily or weekly student journaling to enhance the dynamics of the dialogic space of the seminar room. Upon reading student journals, he would offer insightful responses in the form of questions or comments designed to elicit something new from the student. The dynamics of the dialogic textuality of journaling complement the dynamics of the dialogic space of the classroom. In journaling, the monologue of the student gives way to dialogue with the teacher through which narrative structures continually form and re-form. In dialogic space, dialogue gives way to multilogue, or conversation involving the voices of many through which narratives, including student journal entries, form and re-form under the influence of spontaneous narration. Both the expressions of journaling and of dialogic or multilogic space are free forms whose outcomes are hard to measure and impossible to predict. The incentive for students to perform in these free forms may turn on the joy of dwelling in the in-between, the joy of generating lines of movement between perspectives, the joy of experiencing the not yet, the joy of deepening the bonds of community, the joy of human becoming.

These voices from diverse disciplines help us better understand the dynamics of dialogic and interperspectival space, possibly enabling us to transform that space into a site of living pedagogy, a space alive with transformative possibilities for students. Today, perhaps as never before, students need open and safe spaces to address issues concerning racism, ageism, sexism, privacy, identity, difference, bullying, gadgetry, and abuse. In opening up such spaces for students, teachers create opportunities to follow the "pedagogic good in a caring situation" suffused with mutual respect (Aoki, 1992/2005, p. 191). Early literacy and special-needs students, no less than other students, need such spaces.

At the very least, in light of Aoki's ideas on curriculum, we may conclude that the proliferation of control-driven mandated assessments and related instrumental teaching practices poses a threat to the quality of the curriculum-as-lived. At the district and provincial level, the stewards of public education need to place management interests under the constraint of pedagogical interests. At the school and classroom level, teachers may reassert the curriculum-as-lived and reclaim curricular spaces for improvisation by carefully tracking the manifestations of the interest in control; by distinguishing between necessary instrumentalities that meet the particular needs of particular students and unnecessary instrumentalities that, to some degree, impinge upon improvisation; and by distinguishing between the instrumental use of language and the nuanced language of being. The interest in control may drive defensible practices associated with systemic efficiencies but must not be allowed to become the predominant interest driving the curriculum landscape. It is time to bring under control the interest in control and reassert the interests in understanding and changing the human world. The soul of curriculum is at stake.

A Lingering Note

The *sakura*, or cherry tree, Inazo Nitobe wrote, stands "ever ready to depart life at the call of nature," whereas the rose "clings to life as though loth or afraid to die rather than drop untimely" (as cited in Aoki, 1979/2005, p. 346). In reflecting on this passage, Aoki noted that, for Nitobe, the sakura and the rose symbolized two ways of knowing: the Japanese way of knowing that accepts the dialectic of life and death and the European way of knowing that attempts to "shunt death into the periphery of our vision" (Aoki, 1979/2005, p. 346). As a Canadian of Japanese ancestry, he refused to appropriate either one of the symbols or to hybridize them into a new kind of flower even if, zoologically, that were possible. Instead, he chose to "give meaning to my lifestyle keeping the rose and the *sakura* in view simultaneously," preferring "to see life with the fullness of double or even multiple vision" (Aoki, 1979/2005, p. 347).

I have a photograph of Ted Aoki and his wife, June, standing on a footbridge at Nitobe Gardens in Vancouver in the quiet of a morning in late spring. For me, this scene brings to mind Aoki's idea of the imaginary bridge that stands in the space between cultures, languages, races, classes, generations, and genders. In choosing to linger on this bridge and enter into the dialectic of identity and difference, Ted and June have contributed much to a deepening of our understanding of human becoming. As a teacher, as a human being, as a friend, I see no better place to be than on this bridge.

References

Aoki, T.T. (1978/1980/2005). Toward curriculum inquiry in a new key. In W.F. Pinar & R.L. Irwin (Eds.), *Curriculum in a new key: The collected works of Ted T. Aoki* (pp. 89–110). Mahwah, NJ: Lawrence Erlbaum.

Aoki, T.T. (1979/2005). Reflections of a Japanese Canadian teacher experiencing ethnicity. In W.F. Pinar & R.L. Irwin (Eds.), *Curriculum in a new key: The collected works of Ted T. Aoki* (pp. 333–348). Mahwah, NJ: Lawrence Erlbaum.

Aoki, T.T. (1986/1991/2005). Teaching as indwelling between two curriculum worlds. In W.F. Pinar & R.L. Irwin (Eds.), *Curriculum in a new key: The collected works of Ted T. Aoki* (pp. 158–165). Mahwah, NJ: Lawrence Erlbaum.

Aoki, T.T. (1987/2005). Revisiting the notions of leadership and identity. In W.F. Pinar & R.L. Irwin (Eds.), *Curriculum in a new key: The collected works of Ted T. Aoki* (pp. 349–355). Mahwah, NJ: Lawrence Erlbaum.

Aoki, T.T. (1990/2005). Inspiriting the curriculum. In W.F. Pinar & R.L. Irwin (Eds.), *Curriculum in a new key: The collected works of Ted T. Aoki* (pp. 357–365). Mahwah, NJ: Lawrence Erlbaum.

Aoki, T.T. (1992/2005). Layered voices of teaching: The uncannily correct and the elusively true. In W.F. Pinar & R.L. Irwin (Eds.), *Curriculum in a new key: The collected works of Ted T. Aoki* (pp. 185–197). Mahwah, NJ: Lawrence Erlbaum.

Aoki, T.T. (1993a/2005). Humiliating the Cartesian ego. In W.F. Pinar & R.L. Irwin (Eds.), *Curriculum in a new key: The collective works of Ted T. Aoki* (pp. 291–301). Mahwah, NJ: Lawrence Erlbaum.

Aoki, T.T. (1993b/2005). In the midst of slippery theme-words: Living as designers of Japanese Canadian curriculum. In W.F. Pinar & R.L. Irwin (Eds.), *Curriculum in a new key: The collected works of Ted T. Aoki* (pp. 263–277). Mahwah, NJ: Lawrence Erlbaum.

Aoki, T.T. (1993c/2005). The child-centered curriculum: Where is the social in pedocentricism? In W.F. Pinar & R.L. Irwin (Eds.), *Curriculum in a new key: The collected works of Ted T. Aoki* (pp. 279–289). Mahwah, NJ: Lawrence Erlbaum.

Aoki, T.T. (1996/2005). Spinning inspired images in the midst of planned and live(d) curricula. In W.F. Pinar & R.L. Irwin (Eds.), *Curriculum in a new key: The collected works of Ted T. Aoki* (pp. 413–423). Mahwah, NJ: Lawrence Erlbaum.

Aoki, T.T. (2000/2005). Language, culture and curriculum . . . In W.F. Pinar & R.L. Irwin (Eds.), *Curriculum in a new key: The collected works of Ted T. Aoki* (pp. 321–329). Mahwah, NJ: Lawrence Erlbaum.

Aoki, T.T. (2003/2005). Locating living pedagogy in teacher research: Five metonymic moments. In W.F. Pinar & R.L. Irwin (Eds.), *Curriculum in a new key: The collected works of Ted T. Aoki* (pp. 425–422). Mahwah, NJ: Lawrence Erlbaum.

Boelé, A.L. (2010, April). Review of *Teaching by Numbers* by Peter M. Taubman. *Education Review, 13*, 1–8. Retrieved from http://www.edrev.info

British Columbia Ministry of Education. (2002). *Policy document: Accountability framework*. Retrieved from http://www2.gov.bc.ca/gov/topic.page?id=DCC1C4815C65494E98 F53969B67DA3B4&title=Accountability%20Framework

British Columbia Ministry of Education. (2011). Developing an individual education plan. In *Special education services: A manual of policies, procedures and guidelines* (pp. 12–21). Retrieved from http://www.bced.gov.bc.ca/specialed/ppandg.htm

British Columbia Ministry of Education. (2012). Student response booklet. In *Foundation skills assessment (FSA): General information on samples*. Retrieved from http://www.bced.gov.bc.ca/assessment/fsa/en_samples/12_gr7_sample_resp.pdf

Jardine, D.W. (2006). Foreword: Dreaming of a single logic. In D.G. Smith, *Trying to teach in a season of great untruth* (pp. ix–xvii). Rotterdam, Netherlands: Sense.

Pinar, W.F. (2004). *What is curriculum theory?* Mahwah, NJ: Lawrence Erlbaum.

Pinar, W.F., & Irwin, R.L. (Eds.). (2005). *Curriculum in a new key: The collected works of Ted T. Aoki*. Mahwah, NJ: Lawrence Erlbaum.

Smith, D.G. (2006). *Trying to teach in a season of great untruth: Globalization, empire and the crises of pedagogy*. Rotterdam, Netherlands: Sense.

Sumara, D., Davis, B., & Laidlaw, L. (2001). Canadian identity and curriculum theory: An ecological, postmodern perspective. *Canadian Journal of Education, 26*(2), 144–163.

14

EVOLVING INSIDE THE LANDSCAPE

Fireweed Phenology

Shanna Hagens

Fireweed Forefront

The writing of Ted Aoki on place and situatedness, relationality and tensionality, and the *curriculum-as-lived* (Pinar & Irwin, 2005) opened for me a landscape where I could ground myself as a scholar in the curricular world of the Denendeh. This collection of poems based on the phenology of fireweed demonstrates an organic unfolding of understanding that occurred as I lived and taught along the shores of the Deh Cho[1]. Dwelling there in the Aokian sense, I learned from the natural patterns of the land and traditional lifeways of Dene education that they inform. The Dene, like most place-based cultures, understand life to occur in cycles, the constants in nature forming definite patterns in the ecosystem and repeating themselves over time (Fixico, 2003): the rise and fall of the moon and sun; the cycles of seasons that shape lands, waterways, flora, and fauna according to the Earth's movements.

I write these words in gratitude for the scholarship of Ted Aoki, along with that of a co-arising and co-evolving community of many others, who dwelled with me in the land as I grew more attuned to the dynamics of the cross-cultural situation in which I found myself and more wakeful to the Earth-centered values of connection, relationship, emergence, community, and growth that permeated that place . . .

a seed adrift on the wind

> *moved by currents into*

> > *remote*
> > *terrains*

t
  w
    i
  s
t
  i
   n
    g

and

t
  u
   r
    n
     i
   n
 g

through the trees

this way

and

that way

everywhere to go

taking root

landed in stilled autumn winds
the seed burrows into the soil
threading deeper and deeper into the dark gritty earth

winter sets
life teems quietly below
silent under layers of frozen darkness

nothing is still

seasons and cycles
shift and shape
dawning

elements of change

a shoot emerging

after months of darkness
                                        midnight suns begin to
                warm the cold frozen surface
                                releasing the river to an open and steady flow—

the songs of returning birds carry through
                                the sounds of crystal ice crashing
                waking the land,
                                wind and sky breathe anew—

quietly by the river a stem slowly rises, growing
                                out of the damp, dark
                earthing/unearthing,
                                                leaves split open like a wing.

buds bursting on a flowering spike

swaying
in the shadows of trees
pods of magenta
e
s
i
r
toward the light
nurtured in
a dynamic
network
of
interdependent
relationships

opening magenta

> buds flower
> under midnight suns
> reaching the tip
> standing vibrant against a blue horizon

unseen inside the earth
  roots grow
    rhizomatically below the surface soil

                                        resiliently spreading
                                        through permafrost soils

              silently
  regenerating
        thriving
        flourishing
                    new life

seeds drifting on the wind

reaching maturation

                        seed pods dry and split open

      releasing

hundreds of soft downy seeds

            a   c   r   c   s   s

                        the land

carried by

        cool

           autumn

                b   e   z

              r   e   s

                e

filling the sky

                  with new life

red willows entwine by the river,
breathing in a changing landscape
the river speaks, silent and unseen

References

Fixico, D. (2003). *The American Indian mind in a linear world: American Indian studies and traditional knowledge.* New York, NY: Routledge.

Pinar. F.W., & Irwin, R.L. (Eds.). (2005). *Curriculum in a new key: The collected works of Ted T. Aoki.* Mahwah, NJ: Lawrence Erlbaum.

Note

1. The Deh Cho is known on most maps as the Mackenzie River. The Dene First Nations people of the Denendeh in the Northwest Territories call this river the "Deh Cho," which means "Big River."

15

LIVING PEDAGOGY . . . CRACKS AND IN-BETWEENS

The Messy of Landscapes and Languages

Marylin Low

for Ted Tetsuo Aoki, mentor and friend

Anecdotal inscriptions emerge from dwelling with/in what Aoki calls *living pedagogy*—for me, the cracks and in-betweens of educating and being educated in various landscapes and languages of the Pacific . . . of running a course—a *currere* of pedagogy—where life/work of "the messy" lives. Jagged lifelines of this text are written out of Bhabha's (2002) "spirit of dialogue that is contingent, interruptive, insurgent" (p. x) and generated from a socially ascribed genealogy of matrilineal and patrilineal curricular influences. Multiple and messy kinships are deep, un/bound to each other in history and story . . . embedded in languages and landscapes to which we do (not) belong.

An Aokian ring to an unfamiliar "me." In the world of (my) work, I am told to be clear . . . to write so that others will understand; they will know. Yet, knowing comes not from what I might say but from the reading that takes place in the multilayered messiness of words and their belongings—belongings attached by (invisible) hyphens . . . marginal lines . . . the fraying of colonial tethers that almost set them free.

english words
fall from my tongue
strange and twisted
disturbing . . . disorienting
as if I no longer belong
to this language

Written into fiscal agreements between the United States and the U.S. Affiliated Pacific Islands, the word *accountability* holds no translation. The colonial desire for numbers, not children, lives in the insistence of current systems of data-based decision making. The colonial master demands data. School lives held ransom, tied to a discourse where they become numbers, static and still. Not so for Pacific islanders. Toiling with the responsibility of their children, systems of lineage hold on to the fractured remains of culturally responsive ways—sitting with their children, teaching them to live well at home. Foreign systems impose the unfamiliar— replacing children with scores, numbing any sense of a "living" student. Multiple numbering systems in Pacific societies now reduced to one—the "count" that matters. What does accountability want from Pacific islanders now caught in the cracks and in-betweens of such an unrecognizable, irreconcilable idea? Questions abound about how they should raise the future of their society, ensuring their sons and daughters are educated in the soil and already soiled landscapes of their belonging. Local systems of cultural responsibility are torn apart at the whim of accountability. Surrender is imminent—powerful readings of a master signifier, ac•count•a•bil•i•ty, now legitimated by the impos(t)er.

ac•count•a•bil•i•ty: responsible, answerable.

An Aokian "third" reading (Aoki, 2000/2005) asks "what it may be like . . . living in the spaces of between, marked by the cracks in the words" (p. 321). Through gentle and deeply abstract metonymic moments, Aoki journeys to a space where language is no longer so bold in claiming its *what* but instead trembles in translation and transformation to a *where* that insists on language as "signifying living moments of life" (p. 328).

In conversation with Ted about numbers (personal communication, June 11, 2010) . . .

> T: *There is another story to be told . . . Attaching 82% to a child begins as fixed, yet the moment we name it, it is no longer fixed. . . . Contextual messages spill out . . . reveal . . . open out to life beyond the number 82—the percent is a metaphor for the Western style of representation—to hold firm something that doesn't want to stay still. The heavy weight numbers hold . . . relates to Lyotard's gravity of thought. A metonymic cracking helps to see there are at least two stories to be told here.*

Cracking words has become both a habit and habitat for my colleague Pat Palulis and me—a *rhizsomatic* genealogy provoked by Aoki—as we move(d) into the messiness and difficulty of reading differently (Palulis & Low, 2005). Continuing practices of living the spaces in-between, fault lines open to Taubman's (2009) accountability as assemblages—assemblages that "remove the subject/ object interface, in the sense that they are always reconnecting with the surroundings, forming new assemblages, which can stabilize or dissolve" (pp. 118–119). Pacific Islanders take responsibility for and answer to these assemblages daily . . .

for them a living pedagogy on the move . . . *accountability* with/in the landscapes and languages of the Pacific reroots itself . . . offering different accounts of life in and out of the classroom that live dangerously . . . perilously in new aporetic relations . . . uncertainties that strain and frustrate the colonial I/eye . . . a living pedagogy of accountability/responsibility that envelops assemblages on the move—systems not static or still but living in places where slippery translations abound . . . uncountable lives of children of which Pacific Islanders already carefully and precariously take account . . . lines begin to fray . . . undoing the West(ern ideal) . . . messy work.

> *english demands refuse*
> *the intrigue of*
> *languages of/in the pacific*
> *that inculcate quietly*
> *interacting with/out my knowing*
> *drenched with nuances*
> *in/visible . . . un/certain . . . thresholds*
> *of meaning I can't quite grasp*
> *these language(s)*
> *to which I do (not) belong*

Beginning Rituals

I arrive at the threshold of the classroom door, next to the pulsating waves on the ocean side of the atoll. I am the first one there. Faint lines of chalk remain on the board left from important symbolic interactions of lessons that have come before. I try to decipher the cryptic code, imagining the conversations that might have taken place. I engage in Aoki's "re"—a rewriting that is layered in meaning of (un) conscious knowing . . . in a semiotics of the vernacular and English that cannot be named . . . yet leaves its trace . . . like Henry Miller's picture erased yet never erased. I begin to write English shapes on the board while reading the juxtaposition of the faint and the visible. The background of the board brings a newness to my words that I would not have anticipated. A promise of the legacy of lineage, of this place, of this language, of our ancestors ever folded into the traces wanting to remain.

Slowly the students arrive, some individually, some in groups, and always the stragglers. We greet and comment about the day or the one before in our common language, English, and then they turn to conversation with each other, often in the vernacular, until the clock tells us it is time to begin . . . another foreign practice that never quite fits. It is a writing class with intolerable goals and unpredictable outcomes. They want rules . . . certainties that determine how to write in

FIGURE 15.1 Multiple thresholds of school life on an atoll

predictable ways valued by the testing machine. In collaboration and collectivity, they sought ordered English from me while I sought vernacular invention from them.

> *Another thing I like very much, where I am most successful perhaps, is when I have made a failure. It's usually a very good sheet of paper which I don't like to waste. So I take the watercolor to the pool and scrub it as much as I can. No matter how much I wash away there are still traces left. Then I turn the faded painting around and I paint something entirely different over it. The faint background of the failure makes the picture.*

—Henry Miller in conversation with George Belmont (1971, p. 122)

Moving within language(s), somewhat uninvited, a sacred topography that is neither me nor mine, but me nonetheless. Inscriptions of doubling. I sit with a student laboring in the doubled gestures of her writing—writing into the double folds of another language—and listen. She tells me she wants to write like me . . . a monolingual native speaker of English. I resist. Instead, together we enter a space where the vernacular and English meet—a messy, mesmerizing space that is injurious to our thoughts. It hurts. Two languages encounter the other, each different in the crafting, structuring of meaning imbued with the values of home. Silenced in the struggle, lifewor(l)ds slowly begin to emerge in unpredictable ways—vernacular reverberations that give English a shake, cracking the presumed clarity of a word, calling it into question, questioning its existence . . . a clandestine writing willed to life by a Pacific Islander and a Canadian—hyphenated writing out of the space of the in-between. "I" and "me" do not exist in her ancestral language, only "us" and "we." Conversations abound about how "we" became "me" and the influence that lexical addition has had.

This is my ritual. It is not the sort of thing I would share with others, for what would I say? Instead, I quietly remind myself of the living landscape in which I am always already immersed. Work in pedagogy has always involved my surroundings—a vast network of perceptions and sensations borne by each of us in the classroom readily experienced in daily rituals of time, place, landscapes, and languages.

Oral Traditions and English

Language education policies across the Pacific are motivated by the belief that English is (at) the root/route of the modernizing nation (Huebner & Davis, 1999). In perpetuating the *need* to learn English, some parents refuse to use the vernacular with their children. Reified in education language policies, English is the *Other* medium of instruction in bilingual programs across the Pacific. For Pacific Island teachers and students, classrooms have become linguistic "borderlands" (Mignolo, 2000); sites where language policy/practice relations toil and triumph in "the sensibilities and conditions of everyday life created by colonial legacies and economic globalization" (Mignolo, 2000, p. 46). Pacific Island teachers' linguistic practices carry the burden of living in the borderlands—code-switching practices emerging from their own experiences with/in languages now passed on to the children they teach.

In the Freely Associated States, language policies designate bilingual programs (the local language and English) in various configurations. What meanings are made of the local language policy, and what conditions enable and constrain policy/practice relations? Stories of failed remedies for the "problems" of another linger, resisting what might happen within the messy of linguistic life and learning-teaching borderlands in indigenous classrooms in the Pacific—where children bring "who they are" to learning, valued and legitimate co-inquirers in the languages given to them and learned through experiences at school—experiences of relations fundamental to life, language, and learning (Bishop, 2008). How do we make visible the sociopolitical dynamics at work in current policy/practice relations while calling into question assumptions and perspectives, including my own, around language and its use in Pacific classrooms?

Meanwhile, emerging across a wider global arena for people of oral traditions, are voluble voices that question which languages, whose literacies and learning practices, and for what purposes (Hasebe-Ludt, Chambers, & Leggo, 2009; Huebner & Davis, 1999; Kincheloe & Steinberg, 2008; Skutnabb-Kangas, 2000/2008; Street, 2005). Open to the messy and within this milieu of *métissage,* the movement strategically disrupts/interrupts rather than accepts or rejects the methodological will to clarify and be certain (Lather, 2010). Pacific schools give sway to the allure and presumed global necessity of English and its associated Western assumptions about education—assumptions that continue to reify an epistemology of packaged learning and an accompanying preoccupation with *"predefined content and skills* grounded in extant worldviews" (de Alba, González-Gaudiano, Lankshear, & Peters, 2000, p. 9). Living in tension—between everyday language and literacy practices and the more narrowly defined, traditional approaches to language and literacy learning sanctioned by many policy makers. Reinforced by "quick-fix" programs and accompanying scripted resources for children, they frequently become the de facto curriculum that is often culturally and linguistically inappropriate. Such resources "force" teachers to conform to particular ways, insisting on a particular curricular life in school (school literacy practices) and how it should be lived (taught/learned). While the dominant language of instruction for the early years of schooling is a Pacific language, the

FIGURE 15.2 Lines of obligations for (the) English master(y)

influence of English and its cultural content continues to take a role in ongoing cultural and linguistic change in the vernacular; in addition, English effects what and whose literacy is worthy of learning.

The "truths" for learning to need English that underlie educational language-policy texts and perspectives articulated by Pacific islanders incite local policies and practices—students faltering in both languages give rise to these voices—un/afraid to trouble and be troubled by global/local influences within postcolonial times (Lyotard, 1979/1984; Smith, 2000). As adults query this dilemma, hundreds of students continue to be educated in environments that do not deliver on the promise of the mission (Torres, 2000). How does a community of non-English traditions remain open to generative and difficult spaces of language and learning possibilities that may both benefit and harm the future generation of their nation?

Schooling for Pacific Island children—being and becoming literate—reverberates in global contact . . . the colonial vision inscribed . . . inscripted in the master's words. Situated in contexts of colonial exploration and exploitation, no longer can it be assumed that the local language is the language of home. Linguistic border crossings through media(ted) events such as television, video games, and the Internet are genuinely altering language use and literacy practices in radical ways. The pull of globalization, and its assumed promise of a "better" life, invokes

FIGURE 15.3 South of the equator the master's words linger. . .

deep contradictions as to how life should be lived in language(s). Members of home and school communities struggle to make sense of changing language and literacy practices in and out of school. Cracks widen within and between individuals concerned with issues of local cultural and linguistic sustainability and global "success" that necessitates academic achievement in English.

Lost in Language

Coming from oral traditions in which literacy has had limited use, Pacific children are re-wired . . . mis-wired in ways that spark of difference. Samoan poet Eti Sa'aga makes visible the complexities and blind spots of such experiences, raising questions of English and its cultural impact on reading and writing in the vernacular while exploring what happens when border crossing in languages occurs . . . a space that engenders "loss/t" . . . a place where children and adults alike are living in languages and landscapes of the messy . . . potentially generative spaces of the messy . . . if only such a space was valued for the potential it offers. Sa'aga (2009, p. 31) writes,

> I always mix my tenses
> every time I use
> the English language.
>
> I cannot seem to know
> Where to separate the past,
> end the present,
> and begin the future.
> When I write,
> the past creeps in
> to remind me that
> the present is somehow
> not arrived,
> and that the future
> might slightly
> be delayed.

What would happen if our conversations with children dwelled in the mixing and messy of two languages? Where might that take us?

People at the grass roots, living in isolated island villages, have learned to accept and resist messy landscapes and languages in differing ways. Some are reclaiming and regenerating their new locations; others leave the islands for the urban center of their entity or the mainland where enclaves of Pacific Islanders have relocated for economic benefit. For those that remain, the more creatively they regenerate their commons, the more easily they go beyond education, freeing themselves from a reactive stance, becoming more proactive in their acts of transformation—living out a deep pride in their own values, tradition, and wisdoms. Through the cracks and in-betweens, they call for generative ways of knowing and doing that are needed to survive locally and globally . . . and resist any acts of achieving one at the expense of the other.

Visions of a place to be Pacific continue to circulate throughout conversations in the region. Yet, schooling remains for too many children a ritual—a blocked right of passage—a disinterest of any meaningful relation to the place where learning occurs. School often leads nowhere (or everywhere but home)—an unresolved injustice that wounds. Education as disenfranchisement prepares young people to give up or leave their islands . . . static ideas about schooling reified . . . while cracks and in-betweens engendering spaces of living pedagogy are left untouched—landscapes and languages of the messy unwanted in school.

> And the naming of the intolerable is itself the hope.
>
> —John Berger (1991, p. 18)

> Calling us to reconsider "places of learning," Ellsworth (2005, p. 2) speaks of pedagogy as the impetus behind particular movements, sensations, and affects of bodies/mind; brains in the midst of learning . . . the embodied experiences that pedagogy elicits and plays host to: experiences of being radically in relation to one's self, to others, and to the world.

Encounters with such places of learning invoke a living pedagogy—a coursing *currere* that sets a learning self in motion . . . invites Pinar's (2004) *complicated conversations* . . . Jardine's (2000) *ecopedagogy of place* . . . getting lost with Lather (2007).

Warning

Dwelling in living pedagogy—in its richness and its rot—is messy work.

References

Aoki, T.T. (2000/2005). Language, culture, and curriculum . . . In W.F. Pinar & R.L. Irwin (Eds.), *Curriculum in a new key: The collected works of Ted T. Aoki* (pp. 321–329). Mahwah, NJ: Lawrence Erlbaum.

Belmont, G. (1971). *Face to face with Henry Miller*. London, United Kingdom: Sedgwick & Jackson.

Berger, J. (1991). *And our faces, my heart, brief as photos*. New York, NY: Vintage.

Bhabha, H. (2002). Foreword. In D. Chakrabarty, *Habitations of modernity* (pp. x–xiii). Chicago, IL: University of Chicago Press.

Bishop, R. (2008). Te Kotahitanga: Kaupapa Maori in mainstream classrooms. In N.K. Denzin, Y.S. Lincoln, & L.T. Smith (Eds.), *Handbook of critical and indigenous methodologies* (pp. 439–458). London, United Kingdom: Sage.

Ellsworth, E. (2005). *Places of learning: Media, architecture, pedagogy* New York, NY: RoutledgeFalmer.

Hasebe-Ludt, E., Chambers, C., & Leggo, C. (2009). *Life writing and literary métissage as an ethos for our times.* New York, NY: Peter Lang.

Huebner, T., & Davis, K. (Eds.). (1999). *Sociopolitical perspectives on language policy and planning in the USA.* Amsterdam, Netherlands: John Benjamins.

Jardine, D. (2000). *Under the tough old stars.* Brandon, VT: Foundation for Educational Renewal.

Kincheloe, J., & Steinberg, S. (2008). Indigenous knowledges in education: Complexities, dangers, and profound benefits. In N.K. Denzin, Y.S. Lincoln, & L.T. Smith (Eds.), *Handbook of critical and indigenous methodologies* (pp. 135–156). London, United Kingdom: Sage.

Lather, P. (2007). *Getting lost.* New York: State University of New York Press.

Lather, P. (2010). *Engaging science policy: From the side of the messy.* New York, NY: Peter Lang.

Lyotard, J.-F. (1979/1984). *The postmodern condition: A report on knowledge* (G. Bennington & B. Massumi, Trans.). Minneapolis: University of Minnesota Press.

Mignolo, W. (2000). *Local histories/global designs.* Princeton, NJ: Princeton University Press.

Palulis, P., & Low, M. (2005). The (im)possibilities of collecting conversation(s): A material event that refuses closure . . . *Journal of the American Association for the Advancement of Curriculum, 1.* Retrieved from http://www2.uwstout.edu/content/jaaacs/vol1/index.htm

Pinar, W.F. (2004). *What is curriculum theory?* Mahwah, NJ: Lawrence Erlbaum.

Sa'aga, E. (2009). *Me, the laborer.* Apia, Samoa: Malua Printing Press.

Skutnabb-Kangas, T. (2000/2008). *Linguistic genocide in education—or worldwide diversity and human rights?* New Delhi, India: Orient Longman.

Smith, D.G. (2000). The specific challenges of globalization for teaching and vice versa. *Alberta Journal of Educational Research, 46*(1), 7–26.

Street, B. (Ed). (2005). *Literacies across educational context.* Philadelphia, PA: Caslon.

Taubman, P. (2009). *Teaching by numbers.* New York, NY: Routledge.

Torres, M. (2000). *Literacy for all: A United Nations literacy decade (2003–2012).* Paris, France: United Nations Educational, Scientific, and Cultural Organization.

16

HARAAM

Sheila Simpkins

In the poem "Stormtide," penned by the Kurdish poet Sherko Bekas, a fisherman asks the tide why its waves are in a rage; the tide responds,

> *I am for the freedom of the fish*
> *and against*
> *the net*

Haraam[1]

> The panel commends the care with which ethical issues have been presented and considered using the very thorough processes for this purpose at the home University. There are particular issues surrounding the conduct of research using students at the University of Kurdistan-Hawler, and in regard to the Kurdistan culture, which need to be addressed. Your research project at the University of Kurdistan has been approved pending the following changes:
>
> That the complete anonymity of the participants be preserved in the publication of material from the project by using pseudonyms in any such material. . . . As a result of these changes, the YES box in Section 17b [of the ethics application forms] need be ticked to show that participants will be anonymous in the dissemination of results. (Personal communication, Research Ethics Committee at the University of Kurdistan-Hawler, Iraq, 2010)
>
> I am shocked, dismayed.

Graduate work was something of a spiritual conversion for me. What wonder, what marvel, the discovery . . . music, poetics, narrative, photography, storytelling, drawing, drama, *métissage*, autoethnography, incorporating artistic modes, violating prescribed conventions, *sonare* re/siding with *videre*,[2] inquiry, sensual pleasure . . . how divine a revelation. I rejoiced in the rebellion and rejection of the traditional, the positivistic, the scientific, the impersonal, the unembodied, the insensible. I have become a seeker of pleasure, seeking and finding pleasure in my research and writing. I have embraced this newness like a new religion. And like any zealous convert, I have turned my back on the old ways. The planning of my research and dissertation was a celebration of the new, a passionate endeavour.

My research involves practicing narrative métissage to foster empathy and understanding in a postconflict society. Métissage "weaves disparate elements into multi-valenced, metonymic, and multi-textured forms, unravelling the logic of linearity, hierarchy, and uniformity" (Hasebe-Ludt, Chambers, & Leggo, 2009, p. 35). And so, I planned to write up the dissertation in a way that re/presented métissage; it would be polyvocal, polyphonic, a mingling of texts and genres and voices. Photography, painting, collage, and audio and digital recordings would be incorporated into the dissertation in celebration of the oral, literal, visual, and embodied ways we humans have of engaging in the world.

Obtaining ethics approval to use auditory and digital recording along with autobiography had required much back and forth conversation with ethics advisors, many revisions, careful wording, painstakingly finding a way through the maze of obstacles to be able to carry out my envisioned research/dissertation.

And now this. Complete anonymity of participants? But . . . that means . . .

> . . . *no audio recording* . . .
> . . . *no digital recording* . . .
> . . . *no photographs* . . .
> . . . *my research project is now dismantled* . . .
> . . . *my carefully laid plans all for naught* . . .
> . . . *painstakingly completed ethics forms null and void* . . .
> . . . *the core is gutted* . . .
> . . . *the dissertation has been demolished* . . .
> "*And so?*" *I can hear you ask.*

I am embarrassed, chagrined, to say that I reacted quite badly. Oh, don't get me wrong. I didn't lament, didn't get angry, didn't say anything. The situation was too precarious. I felt too vulnerable. But . . .

What I kept thinking was, *What the hell!!* And, *Surely, if it's good enough for the University of Victoria's ethics committee, it's good enough for the administration at the University of Kurdistan!* And, *My God, these people don't even have an ethics board.*

And, *God knows the ethics board at UVic is very thorough!* And, *Who do they think they are?*

I am more than embarrassed, more than chagrined. I am shamed. For these sentiments are wrapped up in cultural superiority; Western-conceived research wrapped up in Western values wrapped up in Western ethics committees wrapped up in *If it's good enough for the West, it's good enough for everywhere*. But . . .

The shame goes deeper than that. After the dust of the umbrage, the offence, the disappointment, the devastation settles, I am aware that I have been painfully, disturbingly, caught out. I should have known better. After all, I had spent a year here, teaching and living in Kurdistan.

The shame is bone deep. For I begin to remember what it is I know about Kurdistan and the danger of the pen. The danger of speaking, and of writing and of naming.

I know . . . that independent journalists are exposed to extreme danger in Kurdistan. Freedom to write, to speak, to have an opinion has boundaries. There is a culture of harassment, intimidation, physical assault, beatings, violence, hate mail, death threats, and arrests carried out by police officers, government security guards, and the ruling party security forces sanctioned by the courts. Harassment in the form of lawsuits and defamation charges brought against editors and newspapers and journalists by influential politicians are par for the course. Newspapers and independent journalists practice self-censorship on topics that seem very benign to a Westerner. There are many lines that can't be crossed, subjects that are off limits: religion, sex and/or sexual orientation, tribal/historical leaders, corruption and nepotism, critique of the Kurdistan Regional Government (KRG) are *haraam* . . . really *haraam* ("Attacks on the Press," 2010; Home Office: UK Border Agency, 2009; "Iraq," 2010; "Press Conditions Deteriorate," 2010; Reporters Without Borders, 2010; United Nations Human Rights Committee, 2010).

I know . . . that to get a death threat means that sometimes it is not just a threat.

I know . . . about Sardasht Osman. Sardasht was a 23-year-old English language student at the University of Salahaddin in Erbil, Kurdistan. He was also an independent journalist who often wrote about public issues such as corruption and nepotism, and he was critical of the KRG, local politicians, and the security forces. He had been "warned" on numerous occasions to stop his investigative journalism. In April 2010, Sardasht crossed over the line, into the forbidden, when he wrote a satirical poem, "I am in love with Massoud Barzani's [President of Kurdistan] daughter" (Osman, 2010). It was an indictment against the nepotism, elitism, and family/tribal privilege that is prevalent in Kurdish society. It cleverly critiqued high unemployment rates and lack of social services. He wondered how his life, and that of his family's, would change if he were married to the president's daughter. For this rhetorical wondering, Sardasht began receiving death threats. On May 4, 2010, security soldiers kidnapped him outside the gate of Salahaddin University. His tortured and slain body was found 2 days later.

I know . . . that complete anonymity of my participants is a necessary precaution. I am not experienced enough. This is not my culture. I am in over my head. My participants are too young. What would be crossing the line? What would be off limits? What would be *haraam*?

There is tension in dwelling in ' the space in between" two cultures (Aoki, 1991/2005). It is trying and difficult Ted Aoki (1991/2005) exhorts me not to try to rid myself of the tension, "for to be tensionless is to be dead like a limp violin string" (p. 382). He encourages me rather to "seek appropriately attuned tension, such that the sound of the tensioned string resounds well" (p. 382).

How do I re/at/tune the tension so that the string re/sounds well?

I hear the sound of the waves crashing up against the shore, I feel the firm sand under my feet, the cold wind on my face. I taste salt in the air. And I say with Sherko Bekas . . . I am for the freedom of the fish.

References

Aoki, T.T. (1991a/2005). *Sonare* and *videre:* A story, three echoes, and a lingering note. In W.F. Pinar & R.L. Irwin (Eds.), *Curriculum in a new key: The collected works of Ted T. Aoki* (pp. 367–365). Mahwah, NJ: Lawrence Erlbaum.

Aoki, T.T. (1991b/2005). Taiko drums and sushi, perogies and sauerkraut: Mirroring a half-life in multicultural education. In W.F. Pinar & R.L. Irwin (Eds.), *Curriculum in a new key: The collected works of Ted T. Aoki* (pp. 377–388). Mahwah, NJ: Lawrence Erlbaum.

Attacks on the press 2009: Iraq. (2010, February 16). *Committee to Protect Journalists.* Retrieved from http://www.cpj.org/2010/02/attacks-on-the-press-2009-iraq.php

Hasebe-Ludt, E., Chambers, C., & Leggo, C. (2009). *Life writing and literary métissage as an ethos for our times.* New York, NY: Peter Lang.

Home Office: UK Border Agency. (2009). *Country of origin information report: Kurdistan regional government area of Iraq, May 21, 2009.* Retrieved from http://www.rds.homeoffice.gov.uk/rds/pdfs09/iraq-kurdistan-220509.doc

Iraq: Kurdistan authorities must investigate abduction and murder of journalist. (2010, May 8). *Amnesty International.* Retrieved from http://www.amnesty.org.nz/news/iraq-kurdistan-authorities-must-investigate-abduction-and-murder-journalist

Osman, S., (2010). I am in love with Massoud Barzani's daughter. *Kurd Net.* Retrieved from http://www.ekurd.net/mismas/articles/misc2010/5/state3816.htm

Press conditions deteriorate in Iraqi Kurdistan. (2010, May 24). *Committee to Protect Journalists.* Retrieved from http://www.cpj.org/2010/05/press-conditions-deteriorate-in-iraqi-kurdistan.php

Reporters Without Borders. (2010). *Mission report, between freedom and abuses: The media paradox in Iraqi Kurdistan.* Retrieved from http://en.rsf.org/irak-between-freedom-and-abuses-the-03–11–2010,38736.html

United Nations Human Rights Committee. (2010, August 10). *Ruling party threat to freedom in Iraqi Kurdistan. Refworld.* Retrieved from http://www.unhcr.org/refworld/country,,,,IRQ,,4c64f1271e,0.html

Notes

1. *Haraam*: adj. hä-'räm: Is an Arabic term meaning "forbidden." It is also used in Kurdish. *Haraam* has, over the years, accumulated additional nontraditional uses to it; *haraam* can mean "shame."
2. Ted Aoki (1991a/2005) explains, "It is imperative that the world of curriculum question the primacy of *videre* and begin to make room for *sonare*" (p. 373). *Videre* is the disembodied objective world of what the eye can see. *Sonare* is embodied knowing, feeling, and emotion.

17

PALEOGRAPHIES OF AOKIAN DISCOURSE

A Genealogy of Border Pedagogies and Generative Possibilities

Patricia Palulis

> Living at the borders means that one constantly treads the fine line between positioning and de-positioning. The fragile nature of the intervals in which one thrives requires that, as a mediator-creator, one always travels transculturally while engaging in the local "habitus" (collective practices that link habit with inhabitance) of one's immediate concern.
> —Trinh Minh ha, from *Elsewhere, Within Here*

This opening quotation is taken from Trinh Minh-ha's recent work titled *Elsewhere, Within Here*, an exquisite title for treading fine lines . . . for risking border pedagogies . . .for in-dwelling with Aokian discourse . . . and for detours . . .

. . . In-Dwelling Midst a Detour . . .

Driving along Highway 24 heading southeast of Calgary, I am suddenly startled by the roadside signification of a Hutterite colony. Recollections of an Aokian narrative are sweeping through like the prairie winds drifting across the frozen landscape of southern Alberta. I have just departed from a conference on "Re-writing Lyotard" at the University of Alberta. Ted Aoki introduced us to Jean-François Lyotard's postmodern condition in the summer class of '96. The chair of my session was jan jagodzinski. Proper names become entangled in storied recollections—as nostalgic in-dwelling with the winter winds sweeping across shimmering prairie grasses on a lunar landscape. We pass Brandt and are heading for Vulcan to pick up supplies for an overnight stay in a cottage on Little Bow Lake. I am traveling with an old friend, and we are reminiscing about our long-ago Arctic teaching assignments on Baffin Island in Nunavut. I am here following the conference to escape the tensions of academia, but the storied journey keeps on writing. Aoki was interned in the prairies and wrote his way out of camp and into a school. I have been camping out in the nation's capital and escaping here in the circulation of groundswelling grass sweeping prairie winds. Inspirited by exquisite silent resonances. We are journeying through a landscape that opens to nowhere and everywhere . . . I am reminded of Cynthia Chambers and a curriculum of place as "wayfinding."

. . . A Teacher as a Material Event . . .

Reading Ted Aoki as a material event, I want to trace a multiplicity of inter-woven threads through what Arendt (1968) articulates as a *paleography* of script and commentary. Arendt is referring to the work of Walter Benjamin. I transpose the paleographic traces transculturally in a re-positioning and de-positioning to Aoki: reader, writer, scholar, teacher, friend. Writing his way out of the internment camps and becoming an internationally acclaimed curriculum scholar, Ted excited and incited his students, encouraging us to work in hybrid in-between spaces. We thrived in the generative spaces that he opened up for us. My transition from student to professor has been a difficult liminal passage. The adventure of lived experience at the borders of pedagogy has been about bringing Aokian discursive doublings to the nation's capital and tracking the (mis)adventures that follow.

Smith (2003) articulates Ted's way as "the place of no-place, and so his classes were a haven for the dispossessed, the homeless, the bruised, the sufferers of exclusion, and really that includes us all, and that is the point" (p. xvi). Smith goes on to say that "Ted's pedagogical genius was (is) to construct a place safe enough for each of us to explore this Other side of ourselves" (p. xvi). I arrived in his class in the summer of '96 as a wounded writer. Ted opened a space for de-centering and re-writing of selves. A space opening to generative possibilities. Reading the work of Hélène Cixous, I was delighted to find a genealogy of time/place in-between-ness. Shurmer-Smith (2000) draws our attention to Cixous's "terrifying ability to write placeless spaces" (p. 155). At the spring convocation of 1992, at the University of Alberta, Aoki and Cixous received honorary doctor of laws degrees. Readers recognized that honours should be bestowed upon these two provocative scholars of outlaw genres in a *place of no-place* and in *placeless spaces*. An extraordinary recognition, and I poach the words from a Derridean (2006) title: *geneses, genealogies, genres, and genius*. Could this be where Trinh (2011) is treading? In the genealogies of border pedagogies, in the in-between of place and no-place, there might be found an interval in which possibilities might thrive.

. . . Teaching as Estrangement . . .

Aoki (1979/2005) recollects his first teaching assignment:

> What job did I choose? I actually had no problem in deciding. I found that no real alternative faced me. I accepted the job at the Hutterite school—as caretaker, teacher, principal, all wrapped up in one package—and

launched a pedagogical career—a move that by the way, I have never regretted taking. (p. 341)

He found, however, that "teaching on a Hutterite colony was a stranger's existence . . . with little contact with fellow teachers or the mainstream of the community's social world" (p. 341). My current position at the University of Ottawa is likely my last post, and yet my estrangement shares a resonance with Ted's *stranger's existence*. Perhaps it is about arriving too late or getting off at the wrong stop. I attend to Trinh's articulation *of the fragile nature of the intervals in which one thrives* as one seeks out the border pedagogies that designate an in-dwelling *elsewhere, within here*. And slowly but with intensity, however fragile, *one thrives*—in the midst of discursive tensions—in-dwelling on a fault line—within the gap in-between incommensurable positionings.

. . . (Un)homely Departures . . .

Strangely, the graduate(d) student is unlikely to find a position at home. We always leave home as a prerequisite in the transition from student to professor. A fragile de-positioning. According to Shurmer-Smith (2000), "All the residents of Academia . . . are refugees from somewhere else" (p. 154). When we arrive, perhaps we need to ask with Cynthia Chambers (2008): "Where are we?" And I want to ask, are we not exiled from our academic homeland? Tenure-tracked and awaiting the passport to cross the tracks, we are in the *place of no-place*—a terrifying *placeless space*. The richly textured discursive traces of a graduate-student experience struggle to survive in the strange land of academia. I am reminded repeatedly of what I have lost, and yet the liveliness of ex-static remains has me scrambling and rummaging to gather the paleographic remnants, the tatters and the scraps, the eccentricities of script and commentary as *bricolage*. As an academic refugee, I camp out in temporary tenancies (un)settled. I seek readings from Boutros and Straw (2010) in their edited collection of essays on urban culture. Boutros and Straw draw from Jörg Heiser on contemporary culture as "fluctuating relations between forms as they move through social space" (Heiser, as cited in Boutros & Straw, 2010, p. 3). Transposed to another time and place, I am drawn into this *fluctuating* momentum and must navigate my way through the local currencies of social space—circulating and resisting at the same time. Reading with Trinh, *one always travels transculturally while engaging in the local "habitus"*—a difficult journey fraught not only with hazards but also with the possibilities of unexpected intervals in which one might *thrive*—those intervals happen as events of the unexpected. Sometimes students lead us into *elsewhere* spaces.

. . . The (Im)Possibility of Grounding Aoki . . .

Writing with Marylin Low in an essay on the collected works of Ted T. Aoki, edited by Pinar and Irwin (2005), we were asked by our reviewers to further ground Aoki in the work (Palulis & Low, 2005). Initially resistant, we finally consented to grounding Aoki without Aoki. We took courage from Ted's consenting to teach a course at McGill if he could do foundations without foundations. I have since learned that this is serious play. When my dossier was evaluated for tenure, this peer-reviewed publication was declared not peer-reviewed. Peer-review without peer-review. As a boundary event. There is always a tension between gathering and dispersion through a frontier control. As Derrida (2005) cautions, to protect a "home," we must "control the flow" (p. 66). Derrida reminds us that Stéphane Mallarmé "designates the reader as a 'guest'" (p. 9). Some guests can be demanding. They can create a lot of trouble wanting to re-arrange the words and their authors all the while counting and discounting. Derrida contends that "like the presence of the Greek *tithenai* ('to put') . . . the act of *putting, depositing*" becomes also the act of "stabilizing immobility" (p. 7).

In times of deep distress, I turn to the writings of Morris (2009), who cautions, "We must not let them win . . . the scholar who cannot psychologically manage the force of the intrusive mother (the academy) loses the battle" (p. 228). Morris insists that we are fighting a war of words (p. 217). I am confronted repeatedly with my own naïveté. I expected to arrive, unpack Aokian discourse, and disperse fragments inciting capital events. I find myself, instead, seeking a *hospes* in Aoki's (1993/2005) positioning and de-positioning of humiliation "polyphonically in *humour* and *human* and *humus* and *humility*" (p. 300). A compost heap becomes an in-site of generative possibility.

. . . Ruptures of Time and Place . . .

"Countering both the nostalgic desire for a retrieval of rooted, place-bound identities on the one hand, and that antinostalgic embrace of a nomadic fluidity of subjectivity, identity, and spatiality on the other," Kwon (2004) opens up to "a theorization of the 'wrong place,' a speculative and heuristic concept for . . . belonging-in-transience" (p. 8) based on (un)sitings of "absence, distance, and ruptures of time and space" (p. 9). Kwon is reading Don DeLillo's play titled *Valparaiso,* in which the protagonist on a business trip to Valparaiso, Indiana, ends up in Valparaíso, Chile. This is DeLillo's "fictional critique of the postmodern condition" whereby "the disruption of a subject's habitual spatiotemporal experience propels the liberation and also the breakdown of its traditional sense of self" (as cited in Kwon, 2004, p. 160). I have found ways to survive and *to thrive* despite the heated template(d) conditions and the frostbitten boundaries. Sometimes it means working out on what Smith (2003) terms the *hermeneutic space,* "the special terrain of Hermes" (p. xvi). Just as Ted wrote his way out of internment camps, I struggle to escape through re-writings from the man-dated templates of academia. Kwon (2004) depicts how DeLillo's protagonist recognizes "a sense of belonging that is not bound to any specific location but to a system of movement" (p. 163). Morris (2009) offers a way out through writing: "When hope is lost, freedom to write begins" (p. 257).

. . . Getting off at the Wrong Stop or At-Work With the Un-Worked, Dés-oeuvré . . .

Getting off at the "wrong place" or, as Kwon puts it, a "belonging in transience" (p. 8), I begin to map my *where* abouts and to build a temporary shelter—a papery shelter—where entanglements might open to Trinh's *elsewhere within here*. Lost in the messiness of *paperies*, my students and I often forget about the templates. We work with Kwon's notions of what is un-worked, *dés-oeuvré* (p. 154). Letting go. It is the very estrangement that has become a generative site for in-dwelling in Aoki's "third" discourse—a doubling momentum of metaphor/metonymy. Of place/not place. Reading Aoki with Derrida the momentum lives on. Derrida (2005) articulates his mode of travel: "I skid and I drift irresistibly" (p. 103). I am adrift in his wake. I am still unpacking my library with Walter Benjamin. Proper names find their way to the special shelves reserved for them. But names begin to *skid and drift* as they become *irresistibly* entangled with each other. Dismantling templates, I seek with Trinh those *fragile intervals* . . .

In the midst of everyday moments, Aoki's metonymic doublings emerge in *interstitial spaces* to startle, to excite, to incite. Arriving late or at the wrong stop is a chance for something else to happen. I have learned with Steedman (2002) that "being wrong" can be "part of the story" (p. 168). The wrong place disrupts the notion of a right place. In the *Dust* of the archival narrative of what cannot be found, "*this* not-going-away-ness" provokes imperishability (p. 165). Steedman contends, "Dust . . . is about circularity. . . . Nothing goes away" (p. 164).

As Kwon (2004) contends:

> Often we are comforted by the thought that a place is ours, that we belong to it, even come from it, and therefore are tied to it in some fundamental way. Such places ("right" places?) are thought to reaffirm. In contrast, the "wrong" place is generally thought of as a place where one feels one does not belong—unfamiliar, disorienting, destabilizing, even threatening. (pp. 163–164)

Camping out as a bricoleur, I build a hut of my own with whatever is at hand—my artefacts from elsewhere. A Tunisian birdcage in the shape of a mosque, framed in olive wood, the clasp left unhinged in the hopes that origami birds in blue and white folds might take flight. Janan and I carried our birdcages through the border zones in between Tunisia and Libya— and now a refugee camp is suspended in the borderlands of two countries. We message back and forth in agonistic insecurities over the fate of Libya—a country that once hosted us as teachers. A rug from Azerbaijan—a whalebone carving from Nunavut—each evocative object wrenching the remnants of an emotive trace. A bluefish sculpture from Lansdowne Market off Bank Street in Ottawa keeps company with a blue wooden dromedary from a folk art shop at Alma and 10th in Vancouver. And I settle into a makeshift sense of homeliness in Ottawa. I am at-work with "wrong" being part of the story, and this not-going-away-ness evokes an unrelenting restlessness. Everywhere is Dust.

. . . Quarrying Midst the Refuse and Refuge . . .

Reading in-between, I seek out the intervals of what Trinh (2011) terms "refuse and refuge" (p. 43). In the refuse and refuge of my *paperies,* I set up camp—on the far side of the Corktown Footbridge over the Rideau Canal. Academia resides across the canal. Academia is a discourse. Aoki cracks it—inviting humility to disrupt the arrogance of academia. Ted always says that you have to stay with the tension, and that has been the most difficult lesson. I am haunted by a multiplicity of voices reminding me of the work yet-to-be-done. I am torn by the desire to escape from the continuing assault of insult and impasse or to linger in Trinh's *elsewhere within here*—the intervals as vibrant spaces of an Aokian "third" discourse rich with generative possibilities and tensionalities. What remains as remains are the openings—the cracks—the seductions of the void—evoking a momentum so that other scholars might *thrive* in the *fragile interval*—quarry in the void midst the refuse and the refuge. The question becomes, how might we create conditions of generosity so that our students might *thrive* and their students might *thrive*? Perhaps that is the (un)homely question that is haunting genealogy. Aoki opens up these spaces for us through traveling *transculturally while engaging in the local.* I invite the reader to attend to Bourdier and Trinh (2011) on vernacular dwellings: "Building is already dwelling . . . this practice so carefully passed from one generation to the next does not impose a restrictive framework; it rather establishes a basis for creativity" (p. 22). And to Trinh's (1991) earlier words,

> To listen, to see like a stranger in one's own land; to fare like a foreigner across one's own language; or, to maintain an intense rapport with the means and materiality of media languages is also to let go of the (masterly) "hold" as one unbuilds and builds. (p. 199)

A passing on of paleographic traces from one generation to the next becomes a fragile interval. Ted Aoki's foundations without foundations would have us indwelling on a fault line. And yet, as Morris (2009) puts it, "Creativity can be born out of that very fragility" (p. 261). Getting off at the wrong stop, you begin to improvise a precarious *inhabitance* in which genealogical traces of Aokian discourse might open to Trinh's *elsewhere within here.* The going(s) on happen *as one unbuilds and builds . . .*

References

Aoki, A. (1979/2005). Reflections of a Japanese Canadian teacher experiencing ethnicity. In W.F. Pinar & R.L. Irwin (Eds.), *Curriculum in a new key: The collected works of Ted. T. Aoki* (pp. 333–348). Mahwah, NJ: Lawrence Erlbaum.

Aoki, A. (1993/2005). Humiliating the Cartesian ego. In W.F. Pinar & R.L. Irwin (Eds.), *Curriculum in a new key: The collected works of Ted. T. Aoki* (pp. 291–301). Mahwah, NJ: Lawrence Erlbaum.

Arendt, H. (1968). Introduction. In H. Arendt (Ed.), *Illuminations: Walter Benjamin 1892–1940* (pp. 1–55.). New York, NY: Random House.

Bourdier, J.-P., & Trinh, M.T. (2011). *Vernacular architecture of West Africa: A world in dwelling.* London, United Kingdom: Routledge.

Boutros, A., & Straw, W. (Eds.). (2010). *Circulation and the city: Essays on urban culture.* Montreal, Quebec: McGill–Queen's University Press.

Chambers, C. (2008). Where are we? Finding common ground in a curriculum of place. *Journal of the Canadian Association for Curriculum Studies, 6*(2), 113–128.

Derrida, J. (2005). *Paper machine.* Stanford, CA: Stanford University Press.

Derrida, J. (2006). *Geneses, genealogies, genres, & genius: The secrets of the archive.* New York, NY: Columbia University Press.

Kwon, M. (2004). *One place after another: Site-specific art and locational identity.* Cambridge, MA: The MIT Press.

Morris, M. (2009). *On not being able to play: Scholars, musicians and the crisis of psyche.* Rotterdam, Netherlands: Sense.

Palulis, P., & Low, M. (2005). The (im)possibilities of collecting conversation(s): A material event that refuses closure. *Journal of the American Association for the Advancement of Curriculum Studies, 1*(1), 1–20. Retrieved from http://www2.uwstout.edu/content/jaaacs/vol1/palulis.html

Pinar, W.F. & Irwin, R.L. (Eds.). (2005). *Curriculum in a new key: The collected works of Ted T. Aoki.* Mahwah, NJ: Erlbaum.

Shurmer-Smith, P. (2000). Hélène Cixous. In M. Crang & N. Thrift (Eds.), *Thinking space* (pp. 154–166). London, United Kingdom: Routledge.

Smith, D.G. (2003). Preface: Some thoughts on living in-between. In E. Hasebe-Ludt & W. Hurren (Eds.), *Curriculum intertext: Place/language/pedagogy* (pp. xv–xvii). New York, NY: Peter Lang.

Steedman, C. (2002). *Dust: The archive and cultural history.* New Brunswick, NJ: Rutgers University Press.

Trinh, M.T. (1991). *When the moon waxes red: Representation, gender and cultural politics.* New York, NY: Routledge.

Trinh, M.T. (2011). *Elsewhere, within here: Immigration, refugeeism and the boundary event.* New York, NY: Routledge.

PART III

Living the Topos

18

CULTIVATING AN AESTHETIC SENSIBILITY IN CURRICULAR SPACES

Five Aesthetic Moments

Wanda Hurren

> *My only agenda is to unearth the very familiar and commonly shared dimensions of our lives that have been neglected in theoretical aesthetics and to appreciate their significance, aesthetic or otherwise.*
>
> —Yuriko Saito, from *Everyday Aesthetics*

Throughout my years in the curricular world, I have continued to move along lines of inquiry that call up visceral and embodied aspects of knowing (in) places. Most recently, I have been paying attention to aesthetics and places where we think and do our work—schools, classrooms, libraries, offices, hallways—any place where we think and do under the category of "work." I am taking up the notion of *aesthetic* as something that would enliven our senses, versus the notion of *anaesthetic* as something that would dull or numb our senses.

While it is generally accepted that aesthetic surroundings enhance creativity, well-being, and even productivity in workplaces, it is often the case that people have very little control over adjusting the aesthetic surroundings of the places where they think and do their work. So, rather than focus on structural renovations, I am intent on inquiring into ways in which we can renovate the way we *think*. I am advocating for contemplating aesthetics and cultivating an aesthetic sensibility in the places where we think and do our (curricular) work. *Cultivating an aesthetic sensibility* is an action that requires slowing down our minds and paying attention to what is right in front of us, developing an appreciation for what we encounter in our everyday worlds. In a delineation of the ideas of various educational philosophers from Plato to Whitehead, Caranfa (2007) links contemplation and quiet thought with the development of an aesthetic sensibility, and he further suggests it is necessary for the good of all, and for optimum living, learning, and working. Cultivating an aesthetic sensibility does not require formal art lessons. It is an activity that people can develop as they go about their daily routines, as long as they are paying attention and noticing. Inviting students or colleagues to walk down a hallway in the early morning and notice the light or the silence or the feelings encountered is an example of such an activity.

Hearing of the recent highest recorded sale of a living artist's work—£21.3 million for a painting titled *Abstraktes Bild (809-4)*, owned by rock guitarist Eric Clapton and painted by Gerhard Richter—I was reminded that my first encounter with Richter's work was through the scholarship of Ted Aoki. Ted wrote a chapter for an earlier curriculum anthology (Aoki, 2003/2005), and as one of the coeditors of that anthology, in relation to Ted's chapter, Erika Hasebe-Ludt and I were tasked with gaining permissions to include the work of two prominent artists—the visual artist Gerhard Richter and poet and singer-songwriter Leonard Cohen.

Ted Aoki was a curricular scholar with a particular aesthetic sensibility—this was evident in both the content and presentation of his work. He had an uncanny knack for calling attention to aesthetic moments in the details of his deliberations. His invitations to linger were most often issued around ideas and notions that held some form of aesthetic component: Japanese kanji, word equations, stories, legends, song lyrics, haiku, jazz music, foods, artwork. Ted's wife, June, appears in several of the stories and deliberations that Ted shared throughout his scholarship, and many of the aesthetic components of Ted's work pay homage to June's presence and her own aesthetic sensibilities and artistic accomplishments; Japanese calligraphy was one of those.

So now, in the spirit of Ted Aoki's call to linger, I would like to invite you to linger with me in several curricular spaces and attend to what I hope will illustrate small, everyday moments that hold an aesthetic dimension. By curricular spaces, I am referring to the physical spaces on the pages of this anthology as well as to metaphorical and geographically referenced spaces where curriculum is deliberated and enacted. Borrowing the format from Ted's five metonymic moments (Aoki, 2003/2005), what follows, then, are five aesthetic moments shared in various curricular spaces, ranging from the large and wide open to the small and intimate.

Aesthetic Moment #1: Opening a Door

I first encountered Ted Aoki's ideas in a paper I read during my master's program, in the early 1990s at the University of Saskatchewan. I don't recall the exact title; I think it may have been a chapter in a collection of papers published by the University of Alberta. I think it was about action research and teacher education. I also saw Ted's name referenced in several papers that I really liked. And I heard about him through other students and curriculum scholars. He was already a bit of a legend in 1992.

Then, in 1995, I moved with my family to Vancouver, to begin doctoral studies at UBC. One of the first people I met was Erika Hasebe-Ludt, and it turned out she was finishing her doctoral program just when I was beginning mine. I was very excited to attend her doctoral defense in the Graduate Student Centre at UBC. The morning of her defense I was running a little late and just about to enter the building, when I could see a little man coming along between two other buildings and heading across the parking lot towards the Grad Centre. He was walking quite quickly, and he was carrying a cardboard take-out tray filled with styrofoam cups; small white creamers were piled up in the centre of the tray. I could tell he wouldn't be able to open the door when he reached it. So I waited for him to cross the parking lot, and I held the door open for him. He chuckled and thanked me, a big smile on his face. It turned out we were both headed into the same exam room, and then I could see that he was joining the committee members at the table. He was one of the university examiners at the defense, and yes, it was indeed Ted Aoki. And *I* had opened the door for *him*.

Aesthetic Moment #2: June

As a doctoral student at the University of British Columbia (UBC), I attended several doctoral defenses wherein Ted was a member of the examining committee. On many of those occasions, June accompanied him and sat at the back of the room. She listened quietly during the examinations and joined in on the outside edges to congratulate students during their celebratory moments following the announced outcomes. She was dressed impeccably, with smart heels, swingy skirts, and beautifully styled hair. I was struck by the way Ted and June were both present in that curricular space, and in this everyday act of togetherness. In fact, in the years that I was a doctoral student, and for several years following, before they moved into a care home, both Ted and June attended conferences, speaking engagements, and various curricular events. I witnessed this as an example of the everyday beauty of two people sharing a life together. It was affirming to me, and touching, that even the solemnness and formality of a doctoral defense could become a space where Ted, a renowned curricular scholar, would insist on and ensure space for a familial presence, that of June.

Aesthetic Moment #3: Swamp Tour

In 1999, I attended the inaugural meeting for the International Association for the Advancement of Curriculum Studies, held at Louisiana State University in Baton Rouge, Louisiana. When the conference finished, several of us stayed on and had a day to explore. Pat Palulis, Marylin Low, and I wanted to take a "real" swamp tour, and we asked Ted and June if they would like to join us. We searched through several brochures, called up a tour company, rented a car, picked up Ted and June from their hotel, and headed for the swamp. We had to wait about three quarters of an hour for the start of our tour. Our pickup point was at a small pub along the bayou. We hadn't had any lunch, so while we waited, we ordered what we could from the bar menu: pickled eggs, beer sausage, beer.

Well, when we got on the swamp boat, the "captain" informed us that we were on a *canal* and not a real bayou. We spent a fascinating 90 minutes boating along a muddy canal, feeding alligators marshmallows and raw chicken parts that the swamp boat captain had tied onto the ends of butcher's string.

At one point during the tour, the captain gave an exasperated answer to my question, what is the difference between a canal and a bayou? He rolled his eyes and said, "Canals are made by men and a bayou is made by"—and he pointed up to the sky and looked at me like I should know the answer to *that*. At first I felt a sense of almost embarrassment that we had dragged Ted and June all the way out there for such a hokey swamp tour, but Ted and June, in their way, honoured that swamp boat captain by asking questions and respecting his answers. It was a most memorable afternoon. "Real" is a relative descriptor.

Aesthetic Moment #4: Lunch With Ted and June

On a couple of occasions, I joined Erika for lunch with Ted and June when they were residents of a care home in Vancouver. If we were coming for a visit, Ted insisted we come to share lunch with them. We sat together at a window table in a smaller dining room off of the main dining area. After lunch, we would head up to their room for a visit. Ted and June had a one-room suite; it was a space with enough room for a few comfortable easy chairs, a dresser that held many family photos, a small keyboard organ, and two twin beds pushed together.

On one of these visits, we shared with Ted the table of contents from the present anthology. He listened very closely, with his eyes closed, and as we named each contributor, he said, "Oh yes." He was keen to hear what each contributor was writing about. June sat and listened quietly, sometimes getting up to straighten a photo, sometimes getting up to look out the window. Several times during our lunch and visit that afternoon, June looked at Erika and me and emphatically stated, with a twinkle in her eye, "Oh, I've never seen such beautiful women."

Aesthetic Moment #5: Ted and June

At the end of a visit with Ted and June at their care home, they insisted on riding the elevator with us down to the main floor entrance to say good-bye. After hugs and good wishes, they remained in the entrance as we left the building, and we turned around for a last farewell wave. That was a moment of mixed emotions.

A jumble of words might illustrate something of what I was holding in my heart and head: *humbleness warmth why don't we do this more often when will we meet again will we meet again emptiness fullness appreciation honouring bittersweet intellect intuition gratitude holiness fragility robustness friendship mentorship.*

•••••••••••

> *Even the seemingly trivial, insignificant everyday aesthetic attitudes and judgments often wield surprising power that can determine the quality of life, the state of the world, or social and cultural ethos in the most literal manner.*
>
> —Yuriko Saito, from *Everyday Aesthetics*

References

Aoki, T.T. (2003/2005). Locating living pedagogy in teacher "research': Five metonymic moments. In W.F. Pinar & R.L. Irwin (Eds.), *Curriculum in a new key: The collected works of Ted T. Aoki* (pp. 425–432). Mahwah, NJ: Lawrence Erlbaum.

Caranfa, A. (2007). Lessons of solitude: The awakening of aesthetic sensibility. *Journal of Philosophy of Education, 41*(1), 113–127.

Saito, Y. (2007). *Everyday aesthetics.* New York, NY: Oxford University Press.

19

THE QUESTION OF COMMUNITY

Community in Question[1]

Terrance R. Carson

Ted Aoki on Community: A Preface

I had Ted Aoki very much in mind as I mulled over accepting an invitation from the Graduate Students' Association to be the keynote speaker for their annual research showcase. In considering this invitation I recalled that the major part of Ted's writing had come in the years after 1985, following his retirement from the University of Alberta and his term as chair of the Department of Secondary Education. I also recollected that much of his subsequent writing had emerged from invitations to speak to various audiences on questions of curriculum and pedagogy. Obviously, Ted had responded affirmatively to invitations such as the one I had received.

I, too, had been chair of the Department of Secondary Education and was now just embarking on my retirement. Although Ted's pedagogical responsiveness set an example that I, and his many other students, admired, most compelling for me was the subject matter of the invitation. I was asked to speak on the matter of sustaining community.

Thoughts on the state of community prompted memories of earlier conversations with Ted. As a doctoral student and then a newly minted assistant professor, I had occasion, from time to time, to discuss the question of community with Ted. Often, I left these conversations perplexed by his ambivalence about the question of community. No doubt, his early life experience of exile from the British Columbia coast and the difficulties he encountered gaining entry to the teaching profession played a part in engendering this scepticism about the inherent benevolence of community. Only recently have I come to this realization. At the time, I recall Ted saying simply, "I would like us to appreciate how difficult it is to form community."

Ted's comment about the difficulty of forming community has stuck with me. His caution helped form the genesis of my presentation, as I thought about the paradoxes of desiring community, lacking community, and already being in a community that we are already unconsciously making and shaping . . .

Introduction

I would like to begin by congratulating the Graduate Student Research Showcase organizers on the choice of the theme: "Sustaining Communities." It is a timely topic for an age where the ties that bind us seem increasingly fragile. And yet, it is a uniquely appropriate topic for interdisciplinary attention from the side of educational research, given the trust placed in education for sustaining memory and preparing future generations. The theme of sustaining communities speaks directly to the trust in education that Madeline Grumet had in mind when she defined curriculum as "the collective story we tell our children about our past, our present, and our future" (as cited in Gough, 1999, p. 50).

Reflecting on the conference theme not only bids attention to the centrality of community in education but also highlights the fact that the meaning of community is in flux. If community is about what binds us together, what does community mean in this time of globalization, instant messaging, wedge politics, and fragmented media?

I have been thinking about this question of community for some time—most recently while on my way to the gym, listening to the Canadian Broadcasting Corporation radio program *Spark,* a show specializing in technology and culture. The host, Norah Young, was interviewing a young British artist by the name of Thomas Thwaites (2010), speaking about his "Toaster Project," in which he tried to make a toaster—literally from scratch. "By scratch" he meant mining the iron for making the steel grilling apparatus, the nickel to make the heating element, the copper for the electric wires, and so forth. Thwaites posted a video on his website documenting the painstaking activities of mining, smelting, and assembling a blobby-looking toaster (http://www.thomasthwaites.com/the-toaster-project/). The website also contrasts his scratch-built creation with a smooth and shiny manufactured toaster that could have been purchased for less than £4.00 from the local big-box store.

Thwaites made several observations about what the toaster project teaches concerning the effects of modern methods of production. One is the arrogant assumption of the superiority of modern production methods. Making a toaster by hand gave Thwaites a fresh appreciation for the skill and ingenuity of early mining and metallurgy. A second more striking observation concerns human relationships. The effort that went into earlier forms of production was the work of human hands, of people we knew, or could imagine. By contrast, while modern culture still depends upon others for the plethora of cheap manufactured goods used in daily life, those others responsible remain invisible in the easy availability of the products we use. This second point says much about the condition of community today. We may depend upon others for our livelihood and welfare, but those others are often invisible in our day-to-day lives. How are we to respond as educators interested in building and sustaining community?

Dwelling in the Question

By way of response, I begin by respecting what Gadamer (1989) terms as "the hermeneutic priority of the question" (p. 362). Gadamer rebukes modern scholarship for its impatience with questions, pointing to our habit of immediately shifting questions into problems to be solved. In Gadamer's view, the difficulty with problem statements is that they already harbour opinions as to the direction of the answer. Opinion, Gadamer argues, "suppresses questions [having] a curious tendency to propagate itself " (p. 366). By contrast, genuine questions have the character of openness—prompted by the desire to know. Questions arrive suddenly, "already a breach in the smooth front of popular opinion" (p. 366). As such, "a genuine question presses itself upon us, . . . [and] we can no longer . . . persist in our accustomed opinion" (p. 366).

It seems to me that what binds us together in community today is just such an insistent question. The world is now replete with many examples of destruction of communities from the disappearance of indigenous languages, and with these, the cultural knowledge and ways of being, to the decline in the legitimacy of familiar social and political institutions in Western democracies, as reflected in the habit of many people choosing not to vote, among other expressions of disinclination to participate in the civic conventions of community.

Gadamer (1989) implies that this tendency to convert questions into problems is merely a form of escape into action. A hermeneutic consciousness begins from a different place, the place of existence. This is the condition of "being thrown" into an already-existing world. As such, our task is not primarily doing, but thinking. Thinking entails the art of questioning and the willingness to engage in dialogue (p. 367). And if we are prepared to enter into dialogue, and to listen, we may begin to understand the conditions of our being—how we are together in this place at this time. Given this perspective, it seems to me that hermeneutics provides an appropriate stance to begin to consider how the matter of "sustaining community" addresses itself to us as educators.

Keeping Open the Question of Community

In the interest of keeping open the question of what it is that binds us together in community, and considering the effects of the invisibility of such ties, I want to offer a couple of observations for your consideration:

Observation #1: Remembering Traditional Community

Davis (2009) provides some insight into traditional community in his 2009 Massey Lecture series. He begins by lamenting the disappearance of indigenous languages, fully half of which will vanish in our lifetimes. This disappearance, Davis asserts, seriously depletes the "ethno-sphere," entailing a loss of ancient wisdom born of a rich variety of ways of life. These varieties of life should not be regarded as failed attempts at being modern, but as part of a "social web of life, an ethno-sphere . . . [representing] the sum total of all thoughts and intuitions, myths and beliefs, ideas and inspirations brought into being by the human imagination since the dawn of consciousness" (p. 2).

Davis's (2009) description of the Barasana people of the Amazon in his third lecture is particularly striking for the insights it brings to the organic sense of community. Here he tells of a people who have "no sense of linear progression of time, destiny or fate" (p. 102). What is remarkable about the example of the Barasana is that it shows a people who live in relationship with the world, and not as exploiters. Within this relationship the shaman has singular importance. Davis explains:

> [It is the shaman's] duty to move in the timeless realm of the *He* (the chaotic violent spirits), embrace the primordial powers, and harness and restore the energy of all creatures. He is like a modern engineer who enters the depths of a nuclear reactor to renew the entire cosmic order.
>
> Among the Barasana, such renewal is the fundamental obligation of the living. . . . Human beings, plants and animals share the same cosmic origins, and in a profound sense are seen as essentially identical, responsive to the same principles, obligated by the same duties, responsive for the collective well being of creation. There is no separation between nature and culture. (p. 109)

From today's vantage point, the world of the Barasana is small, strange, and remote, far away in time and space from a modern consciousness, which has constructed a cosmology built upon divisions between human beings and nature. Modern consciousness has formulated a relationship in which nature itself is objectified and classified, to be understood only in terms of use value—in Heidegger's (1954) terms, as a "standing in reserve" for human use. We need to consider the costs that are exacted in terms of alienation from each other and from a world of meaning, to pay for the obvious material gain resulting from our enframement as beings separated and separate from nature and the natural world.

Observation #2: Dispersal of Subjectivities in Contemporary Community

We are told that networking through Facebook and other social media has the potential to create new forms of virtual communities. Certainly, these innovations are changing the landscape of social intercourse, but what form of community is this to be? Who are we connected with and in what ways? Turkle (2011) observes that while technology sometimes delivers closeness, much of modern life leaves us less connected with people and more connected to simulations of them.

A few years ago, as one of the "seniors" in the faculty, I was asked to comment on the most remarkable changes I had experienced since joining the university in 1982. I immediately thought of the ambivalent effects of e-mail, which has enabled immediate contact with others, while setting up an expectation that one is always available for instantaneous response. This reflex response to e-mail breeds a kind of hyperactivity. We have become busier, but we are busier at home or behind closed office doors, alone in front of our computers and not in face-to-face relationship. This has implications for sustaining communities.

Hyperactivity and individualism are some of the effects created by the material culture of computer technology, described by Borgmann (1993). But Turkle (2011) points in a different direction, away from the effects of computers on culture—an important consideration in itself—and towards the effects of technology on the constitution of the subject. This raises fresh questions about sustaining communities, concerning whom it is that is speaking, and whom it is we imagine ourselves to be with in relationship through technology. This is the territory of the post-human, a field of inquiry that has been emerging in interdisciplinary scholarship and primarily informed by post-structural theory. A central figure in post-structuralism is Gilles Deleuze, known as the philosopher of movement and difference. Deleuzian concepts based on nonrepresentational and horizontal thought have proved to be enormously productive in navigating understandings of multiplicities and destabilized subjectivities in a postmodern condition.

Post-structuralism leads to a third opening to the question of sustaining community: How should we, as educational scholars, now engage with others in our teaching and research?

Observation #3: Curriculum Studies as Currere: Towards Personal and Social Reconstruction

While ancient wisdom and the implications of (post)modern communication technologies are chronologically divergent, they converge around the theme of sustaining communities through the field of curriculum studies. In his award-winning book, *What Is Curriculum Theory?* Pinar (2004) remarks that curriculum studies is the "only academic discipline within the broad field of education . . . unique in hav[ing] its origin in and ow[ing] its loyalty to the discipline and experience of education" (p. 10).

Curriculum studies launched on a new path of scholarship some forty years ago when its putative expertise on curriculum design was largely bypassed during major national curriculum development projects in the United States in the 1960s. As a consequence, the field was, justifiably, declared moribund by one of its leading lights—Schwab (1969).

In response, a reconceptualized curriculum studies has moved the field from an overwhelmingly technical focus on the design and management of the curriculum-as-plan (Aoki, 1986/1991/2005), to curriculum as an active unfolding of the course of life, as expressed in the metaphor of curriculum as *currere,* from the Latin verb "to run." The shift from a narrowly institutional interest on curriculum development to focusing on *running the course of life* opened the field to a multiplicity of informing discourses ranging across autobiography, phenomenology, gender studies, politics, history, psychoanalysis, aesthetics—and including wisdom traditions and post-structuralism. According to Pinar (1974), the project of a reconceptualized curriculum studies is personal and social reconstruction.

Reconceptualism is not without controversy. There are those who feel that in abandoning curriculum design, a reconceptualized curriculum studies has lost focus, no longer serving teachers and public education as it pursues self-absorbed intellectual interests. Our faculty is no stranger to this debate, with curriculum studies sometimes positioned as being "too theoretical" for the practical necessities of teacher education and professional development.

This debate about theory and practice and the place of curriculum studies in a faculty of education speaks directly to the question of sustaining communities and of our responsibilities as educators. Pinar (2004) makes a strong case for curriculum theory in the renewal of American public education as an antidote to a "crippling anti-intellectualism [suffered] as the internalized consequences of decades-long subjugation" seeing in curriculum theory a "renewed "commitment to the intellectual character of our professional labour" (p. 9).

Despite periodic attempts by politicians and right-wing think tanks to import a "crisis" mentality from the United States, support for schools and public education has remained fairly strong in Canada. We should not become complacent, nor should we ignore the larger issue of the relationship between public institutions, such as schools, and sustaining communities. We need only look to the history of Indian residential schools in Canada to appreciate the damaging effects of public institutions on communities.

Returning to the Question of Community

Ultimately, the question of community and our role as educators is not about institutions, but about how we are bound together—how we lend help and depend upon one another. A difficulty we face today in an era of global capitalism is that these others we depend upon are usually invisible. If we need something, we just go shopping—who made the products and the conditions of their work are far from our conscious minds. Even within institutions, face-to-face transactions often take the form of an impersonal relationship of the buying and selling of services. Invisible and impersonal relationships that work against sustaining communities are further complicated as we enter new and unexplored territories opened up by new communication technologies and social networking.

I feel that the project of personal and social reconstruction that drives the reconceptualization of curriculum studies as currere can offer some important intellectual resources for an education concerned with sustaining communities. Vibrant discourses of curriculum such as post-structuralism, postcolonialism, wisdom traditions, and eco-justice pedagogy are critically informative regarding our current conditions and prod our thinking towards creative new directions.

The beginning of inquiry is to recognize that something is questionable. In this regard, I especially want to recognize the work of my friend and colleague David Smith, who has done much to bring the discourses of ancient wisdom to curriculum theorizing. His work has helped foster a new generation of scholarship, influencing thinking in indigenous curriculum studies, postcolonialism, and the connection of these to eco-justice pedagogy. It was David Smith and Ted Aoki who first introduced me to hermeneutics as I began my doctoral studies some thirty years ago. And it is to hermeneutics I want to return to make some closing remarks on the matter of sustaining communities.

Community as Obligation

The hermeneutics to which I now return is a so-called radical hermeneutics, as articulated by the American philosopher John Caputo (1987). A radical hermeneutics is one that is informed by the postmodern condition—that is, a hermeneutics that engages with change and movement without having to resort to metaphysics or transcendental concepts for explanation to escape having to live in the flux. A case in point addressed by Caputo is the question of ethics in postmodernity. Caputo (1993) terms the postmodern condition "disastrous" (p. 6). By disaster, Caputo means literally losing one's star—a dis-aster from the Latin *astrum*, star. In the condition of postmodernity, we do not have ready rules of behaviour, principles, or ideas worked out in advance that can be applied to situations demanding ethics. What we have are *obligations* to one another.

In response, Caputo again summons the Latin roots of obligation as the condition of being bound—from the verb *ligare*. Caputo explains that obligations happen, not of our choosing, but by being called by the other. It is not the generalized other we are called by, but the particular other who has a face. To explain, Caputo references Emmanuel Levinas's invocation of the story of Abraham, who responds to God *me voici*—here you will find me. I call upon Caputo and his poetics of obligation, because the concept of obligation says much about sustaining communities. We do not make communities; we cannot simply will them into existence. Rather, community happens as a result of obligation and how we respond to these obligations.

This does not make things any easier. We all feel many obligations in our lives, probably too many, as we try to juggle obligations to partners, family, friends, students, teachers, colleagues, career, etc. This is the price of autonomy in modern society. Here, Caputo (1993) cites Jean-François Lyotard's remark that "obligation is a scandal to autonomy" (p. 7). It was far easier to be a participating member in a traditional society whose obligations were determined by systems of preordained roles and expectations.

And yet, as we sort through these obligations, deciding to respond, or not, we are already forming communities of one sort or another. The question is, what kind of community is this to be? Teaching in a faculty of education at a university inherently creates conflicting relationships between building an academic career and obligations to the teaching profession. As a former department chair, I have seen this tension up close and worry about the tendency of some to take their cue from the perspective of career advancement rather than from a sense of obligation to public education and the uplifting of the teaching profession. That is a tension worth keeping in mind as you embark on your scholarly careers.

References

Aoki, T.T. (1986/1991/2005). Teaching as indwelling between two curriculum worlds. In W.F. Pinar & R.L. Irwin (Eds.), *Curriculum in a new key: The collected works of Ted T. Aoki* (pp. 158–165). Mahwah, NJ: Lawrence Erlbaum.

Borgmann, A. (1993). *Crossing the postmodern divide*. Chicago, IL: University of Chicago Press.

Caputo, J. (1987). *Radical hermeneutics: Repetition, deconstruction and the hermeneutic project*. Bloomington: Indiana University Press.

Caputo, J. (1993). *Against ethics: Contributions to a poetics of obligation with constant reference to deconstruction*. Bloomington: Indiana University Press.

Davis, W. (2009). *The wayfinders: Why ancient wisdom still matters in the modern world*. Toronto, Ontario: House of Anansi Press.

Gadamer, H.-G. (1989). *Truth and method* (Rev. 2nd ed.; J. Weinsheimer & D. Marshall, Trans.). New York, NY: Crossroad.

Gough, N. (1999). Understanding curriculum systems. In J.G. Henderson & K.R. Kesson (Eds.), *Understanding democratic curriculum leadership* (pp. 47–69). New York, NY: Teachers College Press.

Heidegger, M. (1954). *The question concerning technology and other essays* (W. Lovitt, Trans.). New York, NY: Harper & Row.

Pinar, W.F. (Ed.). (1974). *Curriculum theorizing: The reconceptualists*. Berkley, CA: McCutchan.

Pinar, W.F. (2004). *What is curriculum theory?* Mahwah, NJ: Lawrence Erlbaum.

Schwab, J. (1969). The practical: A language for curriculum. *School Review, 78*, 1–24.

Thwaites, T. (2010). *The toaster project*. Retrieved from http://www.thetoasterproject.org/

Turkle, S. (2011). *Alone together: Why we expect more from technology and less from each other*. New York, NY: Basic Books.

Note

1. This chapter is based on my invited keynote address to the Graduate Student Research Showcase, Faculty of Education, University of Alberta, March 10, 2011.

20

THIS BUT A PRELUDE OF WHAT'S TO COME

Renee Norman

Taking Leave

I have left many places
packed traces and memories
paper relationships
but this time
this time
I did not look back
no fear of turning
into a pillar of salt either
but a way to begin healing

the plant gracelessly bestowed
upon my arrival
new growth all dried up and leaves dead
(a cliché, I know
but it happened)
I tossed with relish
symbolism
into the garbage
remembering my friend's plant
died before she left too
the plant some kind of office psychic

I have walked away from many people
a poet friend once told me

and it's only now I understand
the import of his words
and why

Did You Teach Today?

my mother asks this question
every time I visit
over and over
it is the semantic thread that runs
through our conversations
what binds us
to the leftovers of fried memory
linguistic linguine
how I imagine
the plaque in her frontal lobes

how could you come today?
didn't you have to teach?
defined by that
forever in time a pedagogue
though I am between students
between institutions
between ambitions

my mother's friends
listen closely around the tea table
they seem to retain more
of what I say
do they notice the inconsistencies?
how I rewrite the past?
ignore the future?
play with the present?

no, I'm not at school
I was at a university
then left
(I am AWOL, resigned, fed up, broken)

did you teach today?
I'm on leave

did you teach today?
yes I left early

did you teach today?
no I got a day off

did you teach today?
prevaricate much?
think about
the one tenuous piece
of remembrance that still connects us?

my mother's friends smile
grateful for diversion
they accept
the way my story shifts
changes
reshapes

Why Aren't You in School?
my mother asks again
when I visit
I got out early, I say
the simple answer is best
when you know
you'll have to repeat it
endlessly
repeat it endlessly
endlessly

the truth is longer
more complicated
I haven't taught
in a school
for 2 years
it's questionable
whether she would comprehend
a position at a university
I don't comprehend it either
& I have all my faculties
just not the one
where I've been working
hostility, betrayal, envy
the stuff of the workplace

to my mother
I'm stuck in time
school time
a place I'd gladly time travel

instead
for an hour
I maintain the fiction
the wound

Inspiration

If Nikki Giovanni
can write love poems at 65

talk of her mother
how she made her feel safe

cast Martin Luther King Junior's dream
as a vision for the earth

elevate girls to remind them
all they can be, do

celebrate Obama's win
the beginning of possibility

write her poems
such passion & humility

read her poems aloud
as if they really make
a contribution

believe that writing
makes a difference

if Nikki Giovanni
can capture all of this
with her warm smile
simple words
rich images

down-to-earthness
1 good lung

so can I

Flight

a teacher friend dies
and the world changes
no butterfly this metamorphosis
but memory's wings unfold
in the poem I wrote
about her years ago
the grace she lived with
a disabled son

I watch a movie
about Linda McCartney's death
cry again for my friend
who should have gotten
another 20 years at least
think of what those last months
were for her
her wisdom fluttering
in my mind

the courage it took
to raise that son
mend a broken marriage
fight for children
with special needs

I can't believe she's gone
a mutual friend laments
I feel her
in the bright Monarch ink
I'm writing here
this poem that flies

Home for the Summer

shoes are back
the wooden porch
more leather than wood
cracker crumbs

on the couches   tiny beige
counterpoint to green fabric
dishes
line the counters once again
signal that the dishwasher
has not been unloaded
a waiting game
coffee fallout
appears daily underneath
the cappuccino machine
a Hansel and Gretel trail
of grains to the garbage
beside the unused vacuum

I tidy   shop
and cook
and cook some more
and repeat this process
countless times
mostly with motherly satisfaction
adventurous daughters all temporarily returned
to be honest
a day or 2 of rebellious tantrum
frustration at the fights
but more relief
staving off loneliness

calm and quiet is precious
welcome
restful in appropriate quantities
you do need to hear yourself
talking to your soul

but the requests for mending
DVDing
washing
rides
assistance with forms
and plans
packing
and appointments
that daughter noise
daughter mess
is daughter joy

Teacher

like old times
I sit in the school lobby
awaiting her emergence
instruments once again
cleaned and encased
this young woman
who makes such beautiful music
whose notes are in my blood
on the wind

earlier she chatted animated
with
students
with her mentor
well on her pedagogical transformation
to teacher
marshalling teenagers with instruments
into rows or on stage
an admonishing tap
on a shoulder here
a laugh at a comment
there
synchronized with her mentor
she assists
organizes
plays with the band
that gorgeous low thrum
of her contrabassoon
resonating through
her students' melodies
this but a prelude
of what's to come

I imagine her
in a band room many years ago
working a shammy
through the neck
of a brown and silver instrument
soaking up the spittle
or last year, those sensitive hands

on stage at her recital . . .

and she emerges
dry
glorious
about to burst into song
teacher-to-be
Dazzling Stripes

today I meet with two women
from Beijing
here to learn
about our Kindergartens

what would they say
about yesterday?
I sat with Hayden
who draws zebras
write for me, he demanded
instead we wrote together
his "i" first,
then an admission:
he's worried about the letters
the wrong way

oh, everyone does that at first
I tell him
I did too
don't worry about it now
get your ideas down

I write less
as Hayden writes more
he spells zebra perfectly
I tell him where to find
more books on zebras

today I meet with the two women
from Beijing
I will tell them about zebras
their dazzling stripes
like unformed letters
calling to small boys

For Ted Aoki

always
he will dwell in a place
with roots and rhizomes
I image there
steaming bowls of rice
teriyaki sushi sake
contiguous food metonymy

in the midst of such delicacies
he will embrace his daughter
marvel at her youthful beauty
preserved luminous
whisper how they missed her
how even when he could not see
he held on
to every moment of earthly grace
words forming like flowers
in his ears
in the scent of culture
home
the and/or
and tree roots

21

FIND A SPACE IN BETWEEN FOR INTERCULTURAL ADAPTATION

My Curriculum Cookbook and Ted Aoki

Nicole Nie Bowden

My name is Nicole Ye Nie (Bowden). In 2007, I came to Canada from China to study for my master's degree in curriculum studies. It was my first time coming to a foreign country. Like many international students and immigrants, I had certain assumptions about Western culture. Initially, I struggled with culture shock, dealing with the differences between Canadian and Chinese societies. Now, as I continue to explore this new culture, I am gradually changing my cultural perspectives and emerging more fully into a culturally diverse environment. Over time I have become attuned to many different aspects of Canadian culture. I address and understand this culture through specific things that happen in my studies and my personal life. I consciously compare the differences and similarities between the two cultures. I think deeply about how cultural identity influences people in their intercultural communication and interactions.

In 2009, I conducted an autobiographical study and wrote a master's thesis titled *My Curriculum Cookbook: An Autobiographical Study on Understanding Curriculum From a Cross-Cultural Educator's Perspective* (Nie, 2009). The autobiographical study relates my personal experiences as an international student in Canada to curriculum theory and issues in multicultural education. The study takes a creative, cookbook-journal format, using a selection of recipes for exploring cross-cultural experiences and making connections between self and the multicultural environment, and between curricular theories and educational practice. While sometimes recipes refer to simple instructions, the curriculum recipes in this study do not provide simple solutions but rather creative ways of thinking about curriculum. The research question guiding my study was, *how can we understand multicultural curriculum so that majority groups (the host people in Canada) and minority groups (the people from other cultures) acknowledge a space of shared responsibility for intercultural adaptation, and so that there are not two sides or positions for people when crossing cultures, but a space in between where people dwell together?*

Ted Aoki's (1991/2005) work was an essential influence regarding my chosen research topic. As a Japanese Canadian educator, he paid close attention to multicultural issues in education. In his work he related his unique perspectives of both Eastern and Western cultures to curriculum, and he discussed notions of cross-culturalism and interculturalism in curriculum. He advocated for a notion of "dwelling in" (p. 385) the space between cultures. This is an inspiration to many curricular scholars including myself.

How I became interested in the idea of *a space in between* was quite interesting. As an international student struggling with a poor financial situation, I found a family to stay with, and in exchange for cooking dinner for them, I received free room and board. They were a French Canadian family, and their daily diet consisted of typical Western food. I was initially concerned about my Asian cooking style. I knew I needed to figure out a way to make my food appropriate for two different tastes, Eastern and Western.

Finally, I was able to find some common ground: chicken curry; we all loved it. My chicken curry is not the original Asian recipe. The authentic version is far spicier. Here in Canada I put in less curry paste and a lot of coconut milk. Also, I leave out the peppers and add eggplant instead. The reason I adapted my original recipe was to make it more suitable for the Western tastes of my host family while maintaining a taste that I enjoy.

From my personal food experience, I realized that we need to look for *a space in between* for intercultural adaptation. Many people from other cultures (minority groups) try as hard as they can to change themselves to fit into the environment essential for "survival" in a foreign culture. They focus only on *fitting in*. For example, they change their diet to Western and they make friends only with English speakers to improve their English. Meanwhile, some host people in Canada (majority groups) have the assumptions that intercultural adaptation is the responsibility for guest people only.

However, intercultural adaptation is the fit between individuals and their environment (Gudykunst & Hammer, 1988) but not the case of one fitting *into* another. Guest people enter a new cultural environment and adapt to fit into it. The cultural environment also changes because of them and for them. Host people, sharing the multicultural environment with guest people, are influenced by the change of the environment and make adaptations too. This mutual adaptation leads both guest people and host people to a collective understanding toward their coexistence in the multicultural environment.

The interactions between my host family and me provide a vivid example of intercultural adaptation from both sides. My host family's eating conditions have changed since I joined them. I had to adjust my cooking styles to suit their needs, but they didn't push me to learn to cook Western food. Instead, they let me discover it on my own. During this time of curiosity and discovery, I thought about not only my host family's tastes but also my own likes and capabilities.

I made a balance between the West and the East by adding my interpretation of Western and Eastern styles of cooking and eating. On one hand, I adapted my cooking ways to their needs. On the other hand, they adjusted their tastes to accommodate my cultural cuisine. Our mutual interactions changed our traditional dining environment to a mixed cultural experience rather than an environment that one must *fit into*. Together, we contributed to the adapted dining environment and experience and found a space in between where we could *dwell* together.

Aoki (1995/2005) discusses the concept of space in his work many times. As a scholar who cared deeply about community and cultural diversity, he advocated for a space for the "community as difference" instead of "community as diversity." He saw "inscribed in the word 'community' the words 'common' and 'unity'" (p. 306). In this community, diversity masks difference. Corresponding with his ideas, along with Aoki, I strongly ask if it is necessary for everyone, host people and guest people, to look for a space in between, not only "a space between East and West" (p. 316), or a space between guest and host people, but also an "interspace where the otherness of others can not be buried as is done with the imaginary of community as diversity" (p. 308). It would be ideal for guest people to have the space to make their adaptations to the new cultural environment "without losing [their/our] own essential sense of self" (O'Neill & Cullingford, 2005, p. 109). That is, a space for both groups—majorities and minorities—to make their intercultural adaptations with a unique sense of self and a full respect for others. Can we have that space? How might curriculum enable the idea of this space?

References

Aoki, T.T. (1991/2005). Taiko drums and sushi, perogies and sauerkraut: Mirroring a half-life in multicultural curriculum. In W.F. Pinar & R.L. Irwin (Eds.), *Curriculum in a new key: The collected works of Ted T. Aoki* (pp. 377–388). Mahwah, NJ: Lawrence Erlbaum.

Aoki, T.T. (1995/2005). In the midst of doubled imaginaries: The Pacific community as diversity and as difference. In W.F. Pinar & R.L. Irwin (Eds.), *Curriculum in a new key: The collected works of Ted T. Aoki* (pp. 263–278). Mahwah, NJ: Lawrence Erlbaum.

Gudykunst, W.B., & Hammer, M.R. (1988). Strangers and hosts: An uncertainty reduction based theory of intercultural adaptation. In Y.Y. Kim & W.B. Gudykunst (Eds.), *Cross-cultural adaptation: Current approaches* (pp. 106–139). Newbury Park, CA: Sage.

Nie, N.Y. (2009). *My curriculum cookbook: An autobiographical study on understanding curriculum from a cross-cultural educator's perspective* (Master's thesis). Retrieved from http://dspace.library.uvic.ca:8080/handle/1828/2016

O'Neill, D., & Cullingford, C. (2005). Cultural shock or cultural acquisition? The experiences of overseas students. In C. Cullingford & S. Gunn (Eds.), *Globalisation, education and culture shock* (pp. 107–123). Aldershot, England: Ashgate.

22

IN THE DISCIPLINE OF . . . *WIND*

Vicki Kelly

At the beginning of time, it is said that Wind and the Light of Dawn lay upon one another, giving birth to Changing Woman and life. They were one and the same. Then they separated to light the way and to move all things with different breaths of Wind.

—Gregory Cajete, from *Look to the Mountain*

Introduction

As an indigenous artist educator, I have been pondering the tensioned relationship between sight and sound, or what Ted Aoki (1991/2005) called *sonare* and *videre*. I sense that my pedagogical disposition as an educator is moving from a preoccupation with videre, as a visual artist, to that of sonare, as a musician. Like Aoki, I too had "become enamoured of the metaphor of *videre* (to see), thinking and speaking of what the eyes can see . . . to revel in words such as 'images,' 'speculation,' 'insights,' 'visions,' 'supervisions,' and 'light that illuminates our seeing'" (Aoki, 1991/2005, p. 373). I had noted that my curricular praxis was pregnant with such expressions, and when as a musician I began to listen and to hear in new ways through native flute playing, I began to participate more profoundly in the sounding and echoing of the world. I believe that today Ted Aoki's call to action is even more relevant than it was when he spoke to music educators in 1990.

The time is ripe for us to call upon *sonare* to dwell juxtaposed with *videre*. It seems urgent that we come to be more fully sonorous beings than we are. It is imperative that the world of curriculum question the primacy of *videre* and begin to make room for *sonare*. (p. 373)

In my own Anishinaabe heritage, like in many other traditions, there are creation stories wherein the world was created from sound, and there are creation stories that describe how the world was created from light. In this chapter, I explore indigenous understandings of sight, sound, and wind, and I describe how these understandings have shaped what is understood as indigenous education. Juxtaposed within this exploratory text I will place reflections or echoings inspired by Aoki's (1991/2005) article "*Sonare* and *Videre:* A Story, Three Echoes and a Lingering Note." Complementing the singular harmonic songline of the text with "contrapuntal polyphonic tensionality," I hope to create places of resonance, dissonance, a cacophony of immersed voices with "individual characters in its braided polyphony, winding a complex skein that glows white-hot from within" (p. 371).

Indigenous Education

Indigenous traditions have honoured wind as an expression of the breath of life and the essence of thought for centuries. Indigenous people believe it is the breath that represents the most tangible expression of the spirit in all living things. Within indigenous education, many things are sacred and indigenous pedagogy is about learning the true nature of one's spirit (Cajete, 1994). Central to understanding indigenous education is the cultivation of spiritual ecology and the nourishing of the learning spirit.

In the indigenous worldview, all things are sacred. Lifelong learning is following the sacred pathway; from the moment of conception to beyond the moment of death, it is about learning one's true nature, being whole, findings one's life, or becoming complete for life's sake. First comes learning from the environmental ecology into which one was born: the land, the family, the community—in other words, the biocultual diversity that through the pedagogy of place educates. Understanding nature and the more-than-human world, as well as the nature of being human and the role of culture and community—all this was expressed and communicated through the various manifestations and uses of breath in all its forms.

Spiritual Ecology

Indigenous spiritual traditions created a spiritual ecology revolving around seeking life and communicating with the various manifestations and metamorphoses of breath to realize a higher level of completeness in life's journey.

Cajete (1994) describes four concepts or metaphors that inform the expression and cultivation of spiritual ecology within indigenous education. They are "seeking life" and "becoming complete," the concept of "highest thought," the concept of "orientation," and the concept of "pathway" and "tracking" (p. 45). In the following section, I will braid these concepts or metaphors with *echoings* of my own lived experience in order to weave an emerging patterned pathway of finding "the discipline of *WIND*."

Seeking Life and Becoming Complete

The phrases *seeking life, for life's sake, to find life, to become complete, of good heart or thought, in balance and harmony,* and a host of other related variations of metaphors are used by indigenous people to describe themselves, their places, and their relationships. All indicate an intension to enter a process or sacred way of "remembering to remember" as individuals and as a community. They are used as phrases in ceremony, in community cultural events, as part of ritual prayers, and in teaching.

> These shared metaphors reflect an underlying continuity of thought and participation that have profound influence. . . . They imply a journey of learning to know life in all its manifestations—especially those of the spirit—and through this journey experience a state of wholeness. Seeking, finding, being with, and celebrating spiritual ecology is the essential meaning of the phrase "that's the place Indians talk about." (Cajete, 1994, p. 46)

As a guiding metaphor, "seeking life and becoming complete" pervades indigenous views of spirituality and life implicitly and is internalized within much of the cultural life. "Nature and Spirit are the real world, the ground of existence upon which they form a theology of Nature that has evolved and matured over the last forty thousand years" (Cajete, 1994, p. 46). As such, the theology of nature and the metaphor of seeking life form the foundations for all explorations of the spiritual ecology of indigenous education.

Echoings

> The eye takes a person into the world. The ear brings the world into the human being.
>
> —Lorenz Oken, as cited in Aoki,
> from "*Sonare* and *Videre*"

Aoki (1991/2005) describes inviting the jazz musician Bobby Shew to give a curriculum seminar addressing two questions: "When does an instrument cease to be an instrument?" and "What is it to improvise? What is improvisation?" (p. 367). On the given day, Bobby Shew entered the classroom with his trumpet and played a few licks to begin the seminar. Then he began to introduce his pedagogy for teaching the trumpet. He allowed his students only to hold the trumpet behind their backs, which kept them from bringing the trumpet to their lips as he led them through lip and scat-singing exercises. Only when he felt that the trumpet in joining lips would become a part of the body—become an embodied trumpet—would he allow trumpet and lips to meet. He insistently said, "The trumpet, music and body must become as one living wholeness" . . . Thus, Bobby acknowledged that musicianship and "music to be lived calls for transformation of instrument and music into that which is lived bodily." (Aoki, 1991/2005, p. 368)

In response to the question regarding improvisation, Bobby resorted to playing the trumpet and improvising. He spoke of how in improvising he and his fellow musicians respond not only to each other but also to "whatever calls upon them in that situational moment and that for him, no two situational moments, like life lived, are exactly alike. . . . Exact repletion . . . is an impossibility. It's a remarkable feature not to be suppressed" (Aoki, 1991/2005, p. 368).

Thinking the Highest Thought

The indigenous ideal of living a good life also involves the intention or goal of "thinking the highest thought." Thinking the highest thought means thinking of oneself, one's community, and one's environment richly and deeply. It is a respectful and compassionate way of addressing and influencing the environment, individuals, and community by seeking a good and wholesome life. This community of being becomes the centre of the teaching for learning how to live ecologically. Living ecologically is also about living in harmonious relationship to "a place" with respect and reciprocity.

> Through their central myth each Indigenous community identifies itself as a sacred place, a place of living, learning, teaching, and renewal, a place where the People share the breath of life and thought. The community is a living, spiritual entity that is supported by every responsible adult. (Cajete, 1994, p. 47)

Echoings

> The echo is the essence of the thing. . . . The echo has much to teach us. If we listen for echoes, and listen to them, our listening can grow in wisdom.
> —David Levin, as cited in Aoki,
> from "*Sonare* and *Videre*"

Aoki (1991/2005) challenges us as educators to honour and embody educational practices that are polyphonic, integrated, and improvisational, that return us to engaging musically with a complex curriculum composition. He asks, "Shall we integrate the strands into a sonic unity? Shall we allow the strands to sing polyphonically and pray that, on occasion, they glow white-hot from within?" (p. 371). This requires that we learn to listen, honour the ear, and the world of sound.

As a musician, I play the native flute, an instrument that is part of the tradition of the wind in indigenous culture, and as such it is an indigenous knowledge practice. The wooden instruments have a particular tuning that allows them to be played improvisationally. They have an inspiring totem that channels the wind or breath. Ideally, they are played outside in reciprocity with the more-than-human world in dialogue with the spiritual ecology of a place. It is the art of playing within a situational moment and locale, based on a sense of reciprocity and renewal. Here the player takes on the responsibility of honouring the circle of life and the centre of all creation and is seeking to complement or complete the ecology of being present by adding the human voice or flute song to the strands that polyphonically resound in diverse environments. Places have unique ecological signatures and resonance; the intent is to tune or listen deeply to the tonal landscape and to respond reciprocally. Some traditions imagine a prayer eagle soaring on the wind; the gliding and spiralling of the eagle inspires the melody. While playing I have noticed that birds often respond, and the wind, trees, and other sounds create a wonderful polyphonic landscape.

I also play a double native flute where two flutes sing in polyphonic tensionality together. This practice of playing the double flute has acted pedagogically on my ability to hear, create soundscapes, and to take up the study of sonare. This practice has informed my educational praxis; I tune my embodied instrumentality, lean into the wind, and enact a performed improvisation within my various educational contexts. I tune, listen deeply, and then begin playing, improvising on my native flute. This is followed by attempts at inspiriting a pedagogical moment to the end that I am holistically embodying a disposition of curriculum improvisation and ecological integration.

Orientation and Direction

Indigenous education is essentially focused on a learned external orientation to place, one's family, community, culture, and society in general. It is facilitated through circles of relationship by participating in the surrounding environmental ecology. Indigenous education is also about learning an internal orientation to self and to the spirit. Orientation is more than physical context and placement. It is about deeper meanings, a mind-set, ways of thinking and knowing, and an inner sense of direction. It is about how the human spirit navigates and understands itself.

> Traditional forms of . . . education have many expressions of the concept of orientation or "direction." . . . Orientation, with relationship forms a

field for understanding the interaction between the human spirit and other forms of spirit. Spiritual orientation and breath are sometimes explained in conjunction with the origins of wind in the creation/emergence myths among Indigenous people around the world. Mountains and the Winds associated with them appear among some . . . as symbols of orientation. (Cajete, 1994, p. 49)

Echoings

Listen not to me; listen to the Logos.

—Heraclitus, as cited in Aoki,
from "*Sonare* and *Videre*"

As an Anishinaabe person, I understood orientation and the idea of directions in an external sense. However, I have begun an inner practice of beginning my day standing in silence and facing east. When so moved by the wind, I breathe in and I begin to play. I listen to the currents of silence soaring above me, and then my flute melodies glide like an eagle on the currents of wind. I then orientate and listen to the south, the west, and the north to complete the circle of directions. I turn to the centre, orientating to Mother Earth, and bowing slightly I greet her. Rising, I play to all the creatures in the circle of life, and then lifting my flute up I address Father Sky. Finally, I turn to the centre of my world and float on the currents "of the wind that lies within." I let the melody fade and stand as my spirit finds "that place that Indians talk about." I then leave my flute playing to sit silently, to dwell in the centre of my medicine wheel, hearing the echoes of the flute until they lead me into the embrace of silence, the heart of my spiritual ecology. I have learned to lean into orientations, directions, and like leaning into the wind, I have learned to lean into "that place that Indians talk about" as a practice while I improvise on my various flutes. I have also learned to lean into a similar place in my teaching, and I am on the way to learning how to live from that place in all I do. I am cultivating an orientation that honours my spiritual ecology, and as I do, I am finding my way and learning to honour my pathway through the world.

Tracking and Pathway

I knew about the discipline of tracking and being a hunter of good heart. The tracking of anything requires that we undergo a transformation as we learn about that which we track. The aesthetic participation and exact understanding of profound phenomenologies or ecologies was something I had experienced as a child tracking animals, especially through my deep relationship to bears and all that they are in Anishinaabe culture. I knew in pursuing the playing of the native flute I was learning something that profoundly influenced my external life.

However, I was also sensing that this practice was also impacting my inner life. This realization became more of a reality when I encountered Linda Hogan's book, *Dwellings: A Spiritual History of the Living World*. I was stopped in my tracks, as I read the following passage:

> The next time I visited her it was a year later, and again we went through the same prayers, standing outside facing the early sun. On the last morning I was there, she left for her job in town. Before leaving, she said, "Our work is our altar." Those words have remained with me. Now I am a disciple of birds. The birds that I mean are eagle, owls, and hawks. I clean cages at the Birds of Prey Rehabilitation Foundation. It is the work I wanted to do, in order to spend time inside the gentle presence of birds. (Hogan, 1995, p. 153)

Hogan goes on to describe how one green morning an orphan owl perches nervously above her as she cleans the large fenced-in area in which it lives. Fearing her, it suddenly bolts off the perch where it sat and lands by accident on the end of her rake. She then describes how in the moment she felt as if she was waking up the rake and taking up a contemplative practice. This is how she describes her practice:

> The word *rake* means to gather or heap up, to smooth the broken ground. That's what this work is, all of it, the smoothing over of broken ground, the healing of severed trust humans hold with earth. We gather it back together again with great care, take broken pieces and fragments and return them to the sky. It is work at the borderland between species, at the boundary between injury and healing. There is an art to raking . . . raking is a labor round and complete, smooth and new as an egg, and the rounding of the seasons of the world revolving in time and space . . . watching the turning over of life, becomes a road into what is essential. (p. 154)

Echoings

> We do not hear because we have ears. . . . We have ears because we are harkening and need to listen to the song of the Earth. . . . The need to hear the Song of the Earth requires that our hearing be a sensuous one which involves . . . the ears.
>
> —Martin Heidegger, as cited in Aoki, from "*Sonare* and *Videre*"

I too have found myself a disciple of, and am living, the discipline of wind, and the discipline of living inside the gentle presence of sound and silence. I am in the discipline of *WIND*.

References

Aoki, T.T. (1991/2005). *Sonare* and *videre:* A story, three echoes, and a lingering note. In W.F. Pinar & R.L. Irwin (Eds.), *Curriculum in a new key: The collected works of Ted T. Aoki* (pp. 367–365). Mahwah, NJ: Lawrence Erlbaum.

Cajete, G. (1994). *Look to the mountain: An ecology of indigenous education.* Skyland, NC: Kivake Press.

Hogan, L. (1995). *Dwellings: A spiritual history of the living world.* New York, NY: Touchstone.

23

WEARING CURRICULUM AND/OR CURRICULUM WEARING (ON) ME?

Kathleen Nolan

Design Note

Perhaps it is a truism to note that we can wrap our lives in binaries without aware-ness until someone draws our attention to noticing them. Dr. Ted Aoki was that someone.

In the summer of 2000, my binary-wrapped life revealed itself to me when I listened intently to Ted's metonymical musings during the Writing Teachers' Lives Institute held at the University of Lethbridge. Until then, it was easy to imagine two, and only two, sides to every story—there were no in-between spaces in right/wrong, light/dark, presence/absence, is/is not (Interview with Ted Aoki 1999). With that summer institute and Ted's inspiring ideas, the binary slash widened, permitting words, ideas, and images "to dwell in the space between" (Nolan, 2007, p. 67). A welcome ambiguity set in.

That institute—those metonymical moments with Ted—was pivotal in my dissertation work, which followed that year, encouraging me to crack wide open the black/white binary perspective of knowing (in) mathematics and science to expose the full spectrum of colours in between (Nolan, 2001). This was a period of growth, of transition, of hope. I embraced the metonymical slash space not only in my research but in my teaching as well . . . at least for a while. In due course, my metonymical spaces of doubling (Aoki, 2003/2005) gave way to metonymical spaces of doubting.

The following narrative dwells in these doubting spaces. The piece draws on the metaphor of wardrobe to accentuate not-so-comfortable curricular spaces where teacher–student dichotomies are contemplated through fabrics, textiles/textures, and styles of classroom life. "Wearing Curriculum and/or Curriculum Wearing (on) Me?" is a story for teaching of/beyond curriculum.

"Try it on for size," the shopkeeper suggests, gently taking the softcover text with its complementary syllabus off the shelf. She hands me the package, and I wriggle to get into it.

"Well . . . " I whisper uncomfortably. "It seems a little tight around the hips."

"Oh, that's the best part about wearing this curriculum," she chimes enthusiastically. "You can just pull in the straps or let out the seams, so to speak, to adjust to your own fitting. Dwelling in the postmodern encourages multiple fits and styles. Go ahead; tailor it to suit yourself."

Dwelling in the spaces of mind/body, plannable/unplannable, I noticed how freedom and creativity in course design draped ever so gracefully over me during the first few years. When students openly appreciated the way I wore the course and how it gave them ideas for their own styles and learning ensembles, I was encouraged to accessorize with such strategies as creative writing, role play, collages, and reflective journals.

Then one day a student belted out, "What's the *point* of this?!"

Snapping the elastic on my loosely fitting curricular attire, I looked in a mirror and proceeded to justify my style as eclectic and nontraditional.

On another occasion, a student informed me how I should wear curriculum and teaching to better suit *his* stature. Again, I justified my style, only this time in noticeably weaker tones. The glamour of wearing curriculum was fading, and my garments were feeling more confining around my chest.

But the real tear in my fabric came when a student objected to my entire wardrobe and how I wore it. From the moment she entered the room, it was clear that my outfit did not suit her. My outfit was not *her* outfit; it was not cut from the same cultural cloth. Not only did she disapprove of my wardrobe, but I also offended her own taste accessories. Her razor-sharp words cut away all that I had carefully sewn over the years.

And now, I feel the weight of eroding conviction on the binary side of teaching. How might I dwell more metonymically in the wearing, tearing dichotomous fabric of teacher–student relationship? Can I wear curriculum at all, or does it merely wear (on) me?

I am squeezed into not-so-comfortable curricular spaces. Instead of dressing to suit my own style, I am self-conscious about my wardrobe and wonder what the students want me to wear and how they prefer that I wear it. At the same time, however, I wonder if the comfort of "one size fits all" has become the uniform of my students. I wonder if my students are prepared to look closely at their own wardrobe, and consider trying on something new for size in my course. Or, do they prefer to wear nothing (new) at all? Perhaps the students are now the emperor with no clothes, and I am afraid to tell them so.

References

Aoki, T.T. (2003/2005). Locating living pedagogy in teacher "research ': Five metonymic moments. In W.F. Pinar & R.L. Irwin (Eds.), *Curriculum in a new key: The collected works of Ted T. Aoki* (pp. 425–432). Mahwah, NJ: Lawrence Erlbaum.

Interview with Ted Aoki. (1999, Summer). Rethinking curriculum and pedagogy. *Kappa Delta Pi Record, 34*(4), 180–181.

Nolan, K. (2001). *Shadowed by light, knowing by heart: Preservice teachers' images of knowing (in) math and science* (Unpublished doctoral dissertation). University of Regina, Regina, Saskatchewan, Canada.

Nolan, K. (2007). *How should I know? Preservice teachers' images of knowing (by heart) in mathematics and science*. Rotterdam, Netherlands: Sense.

24

LIVED EXPERIENCES OF LOSS

Living Perceptibly as a Teacher in New Familiarities

Candace P. Lewko

> Occupying the lived and educational spaces between . . . one defamliarizes the familiar while making a home out of a strange new land.
> —William F. Pinar, from *Curriculum in a New Key: The Collected Works of Ted T. Aoki*

I am a Canadian teacher of multiethnic origin. I am also a teacher of English as a second or additional languages for adult immigrant and refugee students. The familiar terrain of my teaching world expands as I continue in new dialogues of learning with my students. I enter into dialogue with my heart open to the dichotomous worlds of good and bad, and foreign and familiar. I fuse these worlds together with hope and foresight. I explore my senses of *currere* (Pinar, 1975a) to see, feel, and touch the world that I come from and the cultures that I encounter in my teaching: "I . . . try to uncover layer by layer, from the outside in, from the top to the ground, from the abstract to the concrete place where teaching truly dwells" (Aoki, as cited in Pinar, 2005, p. 17). This interaction reveals what being a Canadian teacher means while living in varied contexts of teaching realities.

I return to places in my heart that remind me how to live in my teaching praxis with courage. My students write about the families and homes they have left behind. Some never look back to see where they have come from. They carry experiences from home in their migration to Canada, where at times, each migration brings more hardship. Sometimes, the stories are not home for my students. It is in this moment that empathy comes forth in the loss of home. Devastation reroutes the heart. The teacher in her listening is not a bystander to the story. Through her listening, the teacher becomes a participant in the events and, from that, a deeper appreciation begins to radiate from the heart. The complexities that the stories present do not silence the voices; rather, the silences resound.

My students hold these experiences close, like precious gifts. These experiences are relived in the classroom in the form of stories. My students' stories enable me to see their worlds and the potential of the teaching self in their worlds. I step into a new pedagogical landscape where I meet my students at the intersection of my classroom and their learning world.

The life events experienced in my students' home countries are remote from the ones found in my own (teaching) life. The stories that my students tell are sometimes indiscernible or discordant to mine. They are stories that, if not listened to carefully, can be interpreted as irrelevant to the teaching situation or to the moment of teaching. The intensity that results from the fusion of contrasting life events determines how I consciously come to a new awareness of the self in my teaching praxis; how I reconcile the meeting of contrasting worlds gives way to a better view of my self in teaching.

The stories of my students' lives are welling inside them waiting to be released. I imagine my classroom as a refuge for these impending stories. The classroom is a place for my students where adversity meets diversity. With our shared experiences, my students and I have met grief; we have faced matters that life and death present with suffering and compassion. However foreign to teaching and living these matters are, they remain close to my heart. I live with/in the narratives of others, which allows me to live acceptingly with the matters that come into my classroom. I situate my self in an embodied curriculum or in *live(d) experiences* of the self and others.

Ted T. Aoki's (1986/2005) conceptualization of the zone between the *live(d) and planned curriculum worlds* of my everyday real-world experiences and pedagogical situation creates a space for me where I contemplate the significance of *being in loss* to my teaching. Loss is an imperceptible place. It conjures up images of obscurity and lifelessness. Yet, on the contrary, the memories associated with it preserve life. What cannot be seen in reality is perceived from the depths of the heart. From the depths of the heart comes compassion. Compassion is a difficult depth to reach. These depths are obscured by fear. Compassion, and then empathy, is one such depth that resurfaces in my teaching reality. It is a place where I become alive as a teacher.

When I consider the multitude of perspectives from which loss could be understood, new plains of understanding emerge and the unforeseen becomes more illuminated than before. I do not return to moments of loss to mourn death but rather to honour and celebrate the new meaning found in the experience of loss. Sometimes in my heart, I return to a family home in these moments and sit in its ruins overgrown with bushes and trees. I contemplate the warmth of the dwelling that once came from the presence of long-ago people who inhabited this home. This home, deep within my heart, is one of acceptance and love. Yet, loss remains deeply located in my heart. Loss reminds me of stories: ones that are rooted in the educational and human-to-human experiences. Aoki (1983/2005) describes a definition of praxis as "a way of knowing" (p. 116). By looking to the world from live(d) experiences, I am able to view the human situation in a teaching praxis as one of embodiment and belonging. Knowing in this way offers possibilities for understanding what meaning is held in being a teacher.

Aoki (1983/2005) discusses through his notion of praxis the value of considering the meaning of being a teacher. He proposes that living in pedagogy is to engage wholeheartedly in a teaching life. Living *heartfully* in teaching opens up ways of seeing the self outside the planned curriculum. Contemplating what *teacher* means to *teaching* (Aoki, 1986/2005) requires one to engage in a self-reflexive process and to consider all the participants in a teaching praxis, such as the students in their own live(d) situations: What is the significance of the other in the pedagogical situation? By standing meditatively outside the planned moment of teaching, the teacher is better able to view the implications for knowing the self as an engaged historical and teaching being. Aoki (1983/2005) quotes Aristotle when he says that the teacher in his or her praxis engages in "holistic activity of the total person—head, heart, and lifestyle, all as one" (p. 116). I make myself present to begin a pedagogical dialogue. The locality of the classroom becomes a setting in which historical circumstances that we have arrived into as students and teachers are waiting to be taken up in the act of reflecting upon the self and the world. In this reflection, new histories come forth in the boundless space of teaching. The educational experience comes to life through a "complicated conversation" with the self (Aoki, 1986/2005; Pinar, 2004).

I am living with the stories that accompany the matters that life brings into my teaching praxis. Aoki (1986/2005) reminds me that as a teacher in my "attunement" (p.165) to the pedagogical situation, the unfamiliar events that can be found in a classroom are places where I can relearn how to live in the experience of being in foreignness. There is foreignness in loss, and with loss suffering manifests into a pain that exists in memories of death, sickness, poverty, vigilantism, or war. Apprehension takes place in the heart. However, when the unspeakable becomes the speak-able, stories are released—stories such as those of attempted assassination, the loss of hearing when a bomb ignites, the loss of a birth name, or the loss of a child. My students carry loss with them in their migration to new lands, and I also carry loss with me as I migrate from pedagogical landscape to heart landscape in my own teaching. Loss is in stories that define the present difficulties in becoming residents of a new country or of past difficulties of abandoning home. I live with experiences of loss, which at times pulls my heart into unknown depths of despair and fear. The past and the present together form a more complete understanding of how living perceptively in loss will revive the will to tell the story in places far from apprehension.

Stories serve to console. Sometimes the matters are so incomprehensible that words are needed to guide and to loosen the hold fear has on the heart. I meet with the human aspect of these stories and contemplate how I can learn to reopen my heart when fear from my own past returns. How can I learn to live with devastating stories of displacement and loss that come into my classroom? How can I dwell without trepidation? I venture into unfamiliar narrative landscapes and seek to join my story with another's.

I live today with the loss of one of my students—a senseless death through a sudden act of violence. I am thrust into this new reality. He was an immigrant to Canada—another home where his life was taken. I am living with my reaction to him not physically present in my life. I embraced his mother the day after his death. I remember her body falling into my arms. Prior to entering the home of the mother, I recall my colleague saying, "We do heart-work; we are not teachers now." What is heart-work in teaching? How does loss appropriate the act of being a teacher? I seek further those possibilities that enable my heart to expand with compassion and love when in moments of loss. Aoki (1992/2005) writes, "And in blindness that accompanies [thinking] we fail to see other possibilities of understanding 'thinking'" (p. 196). Within my student's loss of life lies the possibility for "thoughtfulness as an embodied doing and being—thought and soul embodied in the oneness of the lived moment" (p. 196). I embraced the mother that day not as a teacher but as another mother. I embraced her as our tears fell upon each other's faces. I breathed with her as I relived the hopes she had had for his future and his safety and for solace found within my own compassion for her. The sadness that filled our embrace humbled me. I dwelled with/in her hopes and aspirations, a moment that continues to be an incomprehensible sadness in my own life.

Aoki (1992/2005) speaks to the "lived world of teachers" (p. 197). On this winter day in my present teaching world, the piercing prairie cold provokes me—it reminds me of how the coldness of death can isolate the heart. I feel the solitude the mother lives in now. The moments of sadness in between my world as a teacher and that of a mother bring me into a presence where I am conscious of the grief that overwhelms the heart. At the same time, I allow myself to live in a new awareness of teaching. The story of my student's death allows me the capability to cultivate myself in this new landscape of grief. I am present in this story, which makes it possible to live in this incomprehensible circumstance. I am cognizant of the places far from the heart. I am able to view the world with empathy, which opens paths to the complexity of another's life circumstances.

Aoki's wisdom resonates with me when he says that "I know that what I see and how I see is because of who I am. I am what I see. I am how I see" (Aoki, 1979/2005, p. 348). I stand aside the teacher, my self, whose life is being lived out in the pedagogical situation. Standing *with* becomes an experience that is rich in heart. The sadness of my student's death becomes one comprehensive landscape where the waves of currere (Pinar, 1975a, 1975b, 2004) run cyclically. In the wave of my own currere, the questions persist: What will this landscape of loss look like in this new understanding? What will it have to offer me? What will the hardships be as I venture further into this new landscape of vulnerability? I am further reminded by Aoki (1992/2005) that at this time in understanding what teaching more truly is, [is] to . . . reorient ourselves so that we overcome mere correctness so that we can see and hear our doings as teachers harbored within pedagogical being, so we can see and hear who we *are* as teachers. (p. 197)

I allow my student's memory to live through my own continual and constant growth as a teacher, when I contemplate the relationship of my self to the world.

Still, I cannot make sense of my student's death—violence can maim the heart. But what is born from my own grieving is an understanding of the heart I have for being a teacher. I contemplate Aoki's (1992/2005) question: "What is the voice of teaching that this story speaks" (p. 195)? I ask myself, *what is the heart that this story speaks to?* I further contemplate Aoki's words: "Why is this particular story of a single moment worth remarking? Could it be that that which is re-markable is the indwelling presence of the shimmering being of teaching that is open to those whose listening is attuned aright?" (Aoki, 1992/2005, p. 195). Loss becomes the catalyst for vulnerability. Loss reopens wounds, yet it reminds us of the potential for solace. Loss is re/birth. Loss is a new territory. Loss reorients the heart. Loss grounds the self.

I am open to the unfolding of events and moments that occur within my teaching praxis. *Pedagogical watchfulness* (Aoki, 1992/2005) enables me to step into new landscapes of being a teacher and to critically reflect on what these landscapes have brought to me in the past. My past informs my present. Through *pedagogical thoughtfulness* (Aoki, 1992/2005), I am able to share with the mother outside the realm of being a teacher a shared energy that passes between us—a maternal energy that comes from the core of being a mother. I am present when I console another, and at the same time, I console myself. As I comfort a mother in sorrow, I am mindful of my surroundings. I listen with my heart to her wailing. From deep within, the wailing ignites in me a surge of awareness; it ignites my humanity and, more deeply, my empathy. I am now open to "deeper understand-ings" (p. 195) of loss—and of my self. I keep to love and kindness in this new landscape; I cannot release the mother from my arms. She has become (a) light in my heart; but I feel her heart to be heavy, yet her life remains dim in this possible new light.

Epilogue

The day my student passed away, the fall leaves stopped chattering and the winter cold suddenly arrived to silence what remained rooted in the ground. The season had begun to change at the same time my wide-open heart began to mourn. Now I look at loss through a heart that sings with compassion; my heart is expanding to engage with others in their own experiences of vulnerability. I breathe more heartfully now in my teaching, remembering that each breath I take is a pre-cious one in itself. I am immersed in a teaching situation that is "a lived situation pregnantly alive in the presence of people" (Aoki, 1986/2005, p. 157). I understand the teacher self midst loss. The site of being in foreign experiences such as loss compels me to reflect on my reactions to first encounters with the imperceptible, or the unpredictable. Suffering takes a voice; it is replaced with memories that disturb and, sometimes, prevents new ones being born. But there is light, and the warmth of a mother's love has overcome the cold with forgiveness and compassion.

I embrace what lingers now as the season shifts. The branches weep silently with snow, and the white winter sky is blinding. I surrender to the cold, and ultimately to the sadness. The rhythm of my heart begins like the movement of leaves lightly falling in the wind. I nestle into this moment of loss.

References

Aoki, T. (1979/2005). Reflections of a Japanese Canadian teacher experiencing ethnicity. In W.F. Pinar & R.L. Irwin (Eds.), *Curriculum in a new key: The collected works of Ted T. Aoki* (pp. 333–348). Mahwah, NJ: Lawrence Erlbaum.

Aoki, T. (1983/2005). Curriculum implementation as instrumental action and as situational praxis. In W.F. Pinar & R.L. Irwin (Eds.), *Curriculum in a new key: The collected works of Ted T. Aoki* (pp. 111–123). Mahwah, NJ: Lawrence Erlbaum.

Aoki, T. (1986/2005). Teaching as indwelling between two curriculum worlds. In W.F. Pinar & R.L. Irwin (Eds.), *Curriculum in a new key: The collected works of Ted T. Aoki* (pp. 159–165). Mahwah, NJ: Lawrence Erlbaum.

Aoki, T. (1992/2005). Layered voices of teaching: The uncannily correct and the elusively true. In W.F. Pinar & R.L. Irwin (Eds.), *Curriculum in a new key: The collected works of Ted T. Aoki* (pp. 187–197). Mahwah, NJ: Lawrence Erlbaum.

Pinar, W.F. (1975a). Currere: Toward reconceptualization. In W.F. Pinar (Ed.), *Curriculum theorizing: The reconceptualists* (pp. 396–414). Berkley, CA: McCutchan.

Pinar, W.F. (Ed.). (1975b). *Curriculum theorizing: The reconceptualists*. Berkley, CA: McCutchan.

Pinar, W.F. (2004). *What is curriculum theory?* Mahwah, NJ: Lawrence Erlbaum.

Pinar, W.F., & Irwin, R.L. (Eds.). (2005) *Curriculum in a new key: The collected works of Ted T. Aoki*. Mahwah, NJ: Lawrence Erlbaum.

25

CONTEMPLATING A CANADIAN CURRICULUM THEORY PROJECT

Currere, Denkbild, and Intellectual Genealogies

Nicholas Ng-A-Fook

> *Currere* in recurring movement?
> —Ted T. Aoki, from "Postscript/Rescript,"
> *Curriculum in a New Key*

I was first introduced to the field of curriculum studies and its respective historical discursive trends during a summer course titled "Introduction to Curriculum Studies." The course instructor just happened to be William F. Pinar, a visiting professor that summer term at York University. My *lived curriculum* within this course was indeed an intellectual turning point for me. Bill introduced us to *currere*, as a legitimate form of educational research within the disciplinary structures of schooling. During that summer term he encouraged us to study, to linger, within the verticality and horizontality of the interdisciplinary and international topographies of the field we call "curriculum studies." Bill often stressed that such intellectual study afforded us opportunities to understand the *complicated conversations* already taking place both outside and within what Chambers (1999, 2003) has eloquently and quite succinctly called the *topos* of *Canadian curriculum studies*. Therefore, during our studies with him we asked how our understandings of such historical and intellectual topographies inscribed their disciplinary trends into "our [curriculum] theorizing, as either presence or absence, whether we want them there or not" (Chambers, 1999, p. 148). Moreover, our challenge as burgeoning curriculum theorists and graduate students was in many ways to re-read and re-write the various topographies of our relationships to, and with, an old concept like curriculum.

As a next generation of curriculum theorists, how might we then re-read—both vertically and horizontally (Pinar, 2007)—our lived experiences within interdisciplinary topographies of curriculum studies anew, while remaining unfaithfully faithful to the concept of an old name like *currere,* in terms of its discursive genealogies? And, how might we frame our experimentations with curriculum theorizing as an aesthetic form of *Denkbild,* as *currere,* which works to provoke an *uncommon countenance* within its recurring narrative movements? What *Denkbild* gets us to think *(denken),* as Richter (2007) explains, "is precisely the ways in which it delivers an image *(Bild)* not only of this or that particular content, but always also of its own folding back upon itself, its most successful failure" (p. 13). In response to such provocations, let us turn this narrative toward a curriculum theorist's vertical and horizontal migration, and fold such migrations back upon themselves as an aesthetic form of *Denkbild,* within what we might call *A Canadian Curriculum Theory Project.*

At the Crossroads of *Currere* in Recurring Movements

I first wrote autobiographically for an academic setting on my way to an educational conference in Baton Rouge, Louisiana. The theme of the conference was "In Praise of the Postmodern." The conference celebrated Bill Doll's 70th birthday, as well as his postmodern contributions to the international field of curriculum studies. In February of 2001, I flew from Toronto to New Orleans. Once there, I had a 2-hour layover at the downtown bus station, before taking the next Greyhound for Baton Rouge. While waiting at this southern terminal, I experimented with the aesthetics of writing an educational autobiography for a course paper due the following week.

For the first time, I realized that writing one's educational autobiography provided a place for encountering self and other. In turn, I was able to use a life-writing methodology to graphically represent the psychic dynamics of my educational experiences. Once these experiences were written down, I was able to re-read them, and then analyze their educational significance. During the synthesis of such analysis, I attempted to re-enter the present through questioning how my past educational assumptions continue to manifest themselves in oppressive ways among self and others.

To pose "new" curricular questions and theorize "new concepts," if there is such a thing, as "new" and "old" scholars, one must be aware of the Canadian historical topographies and pay particular attention to how we might trace their intellectual genealogies (see Chambers, 2003; Ng-A-Fook & Rottmann, 2012). And yet, through such study "we must be suspicious," Derrida (1991/1992) reminds us, "of *both* repetitive memory *and* the completely other of the absolutely new of *both* anamnestic capitalization *and* the amnesic exposure to what would be no longer identifiable at all" (p. 19). Nonetheless, within the vertical and horizontal dynamics of this suspicious space is a psychic place where we can experience and share in each other's intellectual otherness.

Through such transnational and genealogical temporal migrations, I began to study the intellectual writings of Walter Benjamin and Siegfried Kracauer, two Jewish exiles with marginal associations to the Frankfurt School before, during, and after their violent encounters with the Nazi regime (Richter, 2007). I sought to understand how the aesthetic dynamics of their philosophical writings might help a next generation of curriculum theorists to provoke a *paleonomic* form of curriculum theorizing such as *Denkbild* (Benjamin, 1978, 1982/2002; Kracauer, 1969, 1995). *Paleonomy,* Derrida (1982) suggests, is "the maintenance of an old name"—like *currere*, for example—in order "to launch a new concept" (as cited in Richter, 2007, p. 1). Perhaps all serious engagement with "philosophical and aesthetic concepts and their political and historical traditions may require," as Richter (2007) suggests, "a form of paleonomic work" (p. 1). So then, before we take up the concept of *Denkbild*, let us migrate anew across the genealogical topographies of an old concept like *currere*.

We can trace *currere* and its vertical topography through one of its many historical genealogies within the field of curriculum studies, that is, toward its Latin infinitive form: *to run the course*. During the 1970s, Bill Pinar and Madeleine Grumet took up the etymological tracings of this old name. They began to pose new questions about curriculum, its discursive genealogical trends, and its respective theorizing. Drawing on autobiography, phenomenology, psychoanalysis, and feminist studies, they sought to disrupt the epistemological narrative sirens of mainstream social science research (Pinar & Grumet, 1976). Curriculum, at least then for Pinar (1975b/2000), was no longer understood educationally as a noun but instead reconceived as a verb, as *currere*.

Pinar (1975b/2000) provides the reader with a methodology for educational research that differentiates itself from the "positivistic, so-called empirical research methodologies" that at the time he believed to occupy center stage within education (p. 416). He introduces us to the crossroads of *currere*, namely: (1) regression, (2) progression, (3) analysis, and (4) synthesis. Might I stress here that *currere* is a methodology and not a method for writing linear narrative progressions from regression to synthesis. Instead, it is, as I will attempt to perform throughout this chapter, a recursive assemblage of autobiographical snapshots taking place within the temporal fluidity of *third space,* and sometimes offering their graphic materialization at the narrative crossroads of these four temporal *signpostings*.

Pinar (1975a/2000) emphasizes the following recursive movements at the crossroads of *currere*:

> First to render one's own educational experience (these terms include what Dewey calls educative and miseducative experience) into words, using associative forms of minding. The second is to use one's critical faculties to understand what principles and patterns have been operative in one's educational life, hence achieving a more profound understanding of one's educational experience, as well as illuminating parts of the inner world and

deepening one's self-understanding generally. The third task is to analyze others' experience to reveal what I call basic educational structures or processes that cross biographical lines. (p. 389)

Pinar (2004) has since refined his initial conceptual framework of *currere*, telling us later that his autobiographical methodology "provides a strategy for students of curriculum to study relations between academic knowledge and life history in the interest of self-understanding and social reconstruction" (p. 35). Today, I stand at the historical edges of our field, pivoting within the recursive temporal movements of *currere*, scanning its horizons for regressive, progressive, analytical, and synthetical signpostings. At its edges, I seek to understand the graphic representations of narrative signpostings, as an aesthetic and graphic materiality of curriculum theorizing.

Back at the crossroads of *currere*, one can read its regressive signposting, as a direction to a side street or an alleyway where one can take autobiographical snapshots of *free associations* and read them against, for example, the panoramic backdrop of an urban landscape. The narrative push for such free associative sightseeing is to try and walk within the random presence of the past, where the rendering of "a genuine photograph [of our memory] precludes the notion of completeness" (Kracauer, 1969, p. 49). *Camera-reality,* as Kracauer (1969) tells us, parallels the reality generated by free associations in terms of its structure and its general constitution. Like camera-reality, free association is partly patterned, partly amorphous—a consequence in both cases, because of 'the half-cooked state of our everyday world" (Kracauer, 1969, p. 58). Our potential autobiographical snapshots of such regressive free associations can be "virtually endless, issuing from a dark which is increasingly receding and extending into an open-ended future" (p. 45). Yet how might we reconstruct our subjectivities in relation to such regressive narrative recessions while looking toward the future in the present?

If we return to the crossroads of *currere*, where time hovers within what Wang (2009) calls the *narrative chronotopes of third space,* we may pivot toward a progressive signposting. Here, there is a narrative cobbled road leading through an archway, infinitely beyond the horizon of our psychic abode, beyond historic time itself. Nonetheless, while pivoting at this signposting, one can look through its archway and get a glimpse of narrative snapshots of the future, always fleeting, but nonetheless taking place within the present.

Back at the center of the crossroads of *currere*, there is also an analytical signposting that leads to an art gallery, where a daguerreotype exhibit narrates the autobiographical past and future, together expressing themselves in the present. Within the interdisciplinary contexts of *currere*, a daguerreotype exhibit is where each autobiographical snapshot has multiple analytical possibilities, and where a curriculum theorist's discursive genealogical assembling of each frame of reference—whether within Marxist, autobiographical, indigenous, postcolonial, and/or queer studies—works in turn to depict a faithfulness authenticated only by the presence of the narrative representation itself (Kracauer, 1969).

The synthetical is another signposting, leading to a coffee shop, a local market, or totem pole just down the street from the crossroads of *currere* "where ghostly signals flash from the traffic and inconceivable connections between events are the order of the day" (Benjamin, 1978, p. 183). Here a curriculum scholar frames past, present, and future narrative snapshots, where images of their limitations and possibilities flash, as we re-enter the present moment, with hope and with a sense of greater self-knowledge in inconceivable ways.

Yet this synthetical framing, as Kracauer (1969) makes clear, "marks a provisional limit; its content points beyond that frame, referring to a multitude of real-life phenomena which cannot possibly be encompassed in their entirety" (p. 59). Much like Wang's (2009) theorization of chronotopes, at the crossroads of *currere*, the narrative directions of these signpostings "are infinitely multiple" and "the plurality of time/space" is always present (p. 2). Furthermore, our autobiographical interactions with "external time, internal time, and pedagogical time" at these crossroads sets into motion what Wang calls "a dynamic of *freeing* the present from its unquestioned assumptions and unaware stuck points in the past and of destabilizing the future beyond" a fixed narration toward a final destination (p. 3). Let us walk away from this genealogical dreamscape of *currere* toward representing its respective narratives as an aesthetic form of *Denkbild*.

Provoking Curriculum Theorizing as a Digital Form of *Denkbild*

On an early Sunday morning, I made my way to the Byward Market in Ottawa, Ontario, with our two sons. I must have walked pass that totem pole on York Street a hundred times—never once noticing the aesthetic of its exiled presence in front of the Ottawa School of Art. On that beautiful day, I took a snapshot of the totem pole and its uncommon countenance reaching up toward the sky. My hope was that in some way the "captured" digital image would encourage our future conceptual experimentations with curriculum theorizing as an aesthetic form of narrative production that in turn might enable us to decipher our intellectual histories as *Denkbild*.

Later that afternoon, I utilized Comic Life to create a digital genealogical cover story with this image for the 4th Biennial Provoking Curriculum Studies Conference program. Prior to assembling this narrative montage, I had utilized the Google search engine to find digital images and documents related to past Provoking Curriculum Studies conferences. I then took screen captures of these digital images and imported them into Comic Life. In turn, these digital narrative montages provided a vertical and horizontal frame of reference around the totem pole at the center of the crossroads of this cover story. Here is also an example how we might experiment with digital images as a form of *Denkbild* to provoke representations of the narrative verticality of Canadian curriculum studies.

Let us now briefly turn to the scholars directly and/or marginally associated with the Frankfurt School, like Walter Benjamin and Siegfried Kracauer, who experimented with *Denkbild* as "a poetic form of condensed, epigrammatic writing in textual snapshots" (Richter, 2007, p. 2). Their philosophical meditations fastened themselves upon seemingly peripheral detail, on marginal topics like a sock in a drawer, a one-way street, an angel of history, an arcade, displacement, exile, extraterritoriality, and homelessness, for example, usually without a developed plot or a prescribed narrative agenda, yet charged with theoretical insight (Richter, 2007).

Benjamin described his friend Kracauer as "a relentless outsider" and "a marginal yet revolutionary ragpicker of history" (as cited in Richter, 2007, p. 116). Might we also envision ourselves as curriculum theorists, standing at the crossroads of *currere*, ragpicking between daybreak and sundown, re-reading the multiple literacies of an urban landscape, translating its historical narrative scraps, and tossing them, while grumbling and growling, into our theoretical carts (Benjamin, 1999)?

As ragpickers migrating across international shorelines, how might we pick up transnational narratives, retrieve them from the ditches and alleyways, and reread the genealogical intellectual topography of an *uncommon common countenance* we call curriculum studies? In response to this curricular question, let us move this narrative setting to the southwest corner of the Byward Market and walk toward its historical signpostings and take a snapshot of a red-cedar totem pole, standing

at its edges, representing indigenous exile within the violent turbulence of past, present, and future colonial times. Here we might ask anew, curricular questions in transnational times.

That afternoon, once I created these screen-capture montages, I then played with the various representational themes in Comic Life, such as Marvel, to reframe the aesthetic representations of the historical digital images generated by Google's re-search engine. However, I had difficulty tracing the various digital topographies of "The Totem Pole of Canada," its uncommon narrative countenances. So on that sunny afternoon, I left the confines of my office, walked downtown to sit on a bench in the Byward Market, and listened to a raven's stories of experiencing colonial immigration and indigenous exile.

This tattooed totem-pole regressive narrative leads us simultaneously across the vertical and horizontal topographies of our country to the Gitanmaax School of Northwest Coast Indian Art in Hazleton, British Columbia. In 1991, the Ottawa School of Art commissioned this community's spiritual guidance for carving the expressions that now make up this "Totem Pole of Canada." The raven and its trickster stories then accompanied this red cedar, as it migrated across our

transnational highway toward this capital landscape. Upon their arrival, and for the right sum, various cultural groups could have their national symbols of origin tattooed across its wooden body. In turn, the aesthetic expressions on this pole, their carved narrations, took 2 years to write. Once finished, Stone (1993) suggests, it became a totem of modern totems representing those that now legitimately and illegitimately inhabit this land.

This "Totem Pole of Canada" was then raised in front of the school as an aesthetic expression, hauled up by modernism and its technology, its wooden narratives bolted to a steel spine, sunk deep into a concrete pad between the sidewalk and street (Stone, 1993). Here is where our raven, a scavenger of narratives, now rests with an uncommon countenance above its shoulders, trading trickster stories of iron/y with the Hudson Bay Company just across the street, greeting tourists

taking snapshots of it sitting within the receding shadows of global empires. Tricking them, telling them that this totem pole is, and is not, a totem pole.

From an alleyway behind the back of the totem pole, I took snapshots of progressive curricular signs. Like the future, the totem back is open, and one can see the steel spine. "This is," Stone (1993) tells us, "because it was made to go against a wall in front of the school, a spot chosen after the organizers looked at a chart of gas lines and underground wires and so on" (p. B6). And thus the unnatural gas lines, and our narrative connections to the recursive exploitation of natural resources, continue to displace the various indigenous communities who have inhabited and still inhabit this urban landscape since time immemorial. The pole then had to be moved out to where you could now see its exposed innards (Stone,

1993). Now freestanding in exile at the crossroads of this global marketplace, it symbolizes a narrative of cultures—indigenous, Greek, German, Dutch, Lebanese, Turkish, and more—bolted together by a Canadian story not yet finished.

In turn, this "Totem Pole of Canada" records what Richter (2007) calls "an historical moment at the same time that it interrupts" colonial history, "perpetuating the very thinkability" of such history, "even as it breaks with the logic" of its historic unfolding (p. 107). While this former red cedar and its current totemic form has found an urban home, its lived curriculum for me represents multiple narrative displacements—now that its historical exile is "captured" as a digital image on the cover of a curriculum studies conference program. In turn, this image tells us of its own departure from history by capturing time most fully by removing itself from the materiality of historic time itself (Richter, 2007). Now this comic narrative representation memorializes this trickster image, by removing it from the temporal flow of historic time within the landscape of an urban abode. Standing at the edges of this theoretical alleyway, pivoting within its space and time, I wonder how we might frame our experimentations with curriculum theorizing, as *currere*, as an aesthetic form of *Denkbild*. In turn, I invite readers to provoke the uncommon countenances of our intellectual histories bolted together in the recurring movements of Canadian curriculum studies now taking place, always unfinished, where their future narratives are still yet to come.

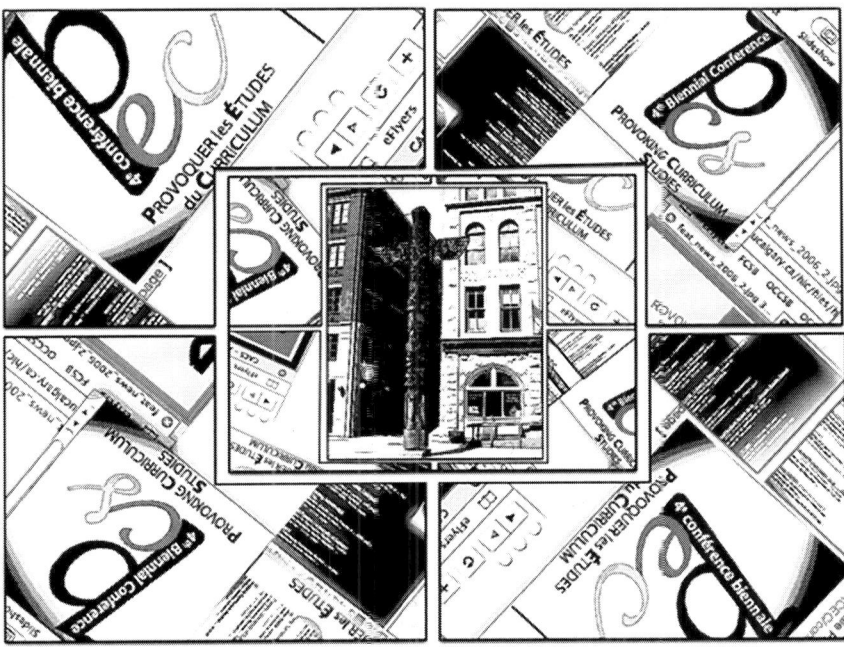

References

Aoki, T.T. (2005). Postscript/Rescript. In W.F. Pinar & R.L. Irwin (Eds.), *Curriculum in a new key: The collected works of Ted T. Aoki* (pp. 453–457). Mahwah, NJ: Lawrence Erlbaum.

Benjamin, W. (1978). *Reflections: Essays, aphorisms, autobiographical writings.* New York, NY: Schocken Books.

Benjamin, W. (1982/2002). *The arcades project* (H. Eiland & K. McLaughlin, Trans.). Cambridge, MA: Harvard University Press.

Benjamin, W. (1999). An outsider makes his mark. In M.W. Jennings, H. Eiland, & G. Smith (Eds.), *Selected writings: Volume 2, 1927–1934* (pp. 305–310). Cambridge, MA: Harvard University Press.

Chambers, C. (1999). A topography for Canadian curriculum theory. *Canadian Journal of Education, 24*(2), 137–150.

Chambers, C. (2003). "As Canadian as possible under the circumstances": A view of contemporary curriculum discourses in Canada. In W.F. Pinar (Ed.), *The internationalization handbook of curriculum research* (pp. 221–252). Mahwah, NJ: Lawrence Erlbaum.

Derrida, J. (1982). *Positions* (A. Bass, Trans.). Chicago, IL: University of Chicago Press.

Derrida, J. (1991/1992). *The other heading: Reflections on today's Europe* (P.A. Brault & M.B. Naas, Trans). Bloomington: Indiana University Press.

Kracauer, S. (1969). *History: The last things before the last.* New York, NY: Oxford University Press.

Kracauer, S. (1995). *The mass ornament: Weimar essays.* Cambridge, MA: Harvard University Press.

Ng-A-Fook, N., & Rottmann, J. (Eds.). (2012). *Reconsidering Canadian curriculum studies.* New York, NY: Palgrave Macmillan.

Pinar, W.F. (1975a/2000). Analysis of educational experience. In W. Pinar (Ed.), *Curriculum studies: The reconceptualization* (pp. 384–395). Troy, NY: Educator's International Press.

Pinar, W.F. (1975b/2000). Search for a method. In W. Pinar (Ed.), *Curriculum studies: The reconceptualization* (pp. 415–424). Troy, NY: Educator's International Press.

Pinar, W.F. (2004). *What is curriculum theory?* Mahwah, NJ: Lawrence Erlbaum.

Pinar, W.F. (2007). *Intellectual advancement through disciplinarity: Verticality and horizontality in curriculum studies.* Rotterdam, Netherlands: Sense.

Pinar, W.F., & Grumet, M. (1976). *Toward a poor curriculum.* Dubuque, IA: Kendall/Hunt.

Richter, G. (2007). *Thought-images: Frankfurt School writers' reflection from a damaged life.* Palo Alto, CA: Stanford University Press.

Stone, J. (1993, April 28). Totem project within reach [Final ed.]. *The Ottawa Citizen,* B6.

Wang, H. (2009). The chronotopes of encounter and emergence. *Journal of Curriculum Theorizing, 25*(1), 1–5.

26

CONTEMPLATING AND COMPLICATING CURRICULUM BY ATTENDING TO LANGUAGE

Twenty-Six Metonymic Moments

Carl Leggo

> In recent years, increasingly, curriculum scholars have opened themselves
> to the realm of language, linguistics, discourse and narratives to understand
> their own field.
>
> —Ted T. Aoki, from *In the Midst of Slippery Theme Words*

As a Teacher, I Am

Aokian
Bakhtinian
Cixousian
Deweyan
Eisnerian
Freirean
Girouxian
Huebnerian
Illichian
Jungian
Kohlian
Latherian
Marxian
Noddingsian
O'Sullivanian
Postmanian
Quindlenian
Russellian

Seussian
Tompkinsian
Underhillian
Vanierian
Whiteheadian
Xavierian
Youngian
Zizekian

Who am I?

a

I first met Ted Aoki in 1994 at a language education conference where I presented some of my poems about language and grammar with postmodern ruminations on how language shapes and composes us in relationships with one another, relationships that are always steeped in imagination, hope, creativity, and love. The paper was titled "Living Un/Grammatically: A Poet's Postmodern Musings on Language Education." Ted responded to my paper with a gift of words that spelled the beginning of a remarkable relationship. For more than 16 years, Ted, by his presence and his words, has inspired and guided me in a creative commitment to contemplating and complicating curriculum by attending to language.

b

The Alphabet

the alphabet we learned
to write in school was Spartan,

pressed between parallel lines,
eschewing swirls curls whirls,

but we need to ask always, all ways,
with tireless wonder,

what lies beyond the alphabet?
for the alphabet, the creation

in letters, is a letter
inviting the imagination

beyond the alphabet in lines
that do not begin, do not end

c

As curriculum theorists, scholars, and educators, we need to attend to language. Like Ted, we need to attend to etymology, diction, grammar, syntax, metaphors, and interpretation. I began school just before my fifth birthday; recently, I celebrated my 58th birthday. All my life I have been a student or a teacher—more than 54 years—and, in all those years, I have been enamoured with the necromancy of the alphabet, the magic of spelling, the alchemy of grammar, the mystery of books—the potent fecundity of language.

d

Spelling

in school I learned to spell words with precise correctness
but I seldom learned the sensuous spell of language

in school I learned the rules and stipulations of grammar
but I seldom learned the glamour, the alchemy of prepositions

in school I learned the conventions of syntax
but I seldom learned the lyrical resonances of connections

in school I learned to chant the teacher's dictums
but I seldom learned the enchantment of poetry

in school I learned facts, fat fatuous facts full of lies,
but I seldom learned the restorative joy of fiction and fantasy

in school I learned to color inside the prescribed lines
but I seldom learned about wild places beyond, elsewhere

in school I learned the denotative definitions of words
but I seldom learned the magic of capacious connotation

in school I learned to be good, an anesthetic obedience
but I seldom learned to ask with aesthetic wonder, what is good

in school I learned to be neat tidy clean even pristine
but I seldom learned to enjoy the body's erotic energies

in school I learned to grow my brain-mind-head like a cabbage
but I seldom heard my heart beat or the heart of anyone else

in school I learned to fear the arts like wild lions, lacking logic,
but I still caught glimpses of dandelions in the cracks of sidewalks

and so I dance with lines, straight and slant, curvaceous and cursive
and I dance with dandy lions, too, no longer fearing their ferociousness

e

Ted was always filled with hope:

> Possibly, just possibly, there might be a new language in the making—
> growing in the middle—a language with a grammar in which a noun is
> not always a noun, in which conjoining words like *between* and *and* are no
> mere joining words. (Aoki, 1993b/2005, p. 215)

Above all, Ted understood how "a view of language is essentially a view of the
world" (Aoki, 1987/2005, p. 238). So he invited us on etymological searches
like Indiana Jones adventures: "Let's play a bit with multiple meanings of *and*"
(Aoki, 1991/2005, p. 259). For Ted, the "curricular landscape" was "a multiplicity of betweens" (Aoki, 1993b/2005, p. 207).

f

Conjunctions

while I once sought the whole
I only ever found holes

because I can never tell
a whole story, I seek fragments

since I am an incomplete sentence
I seek communion with others

like the possibilities of conjunctions
ghosts are everywhere, everywhen

as they call us eagerly to connect
like bridges that lean on light

with invitations to walk in places
where we have been but never been

conjunctions invite us to know inter-
connections, even if our eyes are dim

g

Like Ted, I never grow weary with the possibilities of language for opening up
new ways of seeing and being:

> I revel in the writing space that seems to dissolve beginnings and end-
> ings, that proliferates and disseminates *and* here, there, and in unexpected
> places. I am now thinking, maybe I would like to play in and among
> the *and* for a while, at least for a part of the next 50 years. (Aoki, 1991/
> 2005, p. 260)

Ted understood how "every word has possibilities of multiple meanings and ...
a choice of which meaning is to count is a legitimating process, a political
process, conscious or unconscious" (Aoki, 1992/2005, p. 267). Ted's scholarship reminds me to investigate and interrogate words, but not with the tortur-
ous conviction that words will give up their secrets if sufficiently contorted
and distorted. I investigate words by investing in their hiddenness, learning
to play even (especially) in the concealed corners of words, learning to know
their inexhaustible limits like "an open landscape of multiplicity" (Aoki,
1993b/2005, p. 207).

h

Somewhere I Have Never Travelled

I want to be a verb, since for too long I have
been written a noun only, but no longer satisfied
with being the name, the namer, the named,
I want to name endlessly, be the verb's verve

poetry pushes at edges into spaces
where language refuses clarity, coherence,
composition, even comprehensibility,
amidst literally infinite alliterative possibilities

like holograms, the part in the whole,
rhizome connections in the earth,
the sheer certitude of everything spilling
and spelling out in fractal inevitability

as poems refuse to be consumed, preclude
easy access, even a ready location for readers
who are invited to find, if they can, their positions
for responding in a tantalizing textualizing

as poems invite the words to flow around
the reader, even in and through the reader
who must surrender the desire to hold the text
in place, must carry the memory of mystery

and sift the fragments like hypertextual links
to somewhere untracked to other places,
like e. e. cummings, *somewhere i have never
travelled, gladly beyond*

i

Like Ted, "my interest is in how meanings of words are culturally constituted, and
how the very words and language we are born into may be shaping us" (Aoki,
1993c/2005, p. 284). I write poetically and autobiographically because I am con-
vinced that I need to know who I am in order to understand others, or at least the
otherness of others. This process of knowing myself does not precede the process
of knowing the other—knowing self and other is symbiotic. As Ted explained,
I am concerned about the tension between *I* and *you:*

> We see here the centered self, the narcissistic self, the me-centered egocen-
> trism of the self that relegates others as being secondary to my "I." In such
> a "self *and* other," the "and," pretending conjunctive equality, conceals the
> primacy of the self, relegating the other as object as viewed from the self's
> subjective center. (p. 287)

j

Yo-Yo

I & *you*
the two most used
words in English
full of Buber's
tensile tension

in Spanish
I is *yo*
you is *tú*

I-you   you-I   I-I   you-you   yo-yo

yo-tú   tú-yo   yo-yo   tú-tú   I-I

I know you
you know me

the stranger within
the stranger without

all connected on a string
that knows the limits
of gravity, or at least
its seductive attraction
the constant challenge
of yo-yo tangles

common and idiosyncratic
DNA, in the mirror,
the conjunction AND

everything, all of us
entwined like vines

k

Ted understood how "each one of us is a divided subject, constituted by both self and other" (Aoki, 1993c/2005, p. 289) and how "we are always in the midst of differences, the betweens and ands" (p. 289). Our commitment as human beings in process is to question the taken-for-granted, the seemingly transparent, the familiar obfuscation. Ted investigated the *I* because it boldly, even boastfully and bombastically, declares its importance with inexhaustible insolence: "the subject 'I' is seen as a preexistent ego capable of thinking about the objective world out there, outside the self. This 'I' is saturated with the ego's will to control and master the world through thought and action" (Aoki, 1993a/2005, p. 294).

I

Discourse on Subjectivity
(or, What Kind of I Am I?)
I'm sitting near a coffee vending machine
in the basement lounge of the library
(coffee and a Snickers bar for lunch)

people pass
clones in Klein/Ellis/Hechter clothes
like me
each whispering/proclaiming
I'M ME

in a dark suit and dark blue tie
would I be me?
or not not me?
or another me?

m

I am I/everyone else is you
in a world familiar and strange
where
1 I
+
5 000 000 000 you's
≠
5 000 000 000 I's
+
1 you

if what
I know
of the world
I know
from the subject position
of my I
can I transcend
my I
in order to know
the world
in its fullness/difference

n

epistemological graffiti on the coffee vending machine

to BE is to DO
Kant (the German school)
to DO is to BE

Carlyle (the British school)
DO BE DO BE DO
Sinatra (the American school)
BE a DO BEE
Miss Ann (the Pre-school)

o

a woman in a pink coat
slides to the coffee machine
almost punches
the black coffee button
the light only button
the sugar and light button
turns
eyes like purple orchids in snow
whispers

HOW are you?

I am Homo sapiens
bones, organs, muscles, brain
a melancholy creature
of diverse humours

how ARE you?

Am I?
Am I a phenomenal presence
in a noumenal world?
Am I when alone? not alone?
Perhaps I am not

how are YOU?

Am I a you?
I am me
or at least I pretend
I am me in order to know me
but this you you pretend to know
is a you I do not know

the pink coat is sliding away
I'm fine, you?

away
I'm fine, you?
away
I'm fine, you?
Gone

p

IUIIIIUIIUIII
IIUIIIUIIUI
IUIIIIIUI
IIIUIII
IIIUI
IUI
I

q

I embrace Ted's conviction that "curriculum theorists have begun to consider language as the ground that makes possible the revelation of the life experiences of humans" (Aoki, 1987/2005, p. 235). In my teaching, I have been criticized for being too anecdotal. In reviews of my poetry, I have been criticized for revealing too much, for being too focused on my memories and hopes. In my scholarly writing, I have been castigated for lacking rigour! But in all my teaching and writing and living, I am committed to Ted's conviction about the importance of narrative inquiry: "We in the curriculum world are led to ask about the place of stories and narratives in understanding curriculum or doing curriculum research" (Aoki, 1991/2005, p. 250).

r

Karaoke

in the Ol' Irish Pub in Rovaniemi,
a few kilometers from the Arctic Circle
in Lapland, in the lap of Santa Claus,
drinking Kilkenny alone,
a man asks me for a light
(why do I always feel guilty
when I say no like I have failed
a civic responsibility?)
when Finnish karaoke cracks
the quiet like a line of diamond dust
(everybody wants to be an American Idol),

and I know I should have gone to the pub
named Hemingway's, his images
etched in the windows (didn't he live
in Spain Cuba Africa? I make a note
to read more biographies of Hemingway
or at least Google him when I go home),
and I recall the reindeer I once started
while walking on a warm October night
to the Buck and Ear in Steveston
where I linger on the Gulf of Georgia,
a dozen reindeer in a pen outside the pub
waiting to star in a bad Ben Affleck film,
just eating hay in the moonlight,
and the karaoke kid is now singing
The House of the Rising Sun,
in Finnish since I am in Finland,
not Newfoundland where I first heard it
when the Animals in the late sixties
swept America in the Beatles tailspin
with an old folk song about desire
and debauchery in a New Orleans brothel,
my song when I was his age, and
like an old man with a bad heart
I might burst with the juxtaposed moments
that simply indefatigably defy verb tenses

s

Like Ted, I seek to linger in "the tensioned space of both 'and/not-and,'" which
is always "a space of conjoining and disrupting, indeed a generative space of
possibilities, a space wherein in tensioned ambiguity newness emerges" (Aoki,
1996/2005, p. 318). Ted's scholarship reminds me to look in ways I have never
looked, to see in ways I have never seen. I am fascinated, infatuated even, with
the multiple and fragmentary. My texts are always open, not because I can't write
closed texts, but because I don't want to. I am always questioning, never satisfied,
always confused, never re-solved.

t

Echo

the nymph Echo loved
to talk
and insisted on the last word

until Juno
searching for her wayward husband
        among the nymphs

grew angry with Echo's
chatter   full of wile
(while the other nymphs hid)

and cursed Echo
with the last word only,
always reply, never the first word,

never an original word,
so attracted to Narcissus,
Echo repeated his words only,

words Narcissus heard
        as mimicry, words
that imitated his words only,

words with no promise or deferral,
        only frustration,
and Narcissus rejected Echo

till Echo withered away,
        gaunt and craggy,
a voice in mountain caves,

        the last word only,
never an initiatory word,
the imitative word only

u

Like the poet's penchant for proprioception, Ted understood bridges as liminal
locations for lingering, for contemplating, for dreaming, for conjuring perspective
(p. 316):

                        to cross over

           we are in no hurry   *in fact such bridges*

on this bridge   *lure us to linger*

V

Rambling Rhythms

I jam with the wild lunacy
of the wind tangled in alders,
the day's light in the aspens

&

silence spilled in the forest's arteries
spells the heart's endless desire

&

as the sun falls lower and lower,
the sun chants and I chant with the sun
in ancient blood rhythms

&

the forest presses heavy on the night,
full of hope for names

&

in the whirligig of wild imaginings
I breathe raucous ramblings with no anchor point
like a deflating balloon that never runs out of air

&

the lyrical light fall of rain remembers
the morning star in a heather-blue sky

&

located in the earth, I will learn
to keep the heart calling earth's rhythms
with roots seeking deep and deeper,
the whole earth sung in veins of long light

w

In my writing, I want to escape the constraints of certain ways of knowing, especially epistemologies steeped in the Western Enlightenment traditions of logic and reason. But are all my efforts to escape akin to outrunning my shadow? I am identified with these traditions. If I seek to escape them, I am accused of ignorance and idiocy and impertinence. Ted's scholarship reminds me to attend to "the voice of play in the midst of things—a playful singing in the midst of life" (Aoki, 1993c/2005, p. 282).

x

Prepositions

I write my lines
across
            in
between
            through
over
            inside
on
       under

your lines in dozens
of prepositional possibilities,
a lineal writing, defying
linear measure or equation

y

Like Ted, I reject an instrumental view of language "as a tool to facilitate practical communication in job situations" (Aoki, 1987/2005, p. 237). As a language educator and poet, my whole life has been devoted to Ted's claim that "what seems urgent is the recovery of the fullness of language" (p. 238). Ted's scholarship reminds us that "language is not merely a tool of communication in which thoughts are put into words, nor is it merely a bearer of representational knowledge. Language is a way that humans live humanly in this world" (Aoki, 1991/2005, p. 181). This is my curriculum: learning how to "live humanly in this world" (p. 181). As Ted knew, "the language of the lived curriculum" is "the more poetic, phenomenological and hermeneutic discourse in which life is embodied in the very stories and languages people speak and live" (Aoki, 1993b/2005, p. 207). So, the lived curriculum is a living curriculum, "provoking a discursively live moment" (Aoki, 1991/2005, p. 281).

Z

Vowels

(for Ted Aoki)

with Ted I walk in the moment,
a tangled line of metonymic moments,
making the momentous story
where moments are still and eternal

always in motion, he lingers long
in locations where he stands steady,
sturdy, in the dizzy, always
shape-shifting landscape of holes
like a floating archipelago, best
navigated by memory, and faith
in the mysteries of the alphabet

in his words I am rendered
pneumatic, with feet dangling
in both the earth and the heart's
imagining of poetic possibilities,
still waiting for names

he holds the vowels that breathe
life in our consonants, constantly
ready to know the *I* in our writing,
the metonymic wildness of *I*

he knows the messy texture
of lived experiences, and follows
the line of discipline to know
the oblique, porous, capacious
line that is no line

Ted lives in language, and
language lives in Ted,
drawing us to see what we
overlook, focuses attention
on tension, both tending
and attending, throwing out
lines, here and there, enamoured

with the fecundity of conjunctions
reminds us that grammar, the letter,
the law are chimerical, even comical,
like an alchemist of gramarye,
transforms stone and water
into pigments for re-presenting
the world in words, always
both familiar and unfamiliar,
a seer who teaches us to see

with Ted I walk in the moment,
a tangled line of metonymic moments,
making the momentous story
where moments are still and eternal

References

Aoki, T. (1987/2005). The dialectic of mother language and second language: A curriculum exploration. In W. F. Pinar & R. L. Irwin (Eds.), *Curriculum in a new key: The collected works of Ted T. Aoki* (pp. 235–245). Mahwah, NJ: Lawrence Erlbaum.

Aoki, T.T. (1991/2005). Five curriculum memos and a note for the next half-century. In W. F. Pinar & R. L. Irwin (Eds.), *Curriculum in a new key: The collected works of Ted T. Aoki* (pp. 247–256). Mahwah, NJ: Lawrence Erlbaum.

Aoki, T.T. (1992/2005). In the midst of slippery theme-words: Living as designers of Japanese Canadian curriculum. In W. F. Pinar & R. L. Irwin (Eds.), *Curriculum in a new key: The collected works of Ted T. Aoki* (pp. 263–267). Mahwah, NJ: Lawrence Erlbaum.

Aoki, T.T. (1993a/2005). Humiliating the Cartesian ego. In W. F. Pinar & R. L. Irwin (Eds.), *Curriculum in a new key: The collected works of Ted T. Aoki* (pp. 291–301). Mahwah, NJ: Lawrence Erlbaum.

Aoki, T.T. (1993b/2005). Legitimating lived curriculum: Toward a curricular landscape of multiplicity. In W. F. Pinar & R. L. Irwin (Eds.), *Curriculum in a new key: The collected works of Ted T. Aoki* (pp. 199–215). Mahwah, NJ: Lawrence Erlbaum.

Aoki, T.T. (1993c/2005). The child-centered curriculum: Where is the social in pedocentricism? In W. F. Pinar & R. L. Irwin (Eds.), *Curriculum in a new key: The collected works of Ted T. Aoki* (pp. 279–289). Mahwah, NJ: Lawrence Erlbaum.

Aoki, T.T. (1996/2005). Imaginaries of "East" and "West": Slippery curricular signifiers in education. In W. F. Pinar & R. L. Irwin (Eds.), *Curriculum in a new key: The collected works of Ted T. Aoki* (pp. 313–319). Mahwah, NJ: Lawrence Erlbaum.

LIST OF CONTRIBUTORS

Douglas Sadao Aoki is the *chōnan* 長男 (eldest son) of Ted Aoki. He writes and teaches at the University of Alberta. He also practices and teaches at the Shinki-tai Strathcona karate *dōjō*, along with his own *chōnan,* Alex Aoki, a student of Strathcona High School, in Edmonton, Alberta, and his wife, Lucy De Fabrizio, coordinator of the International Office in the Faculty of Education, University of Alberta.

Christina Audet is a recently retired high-school teacher in a small rural community in southern Alberta. She has undergraduate degrees in English and education from the University of Lethbridge and completed a master's degree in education, also from the University of Lethbridge.

Terrance R. Carson completed his doctoral studies with Ted Aoki at the University of Alberta. He was a member of the academic staff there for nearly thirty years, retiring in 2010. His teaching and research interests include curriculum theory, peace education, intercultural education, and action research.

Wm E. Doll Jr. has taught for over a half century. His latest book is *Pragmatism, Post-Modernism, and Complexity Theory.* He is a Fulbright Senior Scholar and the recipient of an AERA Lifetime Achievement Award. He lectures worldwide with special attention to China and its curriculum reform movement.

Lynn Fels is a writer and associate professor in arts education at Simon Fraser University. She is a former editor of the online education journal *Educational Insights.* Her scholarly essays on performative inquiry and curriculum have been published in journals in North America. Her books include *Living Together: Unmarried Couples in Canada* and, coauthored with George Belliveau, *Exploring Curriculum: Performative Inquiry, Role Drama and Learning.*

Leah C. Fowler is interested in learning and teaching about how we can live mindfully and well together amid difficulty and change. Her research and teaching at the University of Lethbridge clusters around narrative inquiry, teacher development (especially experienced teachers), curriculum studies, Canadian literature, secondary English curricula, and First Nations' teacher education.

Shanna Hagens has lived and worked for over a decade with the Dene First Nations of the Denendeh in the Northwest Territories. Her research interests are in the areas of place-based education, autobiographical inquiry, and cross-cultural teaching and learning. She is a program support teacher and holds an MA from the University of Victoria, British Columbia.

Erika Hasebe-Ludt is Professor in the Faculty of Education at the University of Lethbridge. She teaches, researches, and publishes in the areas of literacy, teacher education, and curriculum studies. Her coedited and coauthored books include *Curriculum Intertext: Place/Language/Pedagogy* (2003), *Life Writing and Literary Métissage as an Ethos for Our Times* (2009), and *A Heart of Wisdom: Life Writing as Empathetic Inquiry* (2012).

Bruce G. Hill was born and raised in Vancouver, British Columbia. He attended the University of British Columbia (BA; teacher education) and the University of Victoria. From 1971 to 2005, he taught in several school districts, including stints as a substitute teacher, classroom teacher, community-school coordinator, PE teacher, and support teacher. In 1987, he was a student of Dr. Aoki and, in recent years, he became a friend of Dr. and Mrs. Aoki.

Wanda Hurren is a photographer and researcher living on Vancouver Island, British Columbia. She firmly believes that the places where we live and work affect who we are and *how* we live and work and vice versa. Wanda is an associate dean at the University of Victoria, where she inquires into links between aesthetics and knowing, especially in places where we think and do our work.

Ingrid Johnston is Professor of English education in the Department of Secondary Education in the Faculty of Education at the University of Alberta. Her research and teaching interests focus on postcolonial literary theories and pedagogies, young adult literature, picture books, Canadian literature, and teacher education. She has published several books and articles on curriculum studies and postcolonial literary studies.

Kathryn Jones was born in Sydney, Australia, and currently teaches English language arts to high-school students for the Calgary Board of Education. In 2012, she graduated with an MA from the University of Calgary. Ted Aoki's work continues to be a great source of inspiration as she contemplates further graduate work.

Vicki Kelly teaches in the areas of indigenous education, art education, and ecological education at Simon Fraser University. She is interested in indigenous knowledges, literacies, aesthetic ways of knowing, holistic learning, integrative art practices, and spirituality and contemplative inquiry. Her current research is in indigenous pathways of learning, Two-Eyed Seeing, the integration of indigenous knowledge in environmental education, and *métissage* as inquiry and curriculum.

Sheena Koops has been a teacher in urban, First Nation, and rural Saskatchewan in private, band, public, and community schools. *Voice of the Valley,* her first novel, and her master's thesis, *Blue Eyes Remembering Toward Anti-Racist Pedagogy,* were both completed in 2006. In the fall of 2012, she began a 200-day walk, meditating on the treaties, blogging and posting pictures along the way. Sheena and her family live in the Qu'Appelle Valley.

Carl Leggo is a poet and Professor in the Faculty of Education at the University of British Columbia. His books include *Teaching to Wonder: Responding to Poetry in the Secondary Classroom; Come-By-Chance; Creative Expression, Creative Education* (coedited with Robert Kelly); *English in Middle and Secondary Classrooms* (coedited with Kedrick James and Teresa M. Dobson); and *Sailing in a Concrete Boat: A Teacher's Journey.*

Candace P. Lewko was born and raised in Lethbridge, Alberta. She received a master of education degree from the University of Lethbridge. She currently is a curriculum consultant at Lethbridge College. Her work as an ESL literacy teacher of immigrant and refugee youth has influenced her life-writing practice, where she continues to reflect upon and write about her live(d) experiences in teaching.

Marylin Low is interested in languages and literacies in a global era, postcolonial subjects, and messy texts of living pedagogy. She seeks difference in her work in the U.S.-affiliated Pacific islands and encourages those she works with to hear in their languages and cultures the limits and possibilities of expression. Highly infected by Aoki's curiosity and brilliant mind, her literate fever continues to be out of control.

Nicholas Ng-A-Fook is an associate professor of curriculum theory in the Faculty of Education at the University of Ottawa. He is the acting director of *A Canadian*

Curriculum Theory Project and the *Developing A Global Perspective for Educators* program. He is the copresident of the Canadian Association for Curriculum Studies. Nicholas has published two books: *Reconsidering Canadian Curriculum Studies* and *An Indigenous Curriculum of Place.*

Nicole Nie Bowden is a cross-cultural educator from China, specializing in multicultural curriculum. Prior to coming to Canada, Nicole worked as a college teacher, director of teaching, and curriculum designer and was the owner of a tutoring center. She holds an MA in curriculum studies from the University of Victoria.

Kathleen Nolan is an associate professor in the Faculty of Education at the University of Regina, where she teaches courses in mathematics curriculum, qualitative research, and contemporary issues in education. Kathleen's research focuses on mathematics teacher education, issues of teacher identity, regulatory practices of schooling, learning and knowing, post-structural readings of scholarly texts, Bourdieu's social field theory, and theories of critical mathematics.

Renee Norman has worked as a teacher, university professor, and a literacy consultant for the Vancouver School Board. She is an award-winning poet and writer whose first (of 3) books of poetry, *True Confessions,* received the Helen and Stan Vine Canadian Jewish Book Award for Poetry. She also was awarded the Canadian Association for Curriculum Studies Distinguished Dissertation Award for *House of Mirrors,* published by Peter Lang, New York.

Patricia Palulis is an associate professor in the Faculty of Education at the University of Ottawa. She teaches English language arts in the Teacher Education Program and graduate courses within the Society, Culture, and Literacies concentration. Her research interests involve language, literacy, culture, and spatiality. She draws from the discursive spaces of postcolonialism, post-structuralism, psychoanalytic theory, and radical feminism.

Alison Pryer received her doctorate from the University of British Columbia, where she taught in the Department of Educational Studies. Alison was awarded the Ted T. Aoki Prize for Outstanding Doctoral Dissertation in Curriculum Studies. She has published numerous articles and poems, as well as the book *Embodied Wisdom: Meditations on Memoir and Education.* Her research focuses on the interconnectedness of body, mind, and spirit in diverse learning contexts.

Ted Riecken is the dean of the Faculty of Education at the University of Victoria. He completed a doctorate in education at the University of British Columbia in the Centre for the Study of Curriculum and Instruction, where he was greatly influenced by the legacy of Ted Aoki's teaching and leadership at UBC.

Sheila Simpkins received her doctorate from the Department of Curriculum and Instruction at the University of Victoria. For her research, she explored how the practice of narrative *métissage* can be used as a peace-education initiative to foster understanding of and empathy for the self/other in the postconflict society of Kurdistan, Northern Iraq. Sheila instructed at universities in China, Turkey, and Northern Iraq. She continues to do what she loves best: teaching.

Michele Tanaka has been an educator for over 30 years. She currently walks alongside preservice teachers as they explore learning-teaching-researching through transformative inquiry. Her research focuses on understanding the nuances of transformative inquiry approaches including the mentoring relationship, rhythms of inquiry, teacher reflexivity, indigenous pedagogy, cross-cultural understanding, and re-visioning educational culture for sustainability.

INDEX